Understanding the Central American Crisis

Central America

MEXICO

Belmopan

BELIZE

GUATEMALA

HONDURAS

Guatemala

Tegucigalpa

EL SALVADOR

San Salvador

NICARAGUA

CARIBBEAN SEA

Gulf of Fonseca

Managua

Corn Islands

PACIFIC OCEAN

COSTA RICA

San José

Panamá City

PANAMÁ

COLOMBIA

Understanding the Central American Crisis

Sources of Conflict, U.S. Policy, and Options for Peace

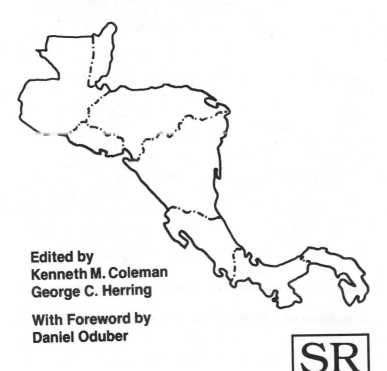

Edited by
Kenneth M. Coleman
George C. Herring

With Foreword by
Daniel Oduber

SR
BOOKS

A Scholarly Resources Inc. Imprint
Wilmington, Delaware

The paper used in this publication meets the minimum requirements of the American National Standard for permanence of paper for printed library materials, Z39.48, 1984.

Scholarly Resources Inc.
104 Greenhill Avenue
Wilmington, DE 19805-1897

Library of Congress Cataloging-in-Publication Data

Understanding the Central American crisis : sources of conflict, U.S.
    policy, and options for peace / edited by Kenneth M. Coleman
    and George C. Herring.
        p. cm. — (Latin American silhouettes)
    Includes bibliographical references and index.
    ISBN 0-8420-2382-8 (cloth). — ISBN 0-8420-2383-6 (pbk.)
    1. Central America—Foreign relations—United States.
2. United States—Foreign relations—Central America. 3. Central
America—Politics and government—1979– 4. United States—
Military policy. 5. Central America—Economic conditions—
1979– 6. Central America—Social conditions—1979–
I. Coleman, Kenneth M. II. Herring, George C., 1936–
III. Series.
F1436.8.U6U53 1991
327.728073—dc20

                                                            91-2974
                                                                CIP

Contents

Part III U.S. Foreign Policy and the Crisis

Foreword

The Central American Crisis, published in 1985, analyzed the sources of conflict in Central America and the failure of U.S. policy. Much has happened since then, and the editors now present a second volume that includes contributions by well-informed analysts, many of whom participated in the first book. It is an excellent study that focuses on the real problems behind the conflicts in Central America.

The greatest effort to pacify the region was made by Latin American democracies in 1985. Mexico, Panama, Colombia, and Venezuela looked for political solutions to end the terrible miseries caused by continued warfare. But war was promoted by groups who believed that only an armed solution was possible in Central America.

The U.S. government paid lip service to those who were trying to promote peaceful settlements by introducing political changes, but it closed its eyes to the military actions taken by the private groups. This was done despite the efforts of the U.S. Congress and the Latin American group known as Contadora—originally formed by Colombia, Venezuela, Panama, and Mexico—to promote dialogue. Slowly, other Latin American nations became democracies, thus enlarging the group to include Brazil, Peru, Argentina, and Uruguay. As the Support Group, these eight countries worked to convince both the Central Americans and the government and public opinion in the United States that the killing should be stopped and political solutions achieved.

The U.S. government, in spite of very clear resolutions by Congress, continued to side with its friends in the area who in turn were allied with the military. The Reagan administration did not want a Latin American solution. Ever since the nineteenth century strong forces within the United States have considered Latin America and the Caribbean a U.S. protectorate.

Since 1985 the interest in Central America of the U.S. government and people has waned dramatically. During the early and middle 1980s the region was the most important issue in Washington's foreign policy. It was prominently featured in the media, and the Nicaraguan problem received greater media attention than it merited. Internal politics had a lot to do with this disproportionate coverage. As the Salvadoran problem had occupied the attention of the first Reagan administration, so the Nicaraguan crisis dominated Washington and the politics of both parties in the second Reagan presidency.

All that has changed in five years. The problems of Central America are worse today than they were in 1985, but they have practically disappeared from view in the United States. The changes in Eastern Europe, the Persian Gulf War, and the disappearance of a bipolar world have reduced the Central American situation to "nothing to worry about." The Nicaraguan elections and the Panamanian invasion were mildly important in their day, but they mean nothing now. Just as the Reagan administration manipulated the Grenada case, so the Bush administration manipulated the Panamanian invasion for internal political purposes, as is clearly analyzed in this book.

We Central Americans have thus once more discovered that the fate of our people will depend only on our own efforts. We must realize that the major powers do not really care about our problems but only about the way they can be manipulated for their own benefit. European, Japanese, or U.S. support for reconstructing and developing Central America and Panama will be minimal, especially considering the problems they presently face in their own countries and regions. Central America must learn to develop by its own efforts.

We also have inherited all the legacies of an erroneous policy. If we examine what has to be done, we will see that conditions are now more difficult than in 1985. External debt, militarism, drugs, ecological disasters, electoral abuses, and other problems are here to stay unless—as we tried to do with Equipulas—we rely on our own efforts and resources.

Much propaganda suggests that democratic elections are the ultimate solution, but there is nothing further from reality. Elections are only one stage in the building of a truly democratic nation. In the majority of Central American countries the alliance of the privileged with the military is stronger than any government, elections or no elections. Obsolete economic theories, imposed from abroad, have created an even greater social gap between the rich and the poor, and a regressive process, insofar as social conditions are concerned, can be noted in all the countries of the area. Freedom of information is determined by the owners of the media. Drug trafficking is carried on by the military, sometimes protected by foreign governments, as was the case with Manuel Noriega, and we could keep on pointing out increasing evils, as is superbly done by the authors of the articles presented here.

This book is for U.S. students, professors, intellectuals, and journalists concerned about Central America and wishing to help eradicate the problems so widely observed these last few years. Readers can help by creating the necessary public opinion to form a unified U.S. policy that would commit itself to promote social democracy in this region, a region that now is being offered entry into an economic community with North America.

Daniel Oduber
President of Costa Rica,
1974-1978

Preface

As the United States involved itself more deeply in Central America in the early years of the presidency of Ronald Reagan, many citizens began to feel uneasy about their nation's role in this troubled area. Some sensed that the prior behavior of the United States had more to do with current problems in Central America than public officials were willing to concede, but few could specify just what had occurred. Wary of the Vietnam experience in which both Democratic and Republican administrations had argued that "we can do only what we are currently doing," many citizens also seemed eager to be exposed to informed discussion of a range of policy options.

The Latin American Studies Program of the University of Kentucky responded to this public anxiety by sponsoring two conferences during the 1983–84 academic year. The first was a series of six lectures given by faculty members from various disciplines at the university and entitled "Central America: Background to Crisis." That series was followed by a two-day conference on "Central America: Policy Options," to which leading participants in the national debate were invited. The presentations in these two conferences comprised the essence of *The Central American Crisis: Sources of Conflict and the Failure of U.S. Policy,* published in 1985. That volume sought to provide for interested general readers and for students in college-level courses a critical explanation of how the United States became engaged in conflict with Central American revolutions. It also proposed alternative policies to deal more effectively with those revolutions. It rejected the assumptions behind the U.S. policies then being pursued in Central America, and it favored accommodating, rather than confronting, the revolutionary government of Nicaragua and the revolutionary movements in El Salvador and Guatemala.

Comprised of six revised and updated essays and five new ones, this book, like its predecessor *The Central American Crisis,* has similar objectives. Much has happened since that volume was published in 1985.

The revolution and civil conflict in El Salvador have dragged on inconclusively, at great cost to the nation and its people. The U.S. involvement in Nicaragua deepened in the mid-1980s, engulfing the Reagan administration in the Iran-contra scandal and Nicaragua itself in civil war. Ultimately, following the lead of Costa Rica's Oscar Arias, Nicaraguans opted for peace. To the shock and dismay of much of the world, in elections held in 1990 they rejected the Sandinista government. The United States thereafter found it expedient to retreat in Nicaragua, but its involvement in El Salvador remained pervasive, and in December 1989 the administration of George Bush invaded Panama to remove the dictator Manuel Noriega. This volume seeks to put these dramatic events in historical perspective.

Like *The Central American Crisis*, this volume also seeks to provide material for an informed public debate on U.S. policy in Central America. The emergence of peace in Nicaragua, apparent U.S. policy successes there and in Panama, the end of the Cold War, and the outbreak of a new, post-Cold War crisis in the Persian Gulf have removed Central America from the forefront of discussion and from the front pages of the newspapers. Yet an unseen crisis persists. Civil war and revolution go on in El Salvador and Guatemala. Throughout the region, a decade of conflict and outside intervention has exacerbated the conditions that gave rise to those conflicts in the first place: poverty; social, political, and economic inequality; debt; political oppression; intraregional disputes; and nationalist rivalries. Washington's policy has contributed to these problems in the past, but it might help resolve them in the future. This volume seeks to explain why unresolved tensions and violence persist and suggests changes in U.S. policy that might help end them.

If there is an underlying political bias to this volume, it is toward the social democratic option. Most of the authors believe that accommodation between the rich and the poor, the landed and the landless, or capitalists and industrial workers would have been possible if political systems controlled by the rich, the landed, and the owners of capital had pursued timely and enlightened policies. Further, the authors agree that certain political systems of Central America failed to do this and that the United States bears some responsibility for these failures.

Even after a decade of conflict, many Latin American specialists still believe that peace is possible in Central America. To achieve that peace, which is attainable only by striking a social democratic bargain between the propertied and the poor, political systems will have to be opened to the political left rather than closed. By its opposition to power sharing in El Salvador and its support of counterrevolution in

Nicaragua, the Reagan administration contributed to the closure of political systems. In Nicaragua, democratic compromise may well have occurred in spite of, rather than because of, Washington.

In terms of national interest the United States seeks primarily peace and stability in the area on its southern periphery. To be true to its ideals, however, it must support democratic forces in Central America. Its economic stake in the region is remarkably small, and it should be willing to accept fundamental economic changes if Central Americans desire to make them. It should identify with those political forces that respect their adversaries and should tolerate those whose views may differ. In instances where extreme polarization has given rise to revolution, the United States should let the Central Americans settle their own conflicts. It should not attempt to prevent left-wing governments from coming to power. Once such governments have attained power, it should remain open-minded and flexible in its policy. If such governments become authoritarian, the United States may wish to remain aloof, but it should not lock itself into a policy of confrontation. Initial impressions of implacable hostility by revolutionary governments may be wrong. Those who come to power by attacking the United States may discover in time the utility of maintaining relations. Thus, accommodation with revolution is possible for and beneficial to the United States.

Historian WALTER LAFEBER's opening essay places the Reagan administration's policies in historical perspective, stressing that they are only recent manifestations of a century-long pattern of U.S. attempts to control social, economic, and political change in Central America through military and political intervention.

Part I focuses on the indigenous sources of the current conflict. Anthropologists BILLIE DEWALT and PEDRO BIDEGARAY examine the way in which recent agrarian trends have exacerbated age-old employment problems and put additional pressure on political systems. Political scientist KENNETH COLEMAN next analyzes the structure of political conflict in the area, distinguishing between conventional, reformist, and revolutionary ideologies of change. He attributes recent conflict in Nicaragua, El Salvador, and Guatemala to the systematic exclusion of reformist groups from power. Sociologist KATHLEEN BLEE examines the role of the Catholic church, especially the ecclesiastical base communities of lay persons, in stimulating popular demands for political and economic change. Finally, one case study considers the internal logic of revolutionary experiences. Political scientist ILJA LUCIAK examines the internal dynamics of the Nicaraguan revolution, presenting a far different perspective of the Sandinistas from that generally available to readers in the United States.

Part II provides case studies of U.S. intervention in individual Central American countries. Political scientist WILLIAM LEOGRANDE looks at the continuing conflict in El Salvador, arguing that U.S. policy under the Reagan and Bush administrations has not been conducive to a settlement and that a change of policy is necessary to end a long and bloody conflict. Historian RICHARD MILLETT challenges the widespread American notion that the Bush administration's December 1989 invasion of Panama was a smashing and unqualified success. He contends that the problems that caused the intervention and resulted from it are far from settled and suggests that, as previously in U.S. relations with the region, it is far easier to remove a government than to install a stable and democratic successor. Last, political scientists HARRY VANDEN and THOMAS WALKER look critically at the Reagan administration's confrontational policy toward the Sandinista revolution, viewing it as an ill-conceived attempt to reimpose hegemony on a legitimate nationalist regime.

Part III examines some often overlooked factors influencing U.S. policies toward Central America. From the beginning of the crisis to its end, much public attention was focused on the analogy between Vietnam and Central America. Historian GEORGE HERRING's essay seeks to show in what ways the analogy was valid and in what ways it was not, and it also suggests how history might be used more profitably in debate on contemporary issues. Political scientist ELDON KENWORTHY shows how Washington's policies in Central America have been influenced by the opinion-manipulation techniques used by U.S. politicians in election campaigns.

In conclusion, KENNETH COLEMAN and GEORGE HERRING synthesize the contents of the volume. Here they offer modest proposals for reshaping current U.S. policies toward a still volatile region.

We hope that this volume will reach some of the many citizens who remain concerned about the wisdom of U.S. policy in Central America. If it helps to rekindle public debate, then it has served its purpose, however readers may assess the merits of the particular views expressed.

George C. Herring and
Kenneth M. Coleman
January 1991

Acknowledgments

We take this opportunity to thank the many people who assisted in the completion of this volume. Our greatest debt is to our contributors, who remained patient while the editors' administrative obligations and the vagaries and vicissitudes of U.S.-Central American relations caused delays in the revision of some articles that originally appeared in *The Central American Crisis: Sources of Conflict and the Failure of U.S. Policy*, this book's successful predecessor. Kathleen Blee, Eldon Kenworthy, and Thomas Walker and Harry Vanden were especially cooperative in meeting one deadline and then reworking their chapters in order to meet another as events dictated.

The University of Kentucky provided financial resources for a series of lectures and a conference on the Central American crisis in the 1983–84 academic year. That money and the collegial environment of the Latin American Studies Program at Kentucky made *The Central American Crisis* possible and provided ongoing assistance to George Herring for the preparation of this volume. Special thanks are due the many individuals who assisted in those earlier efforts: Abraham F. Lowenthal of the University of Southern California; Daniel Oduber of the Republic of Costa Rica; and Michael A. Webb, David F. Ross, Kathleen M. DeWalt, Otis Singletary, and Carol Reardon of the University of Kentucky all made valuable contributions.

Dorothy Leathers of the History Department at the University of Kentucky also provided invaluable assistance of many different kinds at all stages of the preparation of *The Central American Crisis* and especially of this volume.

Kenneth Coleman expresses his appreciation to the Institute of Latin American Studies of the University of North Carolina at Chapel Hill for providing the support essential to complete his assignments on this volume.

Finally, we thank the *Journal of Inter-American Studies and World Affairs* for permission to reprint the article by Richard L. Millett and *World Policy Journal* for allowing us to reprint the article by William M. LeoGrande.

Well over two hundred thousand Central Americans have lost their lives in political and military violence in recent years. All these losses are tragic. Yet, six Jesuit intellectuals and two servants died early on November 16, 1989, precisely because they were committed to academic integrity, tolerance, and reconciliation in El Salvador. We dedicate this volume to the memory of the martyrs of the Universidad Centroamericana José Simeón Cañas: Julia Ramos and her daughter Celina; Father Ignacio Ellacuría, rector; Father Ignacio Martín-Baró, vice rector and director of the University Public Opinion Institute; Father Segundo Montes, dean of Social Sciences; Father Juan Ramón Moreno; Father Joaquín López y López; and Father Amando López.

May those of us who enjoy the protected academic environment of the United States display but a portion of their courage.

G. C. H.
K. M. C.

About the Contributors

Pedro Bidegaray is a Ph.D. candidate in anthropology at the University of Kentucky. A graduate of the Pontificia Universidad Católica in Lima, Peru, he is currently doing dissertation research on a community in highland Ecuador.

Kathleen M. Blee is associate professor of sociology at the University of Kentucky. In addition to her research on the church in Central America, she is studying the role of gender in political movements in the United States, one result of which is a recently completed book on the role of women in the Ku Klux Klan in the 1920s. She and Dwight Billings are also completing a study of the origin and persistence of poverty in rural America.

Kenneth M. Coleman is professor of political science and Latin American studies at the University of North Carolina at Chapel Hill. His recent publications include *Culture and Politics in Mexico* (1988) as well as studies of public opinion in Venezuela and Nicaragua.

Billie R. DeWalt is professor of anthropology at the University of Kentucky. He has served as a visiting professor in Mexico and as a Fulbright lecturer in Ecuador. Among his publications are *Modernization in a Mexican Ejido: A Study in Economic Adaptation* (1979) and *Micro and Macro Levels of Analysis in Anthropology: Issues in Theory and Research* (1985).

George C. Herring is Alumni Professor of History at the University of Kentucky. His recent work has focused on U.S. involvement in Vietnam and includes *America's Longest War: The United States and Vietnam, 1950–1975* (rev. ed., 1985) and *The Secret Diplomacy of the Vietnam War: The "Negotiating Volumes" of the Pentagon Papers* (1983).

Eldon Kenworthy is a member of the government department and Latin American Studies Program at Cornell University. His forthcoming book, *Ads and Intervention*, elaborates on themes introduced in his contribution to this volume. His most recent articles have appeared in *World Policy Journal* and in the second edition of Jan Knippers Black, *Latin America: Its Problems and Its Promise* (1991).

Walter LaFeber is Noll Professor of History at Cornell University. A specialist in the history of U.S. foreign relations, he is the author of *The New Empire* (1963), *The Panama Canal* (rev. ed., 1989), *America, Russia, and the Cold War* (6th ed., 1990), *Inevitable Revolutions: The United States in Central America* (1983), and *The American Age: U.S. Foreign Policy at Home and Abroad since 1750* (1989).

William M. LeoGrande is professor of government in the School of Public Affairs at the American University in Washington, DC. He is the author of numerous articles on U.S. relations with Central America and is the coeditor of *Confronting Revolution: Security through Diplomacy in Central America* (1986).

Ilja A. Luciak is a political scientist at Virginia Polytechnic Institute and State University. He has conducted field research throughout Central America and has taught at the Universidad Centroamericana in Managua. His publications include articles in *Comparative Politics*, *Journal of Latin American Studies*, and *Latin American Perspectives*.

Richard L. Millett is professor of history at Southern Illinois University at Edwardsville. He is the author of numerous articles and books on Central America and the Caribbean, including the widely read *Guardians of the Dynasty: The U.S.-Created Guardia Nacional de Nicaragua and the Somoza Family* (1977).

Harry E. Vanden is professor of political science at the University of South Florida, Tampa. His articles have appeared in the *Latin American Research Review*, *Journal of Inter-American Studies and World Affairs*, *Latin American Perspectives*, and *Annals of the American Academy of Political and Social Science*. His books include *National Marxism in Latin America: José Carlos Mariategui's Thought and Politics* (1986) and *Latin American Marxism, A Biography* (1990). He is currently preparing a study on democracy and socialism in Nicaragua.

Thomas W. Walker is professor of political science and director of Latin American Studies at Ohio University. A specialist on Central America and especially Nicaragua, he is the author of *The Christian Democratic Movement in Nicaragua* (1970) and *Nicaragua: The Land of Sandino* (1981, 1986, 1991); the coauthor of *Understanding Central America* (1989); and the coauthor/editor of *Nicaragua in Revolution* (1982), *Nicaragua: The First Five Years* (1985), *Reagan versus the Sandinistas: The Undeclared War on Nicaragua* (1987), and *Revolution and Counterrevolution in Nicaragua: A Comprehensive Overview* (1991).

Introduction: The Reagan Policy in Historical Perspective

Walter LaFeber

After 1979, U.S. officials changed General Karl von Clausewitz's famous dictum that war is only a "continuation of State policy [that is, a continuation of politics] by other means."[1] In Central America the Reagan administration tried to use war as a substitute for state policy. Diplomacy was replaced by war; military escalation was substituted for politics. More specifically, the Reagan administration used diplomatic discussions as a fig leaf to cover military escalation. In dealing with the Sandinista government in Nicaragua, or the Farabundo Martí National Liberation Front (FMLN) revolutionaries who tried to overthrow the U.S.-supported government in El Salvador, the Reagan administration used war, not diplomacy, as its state policy.

By the time Ronald Reagan left office in January 1989, however, that policy had collapsed. The Sandinistas, impoverished and besieged, grimly tightened their hold on Nicaragua. Their enemies, the contras (who had been equipped and largely created by the United States), had been unable to hold any significant piece of Nicaraguan territory. By 1988 the contras were divided, dispersed, and had largely disappeared as a fighting force. In El Salvador the U.S.-supported government of President José Napoleón Duarte not only had been unable to stop the brutalities against human rights committed by the Washington-equipped Salvadoran army but also rapidly lost popularity to right-wing political parties who supported the army.

U.S. policy had gone awry in the two main arenas of Nicaragua and El Salvador, as well as in neighboring Guatemala, where the Central Intelligence Agency (CIA) had overthrown an elected government and imposed a military regime in 1954. There, the army continued to hold real power despite the election of a civilian president in 1986. The army's control, however, and its use of a violent beans-and-bullets policy (that is, winning over rebellious peasants with beans or killing them with bullets) did not succeed in stamping out a revolution that had existed since the 1960s. And in Honduras, Reagan's closest ally in carrying on the war against the Sandinistas and the Salvadoran revolutionaries, the terrific burden of helping Washington's military policies began to rip apart the society. Once among the most tranquil and liberal of nations in the region, Honduras had been turned into one huge U.S. military base that drained the country's small resources, created widespread venereal disease, produced anti-American terrorism, and turned the southern part of the country—where twelve thousand Washington-supported contras encamped—into virtually a separate, ungovernable nation.

Something had gone seriously wrong with Reagan's policy of using war instead of diplomacy in Central America. A few administration officials had seen it all coming and tried to reverse course. Indeed, the State Department twice tried to modify policy so that a so-called dual track rather than simply a military track would be followed. The dual-track approach was worked out initially by Thomas O. Enders, assistant secretary of state for Inter-American Affairs (1981–1983). Enders was not a dove. While stationed in Southeast Asia during 1969–70, he had established his willingness to use force by guiding (and then helping to keep secret) the covert bombing of Communist bases in Cambodia. As a top State Department official in early 1983, moreover, he warned that "it should be made clear to the Soviet Union and Cuba and Nicaragua that the United States may take direct action if they try to destabilize nations in this hemisphere."[2] Behind the scenes, however, Enders had learned that escalating U.S. military involvement was not solving the key political problems in Central America. The Reagan administration's application of force instead was leading the Nicaraguan and Salvadoran revolutionaries to escalate their military efforts. Enders sought to use the immense U.S. military power as a stick to shape negotiations rather than as a primitive club to drive the Sandinistas and the FMLN into oblivion.

His approach clashed with the administration's determination to overthrow—not negotiate with—the Sandinistas and to destroy—not to discuss power-sharing with—the Salvadoran rebels. Those policies were shaped not in the State Department by Enders but in the National Security Council (NSC). In the White House offices of the NSC, William C. Clark, the president's national security adviser and close friend, combined little knowledge of and less experience in Central

American affairs with an ardent military approach to foreign policy problems. This policy of force was also strongly supported at the U.S. office in the United Nations where Ambassador Jeane J. Kirkpatrick worked out a rationale for supporting right-wing authoritarian regimes in Latin America. Finally, the promilitary policy was encouraged at the Pentagon where Fred Iklé and Nestor Sanchez held die-hard views of the need to oppose Third World revolutionaries by force. (Notably, the uniformed military at the Pentagon often disagreed with Iklé and Sanchez over Central America. Still suffering from the Vietnam involvement, and more concerned with increasing the military budget to deal with the Soviet Union, the uniformed military opposed a Central American policy based on force that could—as it had in Vietnam—slowly but inevitably lead to the increasing use of U.S. troops.)

Against this range of opponents, Enders stood little chance. In May 1983 the White House forced him out of Washington. He became ambassador to Spain, where he could talk with a government that agreed with his dual-track approach. Enders and Spanish officials now could console each other while Clark, Iklé, and Kirkpatrick pushed policy along the single-track military route.[3]

Despite Enders's departure, the State Department did not immediately join the single-trackers. The professionals at State knew Central America and understood the region's dilemmas too well. Enders was replaced by Langhorne Motley, who had been a real estate speculator in Alaska before becoming the rather widely publicized and outspoken U.S. ambassador to Brazil in 1981. Little public evidence indicated that Motley would oppose the single-trackers, but he learned quickly. He continued to support a tough military approach and agreed with the ongoing North American buildup in the region. But, resembling Enders, he also came to understand that, unless the United States aimed for a diplomatic settlement, the use of military power could only lead to a bloody dead end. Worse, that power, instead of frightening the revolutionaries into surrender, was driving them into more rapidly expanding their military strategy. The U.S. military escalation was creating results opposite from what had been intended.

Thus, Motley also began to explore the dual-track alternative. In July and August 1983, however, he and the State Department were dramatically undercut by the White House's announcement that the United States would begin massive military maneuvers in Central America. In conducting the largest peacetime maneuvers in history in the region, U.S. officials planned to deploy as many as thirty thousand troops. The announcement came, moreover, at a time when Washington was rapidly building the military capacity of Honduras as a base for attacking Nicaragua and as the CIA publicly escalated its supplying and direction of the contras. The White House apparently announced the dramatic news without informing either Motley or Secretary of State George Shultz.

Shultz reportedly was furious. His anger exploded, moreover, as Congress and knowledgeable private citizens unloosed a barrage of criticism at the Reagan policy. A political crisis of considerable proportions loomed just one year before the 1984 presidential campaign was to begin. The White House staff, led by the cool chief of staff, James A. Baker, shrewdly gained time by arranging the appointment of a bipartisan commission on Central America chaired by former Secretary of State Henry A. Kissinger. President Reagan charged the commission with examining the region's problems in depth and recommending a course of action. The political crisis temporarily eased, but U.S. military escalation continued. Indeed, that escalation reached new levels during late 1983 and early 1984, just as the Kissinger Commission issued a report that refused to condone any power sharing with the Salvadoran revolutionaries, condemned the Sandinistas, and placed strong emphasis on the need to provide military security and not on diplomatic approaches. Motley's two-track approach was not at all strengthened by Kissinger's report.

Thus, the Central American wars roared on. By 1984, after nearly one full term in office, President Reagan had involved his country in several costly conflicts. The bloodiest in terms of lives lost occurred in Lebanon, where 269 U.S. soldiers were killed within one year. In Central America, North Americans were engaged on three fronts, and a fourth threatened to open.

The first front engulfed El Salvador, where by 1984 about forty thousand government soldiers fought nine thousand to twelve thousand FMLN revolutionaries. In January 1981 the FMLN had launched what it termed a "final offensive" to sweep the government from power, but the Salvadoran army inflicted heavy casualties in pushing back the offensive with surprising ease. About 3,500 FMLN troops remained after the defeat. Over the next three years their numbers tripled. By early 1984 the military situation was so bad that the Kissinger Commission believed the collapse of the Salvadoran army was not inconceivable. Moreover, the government's troops had proven to be poor fighters. Only one out of every ten trained in the United States reenlisted, officers in some key areas were corrupt and ineffective, and important commanders were more concerned with their tasks in the brutal terrorist death squads that killed about forty thousand civilians between 1979 and 1984 than with fighting the revolutionaries.

By the end of Reagan's second term in early 1989 the Salvadoran government had about sixty-five thousand troops, while the United States had spent over $3 billion to keep that government propped up. Washington's aid began to pay more than two thirds of El Salvador's federal expenditures, or about the level at which the United States had supported South Vietnam during the height of that war in the late 1960s. But the FMLN could not be conquered. It closed down large parts of El Salvador by blocking roads and dynamiting power stations. The revolutionaries launched terrorist attacks in 1987–88 within the capital, San Salvador, and made destructive surprise attacks on army bases. The Salvadorans were being ground down in a bloody stalemated war.

Meanwhile, El Salvador's government was losing popularity and legitimacy. It could not pass badly needed land-reform programs because of opposition from the army and the army's longtime ally, the oligarchs (that is, the so-called Fourteen Families that had run the country as a personal fiefdom since the nineteenth century and whose exploitation had largely brought about the revolution). To try to create legitimacy for the government, the United States had sponsored elections. The first, in 1982, created a constituent assembly; the second, in 1984, elected a president. Both fell far short of providing the needed legitimacy, and from 16 to 25 percent of the 1982 votes may have been fraudulent. This fraud helped gain a majority vote for a party (ARENA) that was linked to some of the worst human rights atrocities, so the United States intervened to ensure that this party did not obtain the interim presidency to which the vote entitled it. In neither 1982 nor 1984 did the FMLN participate in the election. Several of their top leaders had been trapped and murdered in cold blood by the Salvadoran army in 1980 as they prepared to discuss terms with the government. No guarantees existed that the personal safety of any politician in the liberal-to-radical part of the political spectrum could be ensured against the death squads' rifles.

In 1984 the United States controlled the election. It used public relations devices and front organizations operated by the CIA which, together with the U.S. embassy in San Salvador, worked out and supervised the election process.[4] Duarte, a graduate of Notre Dame University in Indiana, won the presidency. Because he was highly popular in Washington, Congress opened its pocketbook to him. But by early 1989 he had not been able to carry out reforms or defeat the FMLN, he had failed to control the army or maintain the popularity of his Christian Democratic party, and, tragically, he was dying of cancer.

The elections had been an integral part of U.S. military policy. They were conducted less to create a nationally accepted government than to create a regime that appeared to be legitimate—and thus appeared to be worthy of the billions of dollars of U.S. aid that were necessary to conduct military campaigns.

The second war in the region occurred in northern Nicaragua along the Honduran border. The contras, with about ten thousand men, attempted to launch invasions from Honduran bases into northern Nicaragua between 1981 and 1987. They particularly wanted to declare the existence of a provisional government on Nicaraguan soil, a regime that Washington then could recognize as an alternative to the Sandinista government. To fight the incursions, the Sandinistas built an army of sixty-five thousand troops and reserve militias of about one hundred thousand. In late 1983 the CIA shoved aside the politically inept contra leaders who had failed to achieve their military or political goals. By mid-1984 over $70 million of CIA money had flowed to the contras, but there was little to show for it other than the killing of several hundred persons on both sides and the bombing by the CIA of the Managua airport and the country's major oil refinery and docks in late 1983.

In 1984 news leaked of the detailed CIA efforts, including a manual that discussed assassinating Nicaraguan opponents. An angry U.S. Congress moved to stop the CIA activities and temporarily cut off military aid to the contras. Not until 1986 did Congress restore that aid, which lasted only one year. In 1987 the contras' military and political failures, a spreading peace settlement that took root in the region under the sponsorship of Costa Rican President Oscar Arias, and—perhaps most important—the headline-grabbing revelations that a lowly lieutenant colonel in the White House, Oliver North, had diverted funds from arms sales to the contras' use despite Congress's prohibition of such a diversion, combined to kill their cause in the United States. The contras fragmented. Some returned to Managua to discuss peace terms with the Sandinistas, while a few remained in the jungles and tried to revive the counterrevolution. Most lived in southern Honduras with their dependents and waited for their powerful sponsor to help them move elsewhere—preferably Costa Rica or Miami.[5]

A third war devastated parts of southern Nicaragua along the Costa Rican border. An anti-Sandinista group (with the Spanish acronym ARDE), led by Edén Pastora and Alfonso Robelo, included about four thousand soldiers. Pastora and Robelo had been major figures in the Sandinista movement in the late 1970s, but they left Managua when Pastora did not obtain an important post in the new regime and when both men saw that the Sandinistas intended to carry out a social revolution through authoritarian methods with which Pastora and Robelo had little sympathy. Pastora, nevertheless, adamantly refused to move closer to the CIA or to form a partnership with the contras in the north as Washington urged him to do. He charged that the contras included too many followers of Anastasio Somoza's dictatorship that he had helped throw out of power in 1979. In the spring of 1984 a bomb planted at Pastora's press conference severely wounded him, killed four journalists, and threw his movement into confusion. No conclusive evidence emerged to prove who planted the bomb. As Pastora recovered, Robelo and the CIA tried to reorganize the southern forces so they could fight against the Sandinistas.[6] By 1987, however, this third front was breathing its last.

A fourth war also was being waged in the region, although the United States was involved less directly there than in the other three. The Guatemalan government had been fighting revolutionaries intermittently since 1960. The outbreak changed dramatically in political complexion during the mid-1970s when significant numbers of Indians joined the revolutionaries. Holding a bare majority of Guatemala's population, the Indians have been among the most oppressed and politically quiet people in Latin America. The army-controlled government, however, went too far when it grabbed large areas of land and devastated traditional Indian settlements. The Guatemalan regime responded with such atrocities that, in 1977, President Jimmy Carter threatened to cut off U.S. military aid unless the repression was stopped. The Guatemalan leaders told Carter that they no longer wanted assistance on those terms and continued to slaughter the Indians.[7]

The Reagan administration endeavored to reopen military aid channels for the Guatemalan army, but Congress refused to appropriate large sums of money until the mid-1980s when a civilian president, Vinicio Cerezo, was elected. Cerezo made several small attempts at economic reforms, only to have right-wing members of the army try to overthrow him in May 1988. Cerezo survived, but the reforms stopped. It was clear that the remaining army officers controlled both the president and the country, and human rights brutalities against opponents continued. Nearly one hundred thousand Guatemalans, most of them Indians, lived in camps in southern Mexico where they had fled for safety.[8] U.S. military aid continued to flow to Guatemala, and the Reagan administration apparently asked few questions about how or against whom it was being used.

That the United States was not more fully involved in Guatemala was due less to the restraint of the Reagan administration than to the Guatemalans' passionate belief that they were not going to become like the Hondurans, whose country was being turned into a U.S. military base. The Guatemalan military is one of the proudest and most tightly controlled in Latin America. Its members have exceptional loyalty to their institution and do not care for outside advice, even from the nation that put them into power in 1954. Because of the army's strength and the country's historic influence in the region, and also because of the Reagan administration's desire to form a Central American military front to deal with the FMLN and the Sandinistas (a front that would have to include Guatemalan army forces to be effective), U.S. officials tried to help the Guatemalan forces in every way allowed, and in some cases not condoned, by Congress. Washington hoped to use Guatemala as a fourth front for its "State policy," to use Clausewitz's phrase.

In Guatemala, El Salvador, and the Nicaraguan revolutionary conflict, the United States allied itself with the forces of the past: regimes represented by small elite groups that had exploited their own people for a century or more, by military officers who had lived off their countries for decades and now formed death squads to kill suspected critics, and, in the case of the contras, by army officers and political leaders closely associated with dictatorships.

Such a perspective on U.S. policy raises two major questions. First, how did North Americans, who were once, as John Winthrop of the seventeenth-century Massachusetts Bay Colony (and much later Ronald Reagan) phrased it, to form a "city upon a hill" that shined its light of liberty to the world, end up in such tragedies? Second, what alternatives to the Reagan policy appeared in the 1980s?

The United States did not create the conditions that produced Central American revolutions. When the Spanish colonial rulers involuntarily departed amid the Latin American wars for independence during the first two decades of the nineteenth century, they left behind class-ridden societies, most of which were desperately poor and parochial. Many Central American political leaders were so conservative that they did not want Spain to leave (some feared, correctly, that Guatemala would immediately attempt to extend its power over the area), and they succeeded in killing the nascent union movement of the 1820s and 1830s that might have united the five nations—Guatemala, El Salvador, Honduras, Nicaragua, and Costa Rica—into a self-sufficient unit.

As parochialism triumphed, the oligarch class developed its power in each of the nations except Costa Rica. In that country a more homogeneous racial composition (heavily Spanish with little of the Indian or black blood found elsewhere in the region) and a relatively equitable land-holding system, which survived into the twentieth century, created bases for a more consensual political system than had emerged in the other four nations. With only two major exceptions—the civil wars of 1918 and 1948—Costa Rica developed a democratic and stable government that set it apart in the region and gave its people, the Ticos, a feeling of superiority that made later attempts at Central American cooperation difficult.

In El Salvador, Guatemala, and Nicaragua, on the other hand, control of the land was tightly held by a relative few. Masses of peasants had sunk to depths of poverty and forms of wage slavery by the late 1920s. The elites exploited the laborers and land to produce plantation crops such as coffee, cotton, and bananas for export to industrializing nations. These Central Americans thus became dependent on one or two crops. They were unable to regulate the prices of their products because their exports depended on a world market, not domestic markets where some control might be exerted. Moreover, domestic markets were too poor and wealth too inequitably distributed to ensure a self-sufficient economy.

Honduras underwent a slightly different development. It had more land available than its neighbors. Consequently, its peasants could find room to scratch out a living. The best areas for plantation crops, however, fell into the hands of U.S. banana companies after 1890. Honduras became the prototype of the banana republic, with its land, transportation, communications, and government operated directly (or, in the case of the government, indirectly) by North Americans. Occupying a key strategic location in the region and willing to cooperate with those who held dollars for investment, Honduras acted as Washington's staunch and agreeable ally decades before the Reagan administration used it as a base for U.S. military and CIA operations.

North American policy worked on several levels until the 1930s. On one level, private investors and merchants penetrated the local economies until every nation except El Salvador became highly dependent on the U.S. economy for markets, food staples, or both. El Salvador, which actually had tried to become a state of the United States during the 1820s, escaped Washington's financial control and worked more closely with Western Europe until World War II. On another level, Washington officials frequently dispatched troops to maintain stability. Their objectives were at least twofold: to provide peace of mind for Yankee investors and to ensure that European powers (especially Great Britain and Germany) would not take such police chores into their own hands. U.S. soldiers and sailors had appeared as peacekeepers in the nineteenth century, but, after Theodore Roosevelt began to build the Panama Canal in 1903 and issued his so-called corollary to the Monroe Doctrine in 1904 (a pronouncement in which he told the world that henceforth his country would act unilaterally as a policeman in Latin America), the United States became the supreme military power in the hemisphere.[9]

Most notably the United States used its muscle to maintain order when its forces landed in Nicaragua in 1911–12 and, more particularly, to guarantee that a faction in Managua willing to cooperate with Washington would remain in power. Unfortunately, many Nicaraguans did not care for such a regime, and U.S. troops remained until 1925 to protect the government they had put in power. When the troops left, civil war resumed almost immediately; they returned in 1926 and stayed until 1933. During these later years, however, they signally failed to destroy the guerrilla band of Augusto Sandino. This small, tough nationalist, supported by the peasants, vowed to fight until the Yankees left his country. By 1933 this intervention was becoming too costly and politically embarrassing for officials in Washington. The administrations of Herbert Hoover and Franklin D. Roosevelt pulled out the troops but left behind a new device for protecting their interests: a native National Guard trained by North Americans and commanded by young Anastasio Somoza. A Nicaraguan who had received much of his education in the United States, Somoza promptly used the guard to become dictator. He murdered Sandino when the guerrilla leader came to Managua to make peace, and he controlled the country until an assassin gunned him down in 1956. His sons then took over until the younger Anastasio lost power in 1979 to the Sandinistas.[10]

The lessons of the 1912-to-1933 military interventions in Nicaragua were instructive for those who cared to learn. The first lesson was that the use of force would require a long time to build a viable, pro-United States native regime in Central America. A second lesson was that not even a twenty-year occupation could produce equitable political and economic systems—only a dictatorial regime whose first commitment was to its own stability and pocketbook. A third lesson was that U.S. military intervention actually produced a result that had long terrified Washington officials who had to deal with the Soviet Union, China, and Mexico: mass-based revolutionaries who fought U.S. interests at every turn and who seemed to prosper even more when fresh foreign troops appeared. By 1933 the military intervention had produced exactly the opposite results intended by Washington policymakers.

Unfortunately, those lessons were not well learned. The U.S. military involvement became less direct and public during the Good Neighbor era of President Franklin Roosevelt, but control remained ultimately in North American hands—although this control worked through economic leverage, the common cause of World War II, and the need of the region for North American products and foodstuffs in the 1940s and 1950s. The economic ties, however, did nothing to alleviate the class divisions and inequitable economic situation. Indeed, they worsened these problems. Pressures built toward a series of explosions. One occurred in Guatemala between 1944 and 1954 when a middle-class uprising overthrew a dictatorship and established a reform government that tried to redistribute wealth and institute fair elections. This government incurred the wrath of the CIA and President Dwight D. Eisenhower's administration in 1954.

The breathing room gained by that CIA operation was brief. In 1959, Fidel Castro's revolution suddenly conquered Cuba. No nation in Latin America, not even Nicaragua, had been as fully under Washington's control since the 1890s as Cuba. Castro's success, and his ability to maintain his power despite enormous U.S. pressures (including an attempted replay of the 1954 CIA operation at Cuba's Bay of Pigs in 1961), raised the specter of other Castros seizing power in the region. And Nicaragua, El Salvador, and Guatemala were especially ripe for such revolutions. President John F. Kennedy launched the Alliance for Progress in 1961 to develop an economically just and democratic Latin America that would not need Castro's type of revolutionary change.

The alliance instead became a cause of the revolutions in Central America during the 1970s and 1980s. It did so because the economic aid that the United States poured into the region during the 1960s went to the oligarchs who controlled the distribution points in the economies. As the wealthy profited, the poor multiplied. Even before his death in November 1963, Kennedy understood that the alliance was not working as he had hoped. It was even polarizing some of the Latin American societies. To maintain stability and give the alliance time to work, Kennedy and his successor, Lyndon B. Johnson, launched a series of military policies.[11]

Increased numbers of Central American troops were trained at U.S. bases in the Panama Canal Zone and in the United States itself. Military aid to these forces roughly doubled during the 1960s. Much of this assistance helped to create counterinsurgency forces that soon preyed on their own people. A policy that aimed to build stability for development too often ended with Guatemalan, Salvadoran, or Nicaraguan officers torturing political suspects for the officers' edification and the perpetuation of their own corruption. In 1963–64 the United States even tried to create a Central American military force (CONDECA) that could act as a unit to provide region-wide order. CONDECA collapsed under the national mistrust that divided Honduran from Salvadoran (the two peoples actually went to war briefly in 1969), Guatemalan from Nicaraguan, and Costa Rican from everyone else.[12]

These new policies nevertheless reintroduced a powerful, direct U.S. military presence for the first time since the early 1930s. In historical perspective the Good Neighbor era from 1930 to the 1950s appears as an aberration. As Washington policymakers used troops to maintain stability in much of Central America before 1933, so they now used force to quiet the growing unrest that ironically stemmed from the Alliance for Progress. By the 1970s, President Richard M. Nixon's Latin American policy depended almost entirely on military aid to regimes controlled by the armed forces. Such an approach worked only sporadically. By the late 1970s three revolutionary movements—in Guatemala, Nicaragua, and El Salvador—grew stronger. At the start of the Alliance for Progress twenty years before, only one small revolutionary group in Guatemala had threatened Central American oligarchs.

President Carter attempted to deal with this new insurgency through a human rights program that he hoped would force the oligarchs to make their systems more humane and, moreover, open up those systems before they were overthrown by revolutions. The president's policy, however, contained a fatal contradiction. The oligarch-military complex ultimately had to rule through terror and oppression; it had no other legitimacy. To force it to cease oppression undermined its own authority. Carter's human rights program consequently undermined the status quo, but he proved unwilling to accept such results. In all of Central America except Costa Rica, leftist forces could take advantage of the oligarch-military weakness to propel themselves into power. No center existed. There was no viable Christian Democratic type of party that could present an alternative to the leftist factions. The centrists either had bases too weak to threaten the two extremes, or, as in El Salvador and Nicaragua, they had been killed, exiled, or otherwise kept from political participation.[13]

Carter's ultimate test came in Nicaragua during mid-1979. As the Somoza dictatorship escalated its oppression, including the bombing of slums where Somoza's National Guard mistakenly believed the Sandinistas were hiding, the president forced the dictator to act more humanely. Somoza's change of tactics, however, opened new opportunities for the revolutionaries who rapidly gained power in early 1979.

Carter then resumed sending some aid to Nicaragua and even tried to work out a hemisphere-wide approach that would block the Sandinistas from obtaining power. He apparently hoped to put elements of the National Guard in control until at least the 1981 elections, but he found no support for such intervention. In July 1979 the Sandinistas ruled Nicaragua.[14]

This brief historical survey is necessary for understanding the Reagan administration's policy since 1981. Its emphasis on military force—the preeminence of Pentagon civilians and National Security Council hard-liners willing to use force unilaterally in place of either negotiations or a multilateral approach to resolving the conflicts—was consistent with the history of U.S. intervention in Central America. With the exception of the Good Neighbor era, Washington officials have used military force to try to maintain stability and protect their nation's interests in the region, regardless of the changing nature of those interests. In this sense the Reagan policy is traditional. The history and the tradition it embodies, however, have not been among the happier pages in the story of U.S. diplomacy. Since 1900, Central American nations have become ever more unstable internally, not happier and more stable. Since 1954 (and in Nicaragua since the appearance of Sandino in 1927) revolutionaries in the region have moved ever leftward, not toward the democratic middle. For at least eight decades the United States has been the most powerful force by far in the area; in some cases (for example, Nicaragua, Honduras, and Costa Rica), the smaller nation developed an almost total dependency on its giant neighbor to the north.

Contrary to the Kissinger Commission's claim, it cannot be argued that the United States has paid too little attention to Central America in the twentieth century. The opposite is the case. Nor can it be argued that the United States has been reluctant to use military force, both overtly and covertly, in the region. Here, too, the opposite is the case. Nor can it be argued that the constant application of force and the integration of the North and Central American economies have benefited either side or bought time so that the Central American oligarchs could make their societies more equitable. Indeed, the opposite has been the case.

These events need to be studied in order to break the historical cycle. An alternative to these eight decades of policy were the Contadora proposals formulated in September 1983 and then agreed to by the five Central American nations in January 1984. Those proposals declared that the signatories would deescalate military fighting, reduce their armed forces, reject foreign military forces or advisers, refrain from intervention in the affairs of other nations, carry out open and fair elections, and commit themselves to equitable economic development. The Contadora principles constituted a wish list, and so-called realists in Washington and elsewhere dismissed these principles as empty, if not dangerously seductive, promises. No one could say that they would not work until they were tried, but trying them required that the most powerful nation, the United States, agree to the principles, especially the points on military deescalation and the removal of foreign military forces.

The Reagan administration, however, refused to work with the Contadora nations. By 1985 the two-track U.S. policy had been effectively narrowed to one—military power—and Langhorne Motley resigned from the State Department. He was replaced by Elliott Abrams, a hard-liner who had no interest in a negotiated settlement in Central America. Abrams continued to control policy in the region even after he lied to a congressional committee about his knowledge of how secret funds were sent to the contras despite Congress's prohibition of such aid. Although Abrams became a pariah on Capitol Hill and his policy failed utterly in Central America, Reagan and Shultz kept him in power until the administration left Washington in January 1989.

The vacuum left by the collapse of Abrams's strategy was filled by a plan pushed through in August 1987 by President Arias of Costa Rica. The Arias plan required the five Central American governments to carry out policies of reconciliation with opposing forces, begin a democratization process at home, prohibit use of their land to insurgent forces fighting in neighboring nations, and stop sending aid to such forces. All five Central American presidents signed it, and subsequently—much to the displeasure of top Reagan officials—Arias won the Nobel Prize for Peace. The United States found itself largely isolated in its Central American policies.[15]

The Arias peace plan, without U.S. support and with historic Central American mistrust often paralyzing any progress, was not yet fully in force when President Reagan left office in early 1989. The plan, however, had helped open some political dialogue between opposing forces in El Salvador, and, of special importance, it had helped lead the U.S. Congress to end all military aid to the contras. Arias personally blamed Washington for not fully cooperating with the peace effort, but he also condemned the Sandinistas for refusing to open Nicaraguan society fully to opposing political parties and views. The plan nearly was destroyed in mid-1988 when the Sandinistas jailed several hundred political opponents and closed down critical radio stations. By late 1988, however, many of the prisoners were released, and the radio stations (as well as opposition newspapers) were functioning, albeit warily.

No one could guarantee that the Arias plan would work. Its multi-lateral approach makes it unwieldy, not to mention highly frustrating for Washington officials who traditionally have acted unilaterally and according to U.S. interests alone in the Central American region. But their determination to follow a single-track military policy alienated allies and caused regional Latin American powers to break away from this policy. If the integration of the economies, the use of military force, and unilateral decision making in Washington have been the three characteristics of U.S. policy toward Central America throughout the twentieth century, then the results of that history should convince the supposed pragmatists and realists who formulate that policy that at least a two-track approach, with the larger and stronger track running through the multilateral approaches represented by the Contadora and Arias plans, should become the history of the future. In this case, war has not proven to be a substitute for state policy.

Notes

1. The Clausewitz quotation and a useful commentary are available in Roger A. Leonard, ed., *A Short Guide to Clausewitz on War* (New York, 1968), esp. 11–14.

2. Quoted in Allan Nairn, "Endgame: A Special Report on the U.S. Military Strategy in Central America," *NACLA Report on the Americas* 18 (May–June 1984): 39.

3. Author's interviews, March 1983 and July 1984; *Washington Post*, March 6, 1983.

4. *Washington Post*, February 25, 1984; Timothy Garton Ash, "A Tale of Two Countries," *Spectator*, March 31, 1984; *Central America Report*, March 30, 1984; *Washington Post*, May 4, 1984.

5. Dennis Gilbert, *Sandinistas: The Party and the Revolution* (New York, 1988), esp. 164–67; *New York Times*, June 11, 1984; Commission on U.S.-Central American Relations, *U.S. Military Intervention in Central America* (Washington, DC, 1984), 4–5, 8–12.

6. *New York Times*, June 14, 1984.

7. This section is taken from the extended discussion of these points in Walter LaFeber, *Inevitable Revolutions: The United States in Central America* (New York, 1983), 209–13, 256–61.

8. *New York Times*, September 4, 1988, has a useful overview by Stephen Kinzer.

9. James Daniel Richardson, ed., *Messages and Papers of the Presidents* (New York, 1897–1914), 16:7375–76; Albert Weinberg, *Manifest Destiny* (Baltimore, 1940), esp. 428–29.

10. There is a fine overview in Lester D. Langley, *The United States and the Caribbean, 1900 to 1970* (Athens, GA, 1980), while Neill Macaulay, *The Sandino Affair* (Chicago, 1967), is the standard account.

11. This argument on the alliance is presented at length in Walter LaFeber, "Inevitable Revolutions," *Atlantic Monthly* 249 (June 1982): 74–83.

12. Don L. Etchison, *The United States and Militarism in Central America* (New York, 1975), esp. 64–67.

13. This argument is derived especially from the work of Sandy Vogelgesang, *American Dream, Global Nightmare* (New York, 1980), notably the sections on El Salvador; and Lars Schoultz, *Human Rights and U.S. Policy toward Latin America* (Princeton, 1981).

14. Richard R. Fagen, "Dateline Nicaragua: The End of the Affair," *Foreign Policy* 36 (Fall 1979): 178–91; Arnold Levinson, "Nicaraguan Showdown," *Inquiry* 22 (June 11 and 25, 1979): 13. Robert Pastor, *Condemned to Repetition* (Princeton, 1987), is an insider's account of the sometimes hilarious, sometimes tragic, mistakes committed by the Carter administration.

15. Roy Gutman, *Banana Diplomacy* (New York, 1988), 324–28.

INDIGENOUS SOURCES OF CONFLICT

The Agrarian Bases of Conflict in Central America

Billie R. DeWalt
and Pedro Bidegaray

The current headlines on Central America have provoked many questions concerning the causes of political upheaval in the region. A revolution has succeeded in Nicaragua, revolutions continue in El Salvador and Guatemala, and Honduras is being turned into an armed camp. Even Costa Rica, the only one of the five Central American republics with a significant democratic tradition, has become embroiled in conflict with its neighbors and has experienced internal unrest.

Presented in this essay are some comparative data on the agrarian systems of Central America. The principal objective is to demonstrate that recent agricultural trends, especially the concentration of land ownership resulting from the growth of the cattle industry, have contributed to the conflicts occurring in Central America. Four major points will be emphasized:

1) that the agricultural sector is extraordinarily important in the economies and to the people of Central America;
2) that the agrarian sector of these societies has historically been marked by an emphasis on export commodities;
3) that the export orientation and associated processes have helped to cause an extremely unequal distribution of land and a lack of employment opportunities in Central America; and
4) that these in turn have had a significant role in creating social, economic, and political instability in the region.

It is difficult to obtain accurate current information on the agricultural sector; therefore, the authors have relied largely on data before 1979, a time that predates the Nicaraguan revolution and the latest outbreak of civil war in El Salvador. As we will see, the agrarian processes described here have developed over a long period of time and are still continuing in several of the republics. In other countries the changes that are now occurring are direct consequences of the current revolutionary ferment in the region.

The percentage of the population directly involved in agriculture is still an important segment in all of the countries. In 1980 it ranged from a low of 29 percent in Costa Rica to a high of 63 percent in Honduras, and was over 50 percent in El Salvador and Guatemala. The percentage contribution of the gross domestic product made by agriculture was also substantial, ranging from a low of 18.5 percent in Costa Rica to a high of 33.5 percent in Nicaragua.[1]

While all of the Central American countries have been devoting substantial efforts to industrialization, agriculture has been an important part of their attempts to finance this industrialization. Throughout Latin America, countries count on the agricultural sector to produce staples to feed their rapidly growing and urbanizing populations. Price policies have generally been structured to keep the costs of basic foodstuffs to a minimum. These policies are presumed to serve the needs of urban dwellers and factory workers. However, these "cheap food" strategies have often served as disincentives to production because it is simply not profitable enough for farmers to cultivate basic staples. As Alain de Janvry has shown, the effect of cheap food policies has been increasingly to reduce small farmers to the margin of existence as they are generally the producers of basic commodities. They continue to try to produce enough for their own subsistence but do not find it worthwhile to try to produce a surplus for the market.[2]

Another way in which agriculture is used to finance industrialization is that a substantial part of the Central American countries' foreign exchange is earned from agricultural exports. In 1978 agricultural products comprised well over 50 percent of the total exports in all of the countries, and almost 70 percent in Guatemala and Honduras. This percentage had increased since 1971 in all of the countries except for El Salvador and Honduras where it had declined slightly.[3] At the same time that the governments of Central America have been implementing cheap food policies, they have generally provided subsidies and credit for the capitalist sector of agriculture to try to stimulate the production of export commodities such as bananas, coffee, sugarcane, beef, and cotton. The goal of such policies is to earn scarce foreign exchange.

Cheap food policies and an emphasis on export agriculture are both based on a belief in comparative advantage, the idea that a country should produce those products for which it is most favorably endowed in terms of natural resources, labor skills, cost advantages, or other factors. The concept of comparative advantage is an essential element of the free trade policies advocated by liberal economists since Adam Smith.[4] As will be seen, these policies have not been kind to Central America.

Export agriculture has been a significant part of Central America's linkage with the world market since it was colonized by the Spanish. In many areas of Central America, cacao was a vital export crop as far back as 1540. Indigo was another early export commodity until it was replaced by synthetic dyes in the middle of the nineteenth century.[5] This was around the time that coffee became important. Bananas and other tropical fruits were added around the turn of the century and have been supplemented in more recent times by cotton, sugarcane, and beef cattle.[6] The region has followed policies designed to make use of its comparative advantage—its tropical location—to export products to the rest of the world.

One major problem for Central America has been that these agricultural exports are extremely vulnerable to boom-and-bust cycles; that is, depending on world demand, prices fluctuate wildly. When demand rises, the prices for agricultural products also rise, giving more individuals in more countries an incentive to plant them. This often results in overproduction that will sometimes cause prices to drop precipitously. Because demand for these products is relatively inelastic (as prices drop, consumption does not rise significantly), low prices continue for several years until supply decreases. Further contributing to the instability of demand is that many of these crops are subject to substitution effects. Just as indigo was replaced by synthetic substitutes, the demand for cotton declined as synthetic fabrics were increasingly used in clothing (a process that began to reverse after the steep rises in oil prices after 1973). High sugar prices several years ago led to the increasing use of corn sweeteners, and the world sugar market has been slack ever since.

These bust cycles reduce the profits of the landowners, leading to three economically rational responses on their part. First, those who can afford to do so attempt to expand their holdings still further so that they maintain their profits by earning smaller margins on greater production. Second, they diversify to spread their risks over a larger number of crops. The expansion into cotton, sugarcane, African palm, melons, beef cattle, and other crops may be seen as part of this strategy.[7]

Finally, they seek to reduce their costs of production, most typically by attempting to reduce labor costs through the use of increased technology, such as machinery or herbicides, or by shifting to less labor-intensive crops.

A good example of such processes comes from southern Honduras. This area is inhospitable. The coastal plain around the Gulf of Fonseca is not extensive. There is a dry season from December until May, and there is usually another extended dry period during the rainy season that makes agriculture risky. During the colonial period, indigo and sugarcane were cultivated in this region and some scrub cattle were raised, but the area was a backwater compared with other regions of Central America. Although some coffee was grown in the south, agrarian capitalism and an emphasis on export agriculture did not penetrate this region until after 1950. After this date, sugarcane, cotton, and especially cattle production for the international trade began to change the region's agrarian systems.[8]

Sugarcane and cotton are both crops that, while cultivated by large landowners, provide significant labor opportunities for the small farmers and landless people. The cane is cut by workers using machetes, while the cotton is picked by hand. During the past several years, however, the world market for both of these commodities has been in a bust cycle. The two large sugarcane mills are in danger of closing because of heavy debts, and cotton cultivation has become more and more unprofitable because production requires increasing amounts of pesticides to control insects. This has caused many farmers to continue a trend—the conversion of their lands to pasture for cattle production—which was begun in the late 1950s and early 1960s. Under current conditions, the main requirement for cattle production is having large extensions of pastureland. The expansion of production thus requires clearing all available land for pasture, and, when possible, purchasing and/or renting more land.

The change in land use patterns is dramatic. Between the 1952 and 1974 agricultural censuses in southern Honduras, the amount of land in pasture increased by 50 percent, reaching over 60 percent of the total land area in 1974. This has occurred in both lowlands and highlands. One of the ways in which the process is facilitated is that many landholders rent forestland to the poor who clear it to produce subsistence crops. Pasture is interplanted with these crops so that after a year or two of cultivation the landholder is left with a permanent pasture. The poor have only the option of attempting to rent the increasingly scarce areas of forestland.[9]

Why are landowners so interested in cattle and pasture? One landowner in southern Honduras explained her reasons. She reported that in the past she had grown cotton. In recent years, with the unpredictability of prices on the world market, the high costs of chemicals, fuel, machinery, and the problems associated with hiring workers, she has decided that the crop is too risky and unprofitable. With just three or four hired hands, she can effectively manage a herd of several hundred cattle. Input costs are lower, and, while prices are still unpredictable, it is common practice to hold on to the animals when prices are too low.[10]

The conversion of land to pasture is going on all over Central America. Land utilization patterns for Honduras and Costa Rica show that only a little over 6 percent of the land in both countries is used for export crops such as bananas, coffee, cotton, and sugarcane. While some may criticize the multinational corporations that control the production and/or marketing of these commodities, at least their production employs a substantial amount of labor. However, at present, over 50 percent of the land in both countries is devoted to pasture for cattle, an export commodity that employs relatively little labor.[11]

The growth of cattle production in the five Central American countries has been phenomenal. Between 1959 and 1979 the number of cattle increased by 80 percent, from 6.9 million to 12.4 million head. While meat production in these countries increased by over 185 percent, consumption has barely increased, and per capita consumption actually declined in Honduras and Costa Rica. The reason is that exports of beef have risen even faster (about 500 percent in the last twenty years) than production.[12] The United States is the biggest consumer of exported beef, using it for hamburger, pet foods, and other processed meats.

The effects of turning Central America into a large cattle ranch are profound. Many people have noted the ecological costs, especially the destruction of forests as more and more land is cleared for pasture. In addition, as small farmers and agricultural laborers are displaced from good lands, they are forced into using marginal, often steep-sloped lands in order to produce their subsistence crops. Increased soil erosion is the result. There are no nutritional benefits for the majority of local people; in fact, cattle are competing with poor people for scarce land and food. The pastures to feed cattle replace land that people could use to feed themselves. There are no employment benefits; the main reason for the expansion of cattle production is precisely because so little labor is required. Finally, because cattle production requires extensive amounts of land, larger landholders continue to expand their holdings, thus exacerbating inequalities in access to land.[13]

The result of the concentration on export agriculture, especially beef, is that these Central American agrarian systems are now plagued by the dual problems of extreme inequalities of land distribution and decreasing employment opportunities.

Table 1 indicates the concentration of landholdings that existed in Central America before the Nicaraguan revolution. Although in several cases agricultural censuses have not been carried out for many years and the data are now quite old, in most countries land concentration is growing rather than declining.[14] A small percentage of the landholders has had control over a large part of the land, while the majority of

Table 1. Concentration of Agricultural Landholdings in Central America

Country	Percentage of Landholders	Percentage of Land Controlled
NICARAGUA (1963)[a]		
< 5 hectares	50.8%	3.5%
>100 hectares	5.0	58.8
EL SALVADOR (1971)[a]		
< 5 hectares	86.9	19.6
>100 hectares	.7	38.9
GUATEMALA (1970)[b] (estimates)		
< 4 hectares	83.3	12.3
>350 hectares	.5	42.4
HONDURAS (1974)[c]		
< 5 hectares	63.8	1.8
>100 hectares	9.1	44.1
COSTA RICA (1973)[d]		
< 4.76 hectares	35.0	1.5
>100 hectares	8.4	67.0

[a]J. W. Wilkie and S. Haber, eds., *Statistical Abstract of Latin America*, vol. 22 (Los Angeles, 1983).

[b]World Bank, *Guatemala: Economic and Social Position and Prospects* (Washington, DC, 1978). While these are estimated figures, they generally agree with the data from the 1964 agricultural census, presented in Wilkie and Haber, *Statistical Abstract of Latin America*.

[c]*Censo Nacional Agropecuario 1974, Tomo II, Tenencia de la Tierra* (Tegucigalpa, 1978).

[d]These data were computed from Table 11 of Mitchell A. Seligson, *Peasants of Costa Rica and the Development of Agrarian Capitalism* (Madison, WI, 1980). The data in Seligson's table were originally expressed in terms of *manzanas*, a unit of land that is equivalent to .69 hectare. For this reason I have used lands that are under 4.76 hectares for my comparison.

landholders has had access only to small plots. For example, at the time of the last census in El Salvador only .7 percent of the population controlled almost 39 percent of the land. Meanwhile, almost 87 percent of the landholders were owners of plots of less than five hectares that comprised only 19.6 percent of the cultivated land. In addition, almost 41 percent of the population was completely landless.[15]

A similar pattern prevailed in Nicaragua until the Sandinista revolution. Anastasio Somoza's family owned one half of all the farms over five hundred hectares and controlled about one quarter of all industry. This concentration of land and wealth, and the corruption and abuse of power that went along with it, was one of the principal reasons why so many segments of the populace united to overthrow his regime.[16] The data for the other Central American countries are similar. Guatemala, Honduras, and Costa Rica also have been characterized by an extremely skewed distribution of landholdings.

The revolution that took place in Nicaragua and those in process in El Salvador and Guatemala have roots that go beyond the agrarian issue. Yet the inequalities in the agrarian system are among the most critical stimuli to revolution. One of the rallying cries of the Sandinista revolution was "land for whoever works it!" and agrarian reform is still a major issue there.

Although a proposal of agrarian reform set in motion the CIA-directed coup that toppled the democratically elected government of Jacobo Arbenz in Guatemala in 1954, the U.S. government apparently perceives the necessity of agrarian reform.[17] To try to correct some of the gross inequalities in Central America and to take some of the pressure off friendly regimes, the United States has been providing funds for agrarian reform efforts. This is being attempted in El Salvador despite right-wing opposition, which has extended to the murder of two U.S. government advisers and the head of the Salvadoran Institute of Agrarian Transformation in January 1981. Even in Costa Rica, which thus far has remained an island of democracy in a sea of military dictatorships, agrarian reform has been promoted with the assistance of the U.S. government. As Mitchell A. Seligson has said, "land reform is seen as an imperative for the future stability of the Costa Rican countryside."[18]

The reason why land reform is so crucial is that jobs are not being created in the industrial sector fast enough to absorb either the increasing population or the people who are being pushed out of the rural areas. This is because the process of industrialization in Central America has followed a path similar to that of agriculture, emphasizing capital-intensive rather than labor-intensive development. As Harley

Browning and Bryan Roberts have shown for Latin America as a whole, the percentage of the population employed in industry barely increased, from 18.6 percent in 1950 to only 21.2 percent in 1979.[19] Table 2 demonstrates the same trend for the Central American countries. The percentage of the population engaged in agriculture is declining, and the industrial sector has not expanded at nearly the same rate. In the past twenty years, the percentage of the population in agriculture has dropped as little as 7 percent in Honduras and as much as 22 percent in Costa Rica. The percentage employed in industry in the five countries has increased only between 4 and 7 percent. As a result, the rural landless and the small farmer are caught in a squeeze. They are increasingly pushed out of the countryside into the urban areas in which few decent jobs await them. There they either join the ranks of the unemployed or, more typically, become engaged in the informal service sector of the economy as shoeshine boys, servants, or street vendors. This has been the true sector of growth in Central American economies, especially in Nicaragua and Costa Rica.

Table 2. Percentage Change in the Distribution of the Labor Force in Central America[a]

| | Agriculture | | Industry | | Services | |
	1960	1980	1960	1980	1960	1980
Honduras	70%	63%	11%	15%	19%	23%
El Salvador	62	50	17	22	21	27
Nicaragua	62	43	16	20	22	37
Guatemala	67	55	14	21	19	25
Costa Rica	51	29	19	23	30	48

[a]World Bank, *World Development Report, 1983* (New York, 1983), pp. 188–89.

Since 1979 there have been attempts in both Nicaragua and El Salvador to implement meaningful agrarian reform.[20] In both countries, land has been expropriated from large private holdings in order to distribute it to individual peasants or to cooperatives. This redistribution has been an attempt to respond to the social and political pressure that the landless rural population has been exerting for the past several decades. While it is too early to pass judgment on the relative success or failure of these agrarian reform programs, it is enlightening to compare the experience of these two countries in the initial stages of these programs. This is especially so because the reform in Nicaragua has been undertaken by a regime that came to power as a result of revolution, while the reform in El Salvador has occurred, with U.S. support, as an attempt to undermine the revolutionaries struggling to overthrow the government.

Expropriation and redistribution of land often has been used as a policy partially to alleviate striking inequalities such as those discussed earlier. In addition, agrarian reform efforts have been utilized to address problems of unemployment and poor development of the internal market. The thought is that, through the distribution of land, credit, and technological development, the beneficiaries will become integrated quickly into the productive sphere and increase their purchasing power, thus helping to stimulate national growth through their own production and their ability to consume goods produced in other sectors of the economy. However, using land reform to redress problems of inequality and to stimulate national production can lead to significant political conflicts within the society.

Nola Reinhardt has argued that, although El Salvador and Nicaragua promoted land redistribution under different political circumstances, the initial similarities between the two programs were striking. Policymakers in both countries limited the scope of land expropriation because of considerations having to do with larger economic policy. Both El Salvador and Nicaragua have been faced throughout the 1980s with trying to rebuild economies battered by the world recession and the effects of continuing civil war. The need for generating foreign exchange to make possible economic reconstruction meant that neither country wanted to affect agricultural production for export significantly.[21]

Under these circumstances, government officials were very reluctant to impede or hinder producers of export commodities. In Nicaragua, for example, the government initially concentrated its expropriation efforts on holdings that belonged to the Somoza family and its allies, leaving unaffected individual landholdings that were producing "efficiently." In fact, the Managua government did not set any policy for the maximum allowable size of landholdings until 1985, when increasing popular pressure forced functionaries to widen their expropriation efforts to benefit a larger number of peasant families. During the period from 1979 to 1984 the state attempted to preserve the rights of capitalistic producers who were perceived as potential generators of state income. In El Salvador, the maximum amount of land any individual producer was supposed to own was limited to 500 hectares.[22] The objective was to preserve the medium-sized holdings thought to constitute the heart of the agroexport sector in the country.[23] Thus, in both cases, the social benefits of land reform were in conflict with, and were largely subordinated to, economic considerations.

Working with these somewhat conflicting goals, the Nicaraguan government by the end of 1984 had distributed 44 percent of the total farmland in the country while benefiting 43 percent of the total number of rural families estimated to be eligible to receive land. The proportion of land held by large private estates of more than 100 hectares had dropped from 58.8 percent in 1963 to 11 percent in 1985. The Salvadoran state had affected 22 percent of the total agricultural land, and this was to be distributed among 94,383 families who represented 22 percent of the total number of peasant households in the country.[24] In both cases the results of agrarian reform fell short of the goals originally established. This was particularly true for the Salvadoran reform, which originally was set to benefit 60 percent of the total number of rural families.

The evidence also suggests that land reform in El Salvador faces a much more uncertain future than it does in Nicaragua. Opposition from the powerful right wing in El Salvador has controlled the legislative body, effectively annulling Phase Two of the reform. This second step had proposed to affect all private holdings that exceeded 250 hectares, which could have benefited another 35 percent of the rural population. At the same time, conservative legislators approved the cutoff of the "land to the tiller" program through which sharecroppers and other tenants could claim ownership of parcels they had been working for several years. This program had been enthusiastically supported by the U.S. government. Conservatives, through their control of the Ministry of Agriculture and the support of the military, have continued a policy of political repression and hostility that threatens the effectiveness of the land reform.[25]

The outcome in Nicaragua has been quite different. Because of its origins as a revolutionary government, the state has had to be more responsive to the pressures and complaints of peasant organizations and other peasant producers not satisfied with the initial results of the land reform. As Brockett suggests, by 1985 peasant support for the Sandinista government had started to weaken.[26] Thousands of rural families were still landless, especially in the Pacific region where most of the land had remained in large export states. Managua's response to continuing unrest translated into changes in its agrarian policy. The government's attempts to form cooperatives were reduced, individual ownership was emphasized, the maximum size of private estates free from expropriation was reduced to 85 acres, and the pace of titling was accelerated.[27]

These two different governmental responses to the demands of the rural poor illustrate how programs that are conceived under varying social conditions will conflict sooner or later with the economic and political structure of the country. While both Nicaragua and El Salvador sought to implement land reforms to address social goals, both sought to do so while preserving economic efficiency. In the case of El Salvador, the scope and benefits of these reforms have faltered because of the lack of social support for them and the lack of political commitment by the government. Land distribution in this country has been used exclusively as a social remedy to address problems of unrest in the rural areas rather than as an economic project that could turn the reformed sector into a productive alternative for El Salvador. The fact that the government is continuing to try to preserve the medium-sized agroexport holdings demonstrates the power still held by that sector over policymakers. The state thus has less commitment to the agrarian reform process.

On the other hand, while Nicaragua acted similarly in the first years of the Sandinista revolution, its popular origin required officials to adopt a more flexible attitude to respond to the changing social situation in the country. These officials had to introduce changes in their agrarian policy because their political support was strongly linked to the peasant sector of the population.

With the exception of the recent agrarian reform efforts, the agrarian processes described here have created greater numbers of underemployed urban poor and continue to exacerbate the already glaring inequalities existing in these countries. The agrarian problems of Central America suggest that hundreds of millions of dollars of military assistance, the training of thousands of troops, and the presence and even participation of U.S. troops are not likely to quell for long the revolutionary fires burning in the region.

Much more fundamental social and economic reforms are needed to provide a permanent solution. These include meaningful agrarian reform; price policies that are not antithetical to the production of basic grains; improved distribution of services such as health, education, and water and sanitation; more widespread participation in government and planning; and elimination of corruption and abuse of power. Without such reforms first, economic assistance is only likely to worsen the problem. Walter LaFeber has argued that one of the effects of the immensely popular Alliance for Progress during the Kennedy administration was to make revolutions inevitable. The alliance did result in unprecedented economic growth rates in Latin America, but the growth occurred along the lines of capital-intensive strategies, thus creating fewer jobs for the poor who were and still are the most needy beneficiaries. In addition, the economic benefits were largely usurped by the oligarchs who controlled banks and mercantile businesses. Consequently, economic growth created greater inequality and fed revolutionary sentiment.[28]

Given the prevailing conditions in the Central American republics to which assistance might flow, there is a strong likelihood that money would not help. Those funds most probably would go into developing capital-intensive industries and into expanding export agriculture. For the agricultural sector, this is liable to continue to engender the concentration of landholdings and the investment in commodities and technologies that minimize labor costs. These developments have a greater likelihood of further lining the pockets of the rich and ignoring the fundamental needs of the poor for land and/or jobs with which to earn a decent living.

Notes

1. The percentages of the population involved in agriculture in 1980 may be found in Table 2. Percentages for the contribution of agriculture to the gross domestic product were 18.5 in Costa Rica, 27.5 in El Salvador, 28.3 in Honduras, 28.4 in Guatemala, and 33.5 in Nicaragua. These data may be found in J. W. Wilkie and S. Haber, eds., *Statistical Abstract of Latin America*, vol. 22 (Los Angeles, 1983), 291, 293–95.

2. Alain de Janvry, *The Agrarian Question and Reformism in Latin America* (Baltimore, 1981), 157–73.

3. The actual percentages of exports contributed by agriculture for 1978 were 53.4 for El Salvador, 58.1 for Costa Rica, 58.9 for Nicaragua, 68.2 for Honduras, and 68.9 for Guatemala. See Wilkie and Haber, *Statistical Abstract of Latin America*, 402, 406–7, 409, 411.

4. See Joan Robinson, *Aspects of Development and Underdevelopment* (Cambridge, MA, 1979), 102–3. In her critique of free trade and comparative advantage, Robinson notes that this idea is dependent upon two assumptions, neither of which holds in the modern world. First, the argument is made in terms of comparisons of static equilibrium conditions in which each trading nation is characterized by full employment of resources and balanced payments. Second, because all countries are treated as having the same level of development, unequal exchange is not part of the model.

5. Murdo MacLeod, *Spanish Central America: A Socioeconomic History, 1520–1720* (Berkeley, 1973). This is an excellent source for the early history of agricultural exports in Central America.

6. A very good general reference, particularly on the importance of coffee and bananas in Central American history, is Ralph Woodward, *Central America: A Nation Divided* (New York, 1976), esp. 149–202. More in-depth accounts of the significance of agricultural export commodities may be found in Tommie Sue Montgomery,

Revolution in El Salvador: Origins and Evolution (Boulder, CO, 1982), esp. 34–46; John A. Booth, *The End and the Beginning: The Nicaraguan Revolution* (Boulder, CO, 1982), esp. 20–26; Mitchell A. Seligson, *Peasants of Costa Rica and the Development of Agrarian Capitalism* (Madison, WI, 1980), esp. 14–72; Jefferson C. Boyer, *Agrarian Capitalism and Peasant Praxis in Southern Honduras* (Ann Arbor, MI, 1983), esp. 62–95; and Richard N. Adams, *Crucifixion by Power: Essays on Guatemalan Social Structure, 1944–1966* (Austin, TX, 1970), esp. 353–79.

7. See Montgomery, *Origins and Evolution*, 45, for an account of this in El Salvador in the 1920s.

8. See Boyer, *Agrarian Capitalism*, 59–61; Billie R. DeWalt and Kathleen M. DeWalt, *Farming Systems Research in Southern Honduras*, Report No. 1, Department of Sociology, University of Kentucky, Lexington; and Billie R. DeWalt, "The Cattle Are Eating the Forest," *Bulletin of the Atomic Scientists* 39 (1983): 18–23.

9. See DeWalt, "The Cattle Are Eating the Forest," 20–21.

10. Although this landowner did not mention it, another advantage of cattle is that they are quite maneuverable. Estimates are that 200,000 head of Nicaragua's cattle were smuggled out of the country into Honduras between the beginning of the revolution and mid-1981 (see Joseph Collins, *What Difference Could a Revolution Make?* [San Francisco, 1982], 45). It is also common for Hondurans to smuggle their cattle into El Salvador or Guatemala where prices are higher.

11. These data were obtained from the following sources: for Costa Rica, unpublished accounts from Proyecto de Información Agropecuario del Istmo Centroamericano, Instituto Interamericano de Cooperación para la Agricultura, San José, Costa Rica; and for Honduras, compiled from various volumes of the Censo Nacional Agropecuario, Dirección General de Estadistica y Censos, Republica de Honduras, Tegucigalpa, 1977 and 1978.

12. Between 1959 and 1979 the number of cattle increased by 44.4 percent in El Salvador, 60 percent in Nicaragua, 69.2 percent in Honduras, 100 percent in Costa Rica, and 125 percent in Guatemala. These data are reported in Billie R. DeWalt, "Microcosmic and Macrocosmic Processes of Agrarian Change in Southern Honduras," in Billie R. DeWalt and Pertti J. Pelto, eds., *Microlevel/Macrolevel Linkages in Anthropological Theory and Research* (Boulder, CO, 1985). These percentages are derived from data presented in several U.S. Department of Agriculture foreign circulars entitled "Livestock and Meat" and published between 1959 and 1983.

13. Other discussions of these processes may be found in Douglas Shane, *Hoofprints of the Forest: An Inquiry into the Beef Cattle Industry in the Tropical Forest Areas of Latin America* (Washington, DC, 1980); James Nations and Daniel Komer, "Indians, Immigrants and Beef Exports: Deforestation in Central America," *Cultural Survival Quarterly* 6 (1982): 8–12; Seligson, *Peasants of Costa Rica*, 164; and DeWalt, "The Cattle Are Eating the Forest."

14. For Costa Rica see Seligson, *Peasants of Costa Rica*, 148; for Honduras see Boyer, *Agrarian Capitalism*, 85–96; and for El Salvador see Martin Diskin, "Land Reform in El Salvador: An Evaluation," *Culture and Agriculture* 13 (1981): 1–7.

15. Diskin, "Land Reform in El Salvador," 1.

16. It is interesting to note that in the United States there is a similar pattern of landownership, with about 1 percent of the owners controlling 40 percent of the land. Over 78 percent of the landholders have access to only about 3 percent of the land. The major difference is that in this country there are many more alternative employment possibilities for those who do not have access to land. See Ann Mariano, "A Homesite Is a Lot," *Washington Post National Weekly Edition*, February 13, 1984, 21.

17. On Mexico's continuing agrarian problems see Gustavo Esteva, *The Struggle for Rural Mexico* (South Hadley, MA, 1983); on Nicaragua see Collins, *What Difference Could a Revolution Make?* 79; and on Guatemala see Stephen Schlesinger and Stephen Kinzer, *Bitter Fruit: The Untold Story of the American Coup in Guatemala* (Garden City, NY, 1982), 75–77.

18. Seligson, *Peasants of Costa Rica*, 123.

19. Harley Browning and Bryan Roberts, "Urbanization, Sectoral Transformation, and the Utilization of Labor in Latin America," *Comparative Urban Research* 8 (1980): 86–103.

20. Charles D. Brockett, *Land, Power and Poverty: Agrarian Transformation and Political Conflict in Central America* (Boston, 1988), 7; Carmen Diana Deere, "A Comparative Analysis of Agrarian Reform in El Salvador and Nicaragua, 1979–1981," *Development and Change* 13 (1982): 1–43; Nola Reinhardt, "Agro-Exports and the Peasantry in the Agrarian Reforms of El Salvador and Nicaragua," *World Development* 15 (1987): 941–60.

21. Reinhardt, "Agro-Exports and the Peasantry," 956.

22. Deere, "Agrarian Reform in El Salvador and Nicaragua," 11.

23. Reinhardt, "Agro-Exports and the Peasantry," 953.

24. Ibid., 947.

25. Brockett, *Land, Power and Poverty*, 159.

26. Ibid., 172.

27. Ibid., 173.

28. Walter LaFeber, *Inevitable Revolutions: The United States in Central America* (New York, 1983), 148–55.

The Consequences of Excluding Reformists from Power: The View from 1990

Kenneth M. Coleman

As one looks at Central America after the first eighteen months of the Bush presidency, six different political systems appear to have responded to similar social and economic problems in strikingly different fashions over the twentieth century. In Nicaragua, revolutionaries governed from July 19, 1979, through April 25, 1990, at which point they ceded power in response to an electoral loss. Under pressure from counterrevolutionaries armed by the United States, from Costa Rica's pacifist President Oscar Arias, and from domestic opposition, Nicaragua's revolutionary party—the Frente Sandinista de Liberación Nacional (FSLN)—increasingly transformed the new state into a competitive polity. By late 1989 the "revolutionary" political economy appeared only marginally more socialist than other Latin American societies and considerably more pluralist, with seventeen political parties registered to compete in the February 1990 elections.[1] The election of Violeta Chamorro, a one-time ally of the Sandinistas, as president on the ticket of UNO, a fourteen-party anti-Sandinista coalition, may well have solidified the transition to a competitive party system.

In El Salvador, revolution via insurrection also was tried in the 1980s. The attempt neither succeeded nor failed, and a protracted stalemate ensued. The most recent rebel offensive came in November 1989, striking into previously exempt upper-class neighborhoods in the capital city and leading to death squad reprisals against six Jesuit intellectuals who administered the Universidad Centroamericana.[2] Yet the rebels have neither the popular support nor the military strength to overcome nominally civilian governments armed heavily by the United States. As 1990 wore on, negotiations resumed between the stalemated parties.

In Guatemala, another seemingly "civilian" government came to power through elections greeted with genuine popular enthusiasm in late 1985. But Christian Democratic President Vinicio Cerezo was unable to end polarization; attempts to overthrow him came from right-wing elements fearful of his flirtation with land reform, yet Cerezo himself was largely a captive of the military right. Death squad activity never disappeared during his tenure; consequently, guerrilla opposition refused to disband. Late in the Cerezo presidency, Guatemala remains deeply divided, riven with violence, and a human rights embarrassment to its patrons in Washington.[3]

In Honduras, "civilian" governments come and go while the military and citizens fret over the cost to national sovereignty of the continued presence of Nicaraguan contras in southern Honduras. Neither insurrection nor extensive death squad activity exists. But Honduras is Central America's poorest country, and little progress in addressing its grinding poverty seems to have been made.[4]

In Costa Rica, a close approximation to representative democracy exists. President Arias assumed a peacekeeping vocation, which led to a two-year interlude (August 1987–November 1989) in which his Central American Peace Initiative produced a dramatic lessening of armed conflict, if not a total suspension. Arias's achievement was marred, however, by the inability to produce much compromise in Guatemala, by the momentary resumption of hostilities in El Salvador in late 1989, and by allegations of violations of civil liberties in Costa Rica itself.[5]

Panama proved to be the last holdout for overt military rule, as the reformist leadership of General Omar Torrijos degenerated after his death in 1981 into a "narco-military" regime. But this rule came to an end in 1989. Taunted by strongman Manuel Antonio Noriega, and seemingly unable to count on dissidents in the Panamanian military to overthrow him, President George Bush dispatched twenty-four thousand troops to Panama on December 21, 1989. The U.S. invasion force quickly deposed General Noriega, taking him into custody for trial on drug-trafficking charges, and installed the coalition government of Guillermo Endara, who was seemingly on the way to election on May 7, 1989, when Noriega suspended the electoral process. Panama's political opposition of the late 1980s, now the government, was focused on the attainment of electoral accountability and political liberties. Just how those conditions, once attained, will be used to pursue a vision of the "new" Panama remains to be seen.[6] Unity in opposition to General Noriega may not translate easily into programmatic unity on how to develop the country. Conflicts between conventionalist and reformist visions of change may occur even among civilian leaders.

After a tumultuous decade in which the United States reasserted its role as the hegemonic power in Central America and defined the outer limits of acceptable behavior by using force to punish so-called miscreants, it is tempting to see politics in the region as externally determined. Yet it can be argued that the essential character of Central American political systems is defined locally as a result of long-term political processes.

I have argued previously that there is a correlation between political history and the degree to which revolutionary struggle has advanced (see Table 1). The greater the extent to which reformist elements were excluded from power in the first seventy-five years of this century, the more likely that revolutionary struggle would succeed in the last quarter century. The other side of this equation is that the more important the role that reform elements have played in the political process, the more likely the revolutionaries will be seen as irrelevant. There is truth to the assertion, made nearly thirty years ago by John F. Kennedy, that those who make peaceful change impossible in Latin America will make violent change inevitable.

Let us consider for a moment the worldview of those individuals whom I have called reformists and contrast their orientation with two alternative outlooks commonly found in Central America. To do so, I will borrow from the terminology of Charles Anderson, who distinguishes between what he calls the conventional strategists of development, or reform strategists, and the revolutionary strategists.[7] Each of these is an abstract model that can serve as a benchmark for comparison.

The conventionalists assume that development consists of the elaboration of an existing modern sector of "still imperfectly modernized" economies. They acknowledge that there is a distinction between the capital-intensive, skilled manpower-employing sector of the economy and a sector seen as traditional, labor intensive, and premodern. It is typically assumed that the fruits of growth will eventually reach the premodern community if only the existing modern sector were allowed to expand. For the conventionalist, as Anderson puts it,

Table 1. Relationship between Extent of "Revolutionary Success" in 1990 and Historical Tendency toward Exclusion of Reformists from Power

	Low ——————— Exclusion ——————— High					
HIGH DEGREE OF "REVOLUTIONARY SUCCESS"						
Revolutionaries capture power & govern at length	—	—	—	—	—	Nicaragua
Revolutionaries control territory; can wage fixed battles with national army	—	—	—	—	El Salvador	—
Revolutionaries can disrupt economic and governmental operations but do not control territory and avoid fixed battles	—	—	—	Guatemala	—	—
Occasional revolutionary skirmishes or terrorist acts; no sustained revolutionary activity	—	—	Honduras	—	—	—
No serious revolutionary threat	Costa Rica	Panama	—	—	—	—
LOW DEGREE OF "REVOLUTIONARY SUCCESS"	—	—	—	—	—	—
Reformists define the state	Reformists define the state	Civilian government (1990–), following strong military reformism (1960–81) and U.S. intervention (1989)	Civilian government (1981–), following weak military reformism (1971–74)	Lengthy reform era (1944–54) followed by systemic exclusion; civilian president unable to control military (1985–90)	Brief periods of modest reform followed by exclusion of reformists	Systemic exclusion of reformists from power until triumph of the revolution (1979); revolutionaries govern (1979–90) and move to opposition role as a major political force (40% support)

Capital and technology are the twin keys to the processes of growth. The greatest obstacles to development lie in the inadequacy of investable savings and the fund of technical know-how. Those who hold or could make available such resources must be protected and encouraged.

The role of public policy, for the conventional strategist of development, is to support, stimulate, and protect industry, commerce and market agriculture. . . . Government is to establish a climate propitious for further investment and to provide appropriate . . . services within the modern sector. However, government need not self-consciously concern itself with bringing change to the community defined as premodern. Gradually, the fruits of productivity will "filter down."[8]

Clearly, industrialists, financiers, and agriculturalists in a position to expand because they are creditworthy are among those who stand to profit from such a vision. So are individuals fortunate enough to be employed in an expanding modern sector, including a sizable number of middle-class managers, white-collar employees such as bank tellers, and factory workers in industries large enough to be unionized. Many, however, are excluded from the short-term benefits in this vision of change. The article by Billie DeWalt and Pedro Bidegaray in this volume suggests those whose interests are left out.[9]

In most of Central America, those excluded by the conventional vision of economic transformation as short-term beneficiaries would have to include: 1) the vast numbers of descendants of indigenous communal landholders, whose property historically was gobbled up through reallocations of land by the state to those who promised to become export commodity producers;[10] and 2) those landless peasants today who are driven onto poorer and poorer land by the expansion of the cattle industry, or by other export commodities. These people have lacked political power and have been excluded from the process by which public policy was determined. No one has been forced to listen to those made landless by such policy over the past century. Nor, where the conventionalists have dominated the making of public policy, has there been an attempt to seek out the opinions of the landless. Anderson again suggests the reasons why:

In formulating an approach to that part of the society whose demands are largely uncommunicated to decision-makers, the upholders of the conventional approach usually assume a compatibility between the interests and assumptions of the "invisible sector" and their own. The interest of the "silent individual" is in improving his standard of living. He would live and act as an effective consumer and producer within a modern economic context. He will understand that he can achieve this goal only by the linkage of his own efforts with the gradual extension of the productive capacity of the existing modern sector, *unless he is "misled" by irresponsible agitators who would use the accumulated savings of society not as the wherewithal of productivity, but as a juicy plum to be distributed to their own advantage.* Prosperity must gradually filter down.[11]

Such is the political and economic vision of the conventionalist: no extraordinary efforts must be undertaken by governments on behalf of the landless, the urban poor employed in the service sector, or other economically marginal groups. This vision is that the rich serve the poor best by putting their resources to work in investments. Such investments eventually will work to the benefit of the poor through the diffusion effect implicit in economic growth, which is never bad for anyone and can be produced only by allowing the rich to do what they do best: invest. Those who argue otherwise are demagogues who would squander national resources. Indeed, in some variants of the argument, the demagogues may well be Communists. Such is the logic of those conventionalists not inclined to make subtle distinctions, a genus we shall encounter in our discussions of El Salvador, post-1954 Guatemala, and Anastasio Somoza's Nicaragua. Not all conventionalists are Red-baiters, to be sure; indeed, the vast majority are not. Nonetheless, the politics of at least three Central American states have been structured tragically by such political extensions of a vision of economic change, political inferences that have led to massive violations of basic human rights.

The next group, the reformists, are individuals preoccupied with the discrepancy between the existing modern sector and the traditional sectors. They do not believe that such discrepancies will disappear automatically with the diffusion of modernity. Indeed, reformists see some of the features of economic progress as tending to generate or exacerbate existing inequalities. Yet, they also see hope, if economic change could be guided by public authorities in the proper direction. Anderson puts it this way:

The fundamental problem for the reformer is the poverty of the greater part of the nation, the glaring contrast between the standard of living of the modern sector and the rest of the society. . . . The democratic reformer would "incorporate" those heretofore only marginally affected by the modern political economy "into the life of the nation."[12] This approach to economic change is not so much one of specifying the critical factors in the development process (such as lack of capital and technical know-how that the conventionalists specify). It is rather one of seeking the *terms of compatibility* of the various interests and demands in society under the general rubric of development. The style is essentially *aggregative.* There is a faith that *all* sectors of society have a role to play in the development

effort. . . . Even those groups that have been most reticent . . . have a part
to play in the process of change. . . . From his point of view, he would
save the recalcitrant from the disaster of revolution which would befall
them if change were not wrought; save them, to some extent, in spite of
themselves.[13]

In essence, the reformer seeks a process not of diffusion but of sequential change. He begins by inducing one segment of society to undertake
a change that may be only partially desired. Then, after that first
change, other segments of society may be persuaded, often reluctantly,
to make sacrifices for the long-term collective good of society. The
reformer runs the risk of displeasing most people over time but tries to
induce those who are somewhat myopic to make the changes necessary
to permit everyone to benefit eventually.[14] These changes often involve
redistribution of resources and privilege downward toward the poorest
elements in society. Certain expenditures by the government, which
conventionalists would define as uneconomic and inefficient, are essential to the reformists' vision of change. These reformers hope that
the initial reluctance and displeasure of the privileged can be overcome
in time, as the wider, long-term benefits of reform become apparent to
those who first opposed change.

The economic argument of reformers is that growth can be sustained
only when greater purchasing power is put in the hands of the poor so
that the effective national market increases. The reformist judges that a
very sizable portion of the potential market, often up to 50 to 60
percent, cannot afford the consumer-durable purchases that could
stimulate national industrialization. State action to enlarge the effective
market is required. That implies instituting social welfare and public
works programs, providing credit to small producers, and creating
other activities to be paid for by taxing the rich at a higher rate.
Sometimes the reformist even dares to address the question of property
ownership, pursuing land reforms that take over acreage not in production
or that over a maximum size, often set at the level of 500 hectares
(1,235 acres). Not surprisingly, therefore, the reformist can generate
intense hostility in his efforts to induce the recalcitrant propertied to go
along with schemes for change that the propertied, as natural conventionalists, are not inclined to accept.

The revolutionary shares the preoccupation of the reformist with
the discrepancy between the modern and traditional sectors, but he
differs in two crucial ways. First, he rejects the assumption of the
reformist that a process of sequential change can be identified that will
lead to developmental outcomes, believing instead that a set of dis-
junctive, simultaneous changes is necessary for bona fide development

to occur. The assumption is that the existing social structure is exploitative; that it functions to concentrate land, income, and opportunity upward; and that, for the poor, existing structures are harmful and cannot be otherwise. The revolutionary is inclined to the belief that sequential changes are piecemeal and inadequate; what is needed is a coordinated effort to break through structures of economic and political interaction that oppress human beings.

Second, the revolutionary denies that all elements in society can be induced to participate in activities leading to the common good. Much like the philosophical conservative, the revolutionary has a rather pessimistic assessment of human nature, or at least of human nature under capitalism. The reformist believes that all segments of society can be made to contribute to the developmental effort, while the revolutionary thinks that local capitalists will always subvert modest sequential reforms, if only because of their contacts with outside agents of world capitalism who can intervene to defend property. Therefore, in order to make real progress, political leaders need to break through the limits imposed on national development by local capitalists. The relationships of the nation with the world of external capitalism must be restructured. If this involves incurring the wrath of the capitalist powers, so be it. The revolutionary would look at the development of the cattle industry in Central America and would say:

> Look, it is no accident that such a pattern has emerged. The capitalists will obviously follow the logic of capital accumulation. They will never willingly alter their behavior to accommodate the interests of the poor peasants, whom they exploit as renters to clear pastureland, then whom they cast off their land. Those who attempt a piecemeal reform, such as that of limiting landholdings, or reorienting credit or water toward the poor, will probably provoke violence against the intended beneficiaries, who are not in a position to defend themselves. And if the reformists succeed in the short run, they will induce the propertied to launch an international campaign to oppose their reforms, summoning up a frenzy among the metropolitan capitalist powers, principally the United States. Hence, why bother with piecemeal reform? What you need is *una ruptura*.

Thus, quite the opposite of the conventionalist, the revolutionary sees the modern sector of the economy as the source of the problem rather than as a potential solution. Political compromise between revolutionaries and conventionalists is most difficult since they see the world in such totally different terms.

This compromise can occur, however, if the reformist center comes to play a major political role. Indeed, the probability of political compromise is determined by the size and impact of reform-oriented groups.

Since only reformists seek a role for everyone in the development policymaking process, their role as brokers is essential to the process of forging political agreement. Conventionalists would exclude revolutionaries, and revolutionaries, if successful, would exclude at least some conventionally oriented capitalists. Only reformists entertain the belief that the assets of the rich can and should be employed in the short term to improve the lives of the poor. For different reasons, both the left and the right reject that argument.

Turning to specific cases at opposite ends of the spectrum, first let us examine Costa Rica where the reformist vision has reigned since 1940.[15] In contrast to other Central American states, Costa Rica witnessed the development very early in the postindependence era of a class of small freeholding yeoman farmers, resembling somewhat those of the United States. In both cases the emergence of the yeoman farmer resulted from the inability of indigenous peoples to offer resistance. Eventually, Costa Rica experienced an upward concentration of land since it was unable to resist the seductive siren of export agriculture.[16]

However, Costa Rica started from a different base of land tenure, one that was fundamentally more equal at the time when independence was achieved. While rural landlessness became a social problem that occasioned divisiveness within the country, this divisiveness was more manageable. In the 1940s, first under President Rafael Calderón Guardia, then later under President José (Pepe) Figueres, a series of reformist governments has ruled Costa Rica, motivated by the social democratic vision claimed for itself by the Partido de Liberación Nacional (PLN), the party of Figueres.[17] With an electoral process more respectable than others in Central America, the PLN forces established after 1949 a system of meaningful electoral competition in which the incumbents, including the PLN, are frequently voted out of office only to return later. There is, however, a broad consensus on the outline of public policy and on the need for an activist state that seeks to mitigate social conflict by mildly distributive activity. That consensus has held up for more than forty years, since before the coming to power of the PLN. It was severely tested in the 1980s when the Costa Rican state, now heavily in debt, presided over an economy in which the gross national product contracted in some years. But most Costa Ricans continue to agree on the general direction of public policy. They do not regret that Figueres nationalized the banking system in 1949, immediately upon coming to power, or that the PLN decreed an immediate one-time-only 10 percent tax on assets over 50,000 *colones*. These were seen as limited acts, not necessarily leading toward total socialization of the economy or toward total confiscation of large private fortunes. And, indeed, they were not. They were actions undertaken to launch social reforms necessary to benefit a wide array of Costa Ricans.

The state is today an activist one, in spite of budget-driven efforts in the late 1980s at privatization. To take only one example of this activism, Costa Rica devoted U.S. $28 yearly per rural inhabitant for health care in the late 1970s, compared to $4 in Honduras and $2 in Guatemala.[18] While the per capita income of Costa Rica is higher than that in neighboring Honduras and Guatemala, the ratios of investment in such activities, once adjustments are made for the available gross national product per capita, are still highly favorable.[19] This represents the reformist and social democratic vision of this state. Costa Ricans see some real benefits from their government: they have had a measure of electoral choice for decades (those who lose elections actually give up office), they have had no formal military establishment to exhaust budgetary resources, and they have an extensive governmental apparatus that employed one of every five of their working population entering the 1980s, often in decentralized state agencies that have considerable autonomy from centralized direction.

The shrinking of the Costa Rican state in response to the economic crisis of the 1980s was not effected through the sacrifice of electoral accountability. The broader Central American crisis has strained the country's economy and even eroded its political liberties,[20] but not yet at the cost of the essential character of the system. Costa Rica has functioned rather well over the twentieth century because the reformist vision—in this case, the vision of the social democrats[21]—has been most fully implemented there. Indeed, because Costa Ricans see the linkage between peace and their own prosperity, it was no accident that President Arias took the initiative in seeking peace in the region.

In the Central American Peace Initiative, signed by five presidents in August 1987, the Costa Ricans sought a commitment to regional coexistence between conventionalist regimes, such as that of El Salvador, and revolutionary regimes, such as Nicaragua. This outlook was a logical extension of the reformist perspective. At home, the Costa Ricans typically expand the state to help the poor when possible and contract it when fiscal disequilibriums require sacrifice. At home and abroad, Costa Rican reformism is comprehensive in its scope; it embraces both the bankers and the battered. Such is the route to political success.

By contrast, the reformist vision in El Salvador has been quashed, and the Red-baiters have controlled the political process for decades, polarizing political life between those who would use violence to defend the conventionalist vision of economic change (and thereby the status quo) and those who would use insurrection to overthrow it. Polarization came fifty years ago to El Salvador and has never departed. Stephen Webre describes the origin of polarization in the 1930s:

> General Martínez had no sooner assumed the presidency in 1932 than he faced a crisis whose legacy continues to weigh heavily on the Salvadoran political consciousness. On January 22, 1932, Indian and Ladino peasants in the country's Western zone rose in rebellion under nominal Communist leadership and swept through the district looting, pillaging, and on occasion killing local officials and landowners. Government troops . . . quickly suppressed the movement. Retribution following the restoration of order was swift and brutal. Local civilians lynched some leaders before they could be taken by authorities, but those who fell into official hands fared little better; execution was generally immediate. . . . In most areas it was apparently sufficient proof of guilt to be noticeably an Indian or peasant. . . . The most reliable study concludes that . . . between eight thousand and ten thousand . . . suspected rebels died, probably more than 90 percent of them in the repression, rather than in the fighting itself. By contrast, victims of rebel violence amount to perhaps one hundred, most of whom were soldiers or local officials.[22]

While one need not justify the taking of life in the original uprising, it should be clear that on balance the famous *matanza*, or slaughter, of 1932 involved disproportionately more indiscriminate violence by the political right than by peasants who rebelled on the left. The ratio, according to Thomas P. Anderson, the definitive U.S. historian of this event, was about one hundred killings by rightists to every one by a leftist.[23]

The very audacity of rebellion by the poor in 1932 structured the terms of discourse of Salvadoran politics for the remainder of the twentieth century. Since then the allegation of communism has been employed frequently to discredit those who advocated reform. The case of the late José Napoleón Duarte is instructive. Duarte was the Christian Democrat who served as an appointed president of a civilian-military junta between 1980 and the elections of 1982, and who subsequently served a five-year presidential term after being elected in 1984. He was portrayed by segments of the U.S. press in the early 1980s as a tool of the Salvadoran military, yet he ran as a coalition candidate opposing the military's choice for the presidency in 1972. In the end, that election was apparently stolen from Duarte when early results showed him clearly in the lead. But how was that campaign conducted? According to Webre, "Duarte was the subject of numerous accusations and innuendos that appeared to have two main objectives: 1) to portray Duarte personally as dishonest and incompetent; and 2) to identify him and the coalition in the minds of the voters as Communists."[24]

These verbal attacks were launched because the Christian Democratic party was bold enough in 1972 to propose for the first time a serious land reform program. The campaign platform departed sharply from early party proposals by advocating a legal limit to the size of landholdings and the breaking up of *latifundios*, that is, large underutilized rural estates. Even this program manifested the traditional Christian Democratic caution, however. The government would fix the permissible size of landholdings only after carefully considering in each case the nature of the land, the type of crops being produced, and the efficiency of land use. In fact, only the largest landowners with great tracts of unused acreage were in danger of expropriation.[25]

To what did the Christian Democratic land reform proposals lead? According to Webre, Red-baiting was the initial response. Ultimately, however, electoral fraud was committed against Duarte's candidacy. On the first point he notes:

> Opponents of Duarte's coalition waved the "bloody shirt" of the 1932 peasant uprising, charging that false demagogic promises of agrarian reform (presumably like those the Duarte coalition was now making) had caused that tragic outbreak. The general theme of these attacks was that left-wing deceit of the masses, not oppression or exploitation, led to social violence.[26]

In anonymous advertisements in the press Duarte was attacked as being "the puppet of the opportunistic and deceitful leaders of the Salvadoran Communist Party." Nonetheless, despite such Red-baiting in the 1972 campaign, he seemed well on his way to victory on election night. The truth will never be known, but it was announced by the electoral commission early in the evening, after compilation of the vote in San Salvador—the capital city and home of 30 percent of the national electorate—that Duarte had a 2-to-1 lead over his major opponent. Shortly thereafter the military government banned any further broadcasts of the election results. The next morning, Salvadoran residents awoke to hear that Duarte had been defeated by a margin of twenty-two thousand votes. The London *Economist* noted "how coincidental it was [that] the government's position began to improve only when the results stopped being announced on radio and television."[27]

This was the reality of Salvadoran politics from 1932 through 1980, when the United States began its deep involvement. The electoral process was fraudulent; reformist elements, such as the Christian Democratic party, were systematically excluded from power. Only in the late 1970s and early 1980s, when human rights violations increased markedly, did major elements of the Salvadoran center give up all hope of reform and begin to drift toward the revolutionary movement. Increasingly, leaders of the reformist center concluded that only two options remained: 1) to join with the military that actually governed El Salvador, hoping to institute change from within; or 2) to join the revolutionary insurrection because all expectation of change from within was destroyed. Duarte chose to join a civilian-military junta in 1980. A group of military officers purporting to favor reform had come to power in 1979. Guillermo Ungo, a social democrat, and Rubén Zamora, another Christian Democrat, first served the junta and later chose revolution. In one sense, neither Duarte nor Ungo nor Zamora was happy with his options. Duarte knew that he did not control the military. The others initially preferred reform to revolution, but, given the choice between maintaining a social order they considered devoid of moral authority for its human rights violations and insurrection, they opted for revolution.

What human rights violations, one might ask? Let us consider the case of Mario Zamora, brother of Rubén, who was the attorney general for welfare in the military-civilian government that promised reform in 1979. Yet he was assassinated in his own house by a government-backed death squad linked to Roberto D'Aubuisson, later the speaker of the Constituent Assembly in San Salvador and still later a presidential candidate. The killing was seemingly linked to D'Aubuisson's televised allegation that Zamora was working for the guerrillas, a charge immediately and heatedly denied by him. Thomas Anderson describes subsequent events in the following terms:

> On 22 February 1980, while the PDC leader was conducting a meeting at his house, with such persons as (José) Napoleón Duarte and Héctor Dada, another cabinet member, they were raided by masked right-wing vigilantes. . . . Mario Zamora was singled out, taken into the bathroom, and shot dead. As a result of this incident, both Rubén Zamora, brother of the murdered and a member of the PDC Central Committee, and Héctor Dada resigned from the party and the government, which they criticized for not even being able to protect its own members and for its failure to arrest D'Aubuisson for Zamora's murder.[28]

Not surprisingly, Rubén Zamora soon joined the guerrilla movement. He was for many years a major spokesman in exile for the FDR/FMLN, returning to El Salvador in 1988 to contest the presidential election in support of Ungo's leftist candidacy.[29] He returned only when the Central American Peace Initiative created so much external pressure that such violations momentarily abated.

By early 1989, however, a pattern of human rights violations recurred. The termination of the Duarte presidency (1984–1989) through an electoral process culminating on March 19 did not resolve the human rights issue, especially when Alfredo Cristiani, the candidate of ARENA, a political party created by D'Aubuisson, won the presidency. Salvadoran voters chose the major political option available in the 1989 elections, thus seeking an outlet for their discontent with five years of ineffectual governance by Duarte's Christian Democrats. ARENA, however, seemed to lack either the ability or the disposition to end human rights violations.

Then followed a rebel offensive in mid-November 1989 that brought the war for the first time to the most comfortable bastions of middle- and upper-class life in San Salvador. Journalists estimated that somewhere between four hundred and six hundred individuals, largely combatants, lost their lives.[30] In the midst of that offensive, protected by a curfew prohibiting movement to all but military forces, members of the U.S.-trained ATLACATL battalion were apparently the elements that broke into the living quarters of Jesuit administrators of the Universidad Centroamericana and killed six in their sleep. These included Ignacio Ellacuría, the rector (or president); and Ignacio Martín-Baró, the vice rector and El Salvador's leading public-opinion pollster. These killings were preceded, as has been distressingly customary in El Salvador over decades, by accusations of communism broadcast over the radio in the twenty-four hours before they occurred.[31] The priests favored reconciliation. As the 1980s closed, the peacemakers (and, implicitly, the reformists) were being eliminated by violence, just as Archbishop Oscar Romero had been in 1980 and as has been happening since 1932.

El Salvador remains a divided country, with no clear consensus in favor of the revolutionaries. Election results and public opinion polls by Martín-Baró, the assassinated scholar, make that plain. But electoral processes in which there is no role for a moderate left, somewhat beyond the Christian Democrats, remain suspect, because candidates are afraid to run and citizens are afraid to vote for the left. Just what the Salvadoran people really think cannot be judged fully until their opinions can be expressed in a climate of personal security. Tragically, six decades of polarization and exclusion of the reformist center make that a condition unlikely to be attained in the near future. The Central American Peace Initiative floundered first of all in El Salvador because the legacy of unresolved polarization was longest there.

Let us examine, more anecdotally, another case of the exclusion of reformists.[32] In this instance a reformist politician was first excluded from, and then was admitted to, the political arena on terms that were so disadvantageous that no reform could occur. In 1981 I was invited to lecture in Guatemala at an institute sponsored by the United States

Information Agency. On that occasion I met Vinicio Cerezo, secretary-general of the Christian Democratic party, later to be elected president with 68 percent of the vote in a December 1985 runoff election. Violence reigned supreme in the military governments of Guatemala at that time.[33]

The negotiations leading to my meeting with Cerezo were interesting in themselves. A young free-lance journalist who attended my lectures approached me after four days, having concluded that my political views were not those of the extreme right. He inquired if I would be willing to meet with Cerezo, who had been his classmate at the Universidad San Carlos. I said that I would like to do so but had little time, suggesting that perhaps Saturday morning before I left town would be convenient. I invited Cerezo and his wife, Raquel, a linguist, to meet me at my hotel. Pedro,[34] the journalist, called Cerezo, who demurred that he would rather not meet me at the hotel as "there might be a bit of a security problem." Pedro then relayed this news to me. As I reflected upon the wisdom of going through with the meeting, I wondered: "Am I being set up?"

Nonetheless, I walked across Guatemala City with Pedro on Saturday morning to the house of Cerezo's friends. As we walked, Pedro explained that recent attempts had been made on the lives of the Cerezos, so they were in hiding. Our pace quickened, and I began to exhibit extraordinary interest in all passing vehicles and pedestrians. We arrived and knocked on a solid iron gate with an iron sliding window. The window opened, and a guard with a submachine gun peered out: "Ah, estás tú, Pedro . . . y el otro?"

"No, 'ombre, está bien, Vinicio ya sabe que un profesor norteamericano viene a entrevistarse consigo."

We entered, and I nervously saw a second guard, also with a submachine gun. Then came Cerezo. We greeted each other. Coffee was offered. The gunmen disappeared, and we talked with considerable candor for over two hours.[35]

Cerezo told me the details of the attacks on his person; he was most convincing. He also told me that over seventy leaders of the Christian Democratic party had been killed in the past three years. He expressed the belief that all of these killings were the responsibility of government-linked death squads,[36] adding that members of the government wanted to destroy the center by driving it into rebellion along with the incipient guerrilla movement. If they could prove that some Christian Democrats had joined the guerrillas, then they more easily could justify attacking all Christian Democrats.

"The government is having some success because some of our people are doing just that . . . joining the guerrillas," lamented Cerezo. "But I am not about to give up that easily." He argued for continuing to work within the system, hoping to open it up from the inside, much as Duarte had hoped to do in El Salvador.

"Why do you continue?" I asked. "If people are trying to kill you, isn't this fundamentally hopeless?"

"I love my country," answered Cerezo, "and I believe it can happen . . . that out of a tradition of violence and repression can come democracy . . . such as happened in Venezuela."

On that day in 1981 we debated the replicability of the Venezuelan experience, and then my time was up. As I flew back to Miami, I thought about Cerezo and his beliefs and concluded that they were fundamentally irrational, that the odds of democratic reformism emerging out of the carnage of human rights violations in Guatemala was truly slim or nil. I also concluded that I had just met a patriot, a man who loved his country in spite of all its flaws and was determined, against all reason, to set it right. The man was irrational, but I respected him immensely.[37]

Now, after five years of a Cerezo presidency, it is more difficult to sustain that respect from afar. The human rights violations did not stop under Cerezo. Amnesty International and Americas Watch reported that disappearances and other human rights violations continued at an active pace.[38] As articulate and compassionate as Cerezo seemed to me prior to governing, the institutional structures of violence proved impossible to disassemble during his presidency.

There are few good choices for reformists in the most polarized Central American polities. The cases of Cerezo of Guatemala and of Duarte (who died in 1990) of El Salvador illustrate the hopes of Christian Democratic reformists who attempted to work within military-dominated systems to generate space for democratic dialogue, but who largely failed to do so in governing, and indicate the difficulties of reforming the system of violence from within. The cases of Salvadoran leaders Rubén Zamora (Christian Democrat) and Guillermo Ungo (social democrat), who gave up on the system and joined a guerrilla opposition that could disrupt but could not govern (1979–1990), show how long the road of insurrection may turn out to be. Even if power is attained through insurrection, the case of Sandinista Nicaragua indicates that the transformation of society does not come easily. The opponents of change can take recourse to external resources in resisting the revolutionary reorientation of public policy.

Nonetheless, there are three political systems in Central America where the reformist center has been systematically excluded from the political process: Nicaragua, El Salvador, and Guatemala. These are the cases where revolutionary struggle was pursued most seriously with the greatest success. Nicaragua, under the tutelage of three Somozas between 1934 and 1979, witnessed unrivaled corruption and the systematic exclusion of the political center.[39] In the end, business people, trade unionists, peasants, schoolteachers, and twelve-year-old children rebelled in unison. The Nicaraguan revolution was initially a genuinely popular one. Like all such multiclass mass movements, the participants had dramatically different visions of what would happen after the Somozas were gone, and disagreements emerged early in the new era of government by the Sandinista National Liberation Front. Those crystalized into such a degree of political polarization that, in the 1990 presidential elections, Nicaragua was deeply divided between pro-Sandinista and anti-Sandinista groups. The latter proved victorious. The point is, however, that the revolution succeeded initially because Anastasio Somoza Debayle provided no place for the political center and drove the vast majority of the population, including the hierarchy of the church, into at least tacit acceptance of the armed insurrection. The situation has not been quite so dramatic in El Salvador, where the United States has struggled in vain to resurrect a political center, and in Guatemala, where Cerezo held onto the reins of power but did not really govern. In El Salvador and Guatemala, guerrillas persisted, unable to mount a successful insurrection but consistently able to recruit new members due to the exclusion of reformists from power. As Richard Fagen and Olga Pellicer put it some years ago:

> The politics of reform, at first deeply wedded to electoral strategies, increasingly embraced oppositional strategies of other sorts (strikes, mass protests) and finally was forced to choose between ineffectiveness and possible physical opposition on the other. By the 1980s, the choice for many ex-reformists has become relatively stark: death, exile, alliance with guerrilla movements, or a devil's pact with the military.[40]

In between these situations, in which the reformist center has been excluded, and Costa Rica, where reformists govern, fall Honduras and Panama, where military governments have sometimes tolerated or even encouraged experiments with reform. In Honduras, the signs are mixed. After military governments pursued modest land reform in the early 1970s, civilians have exercised nominal political control since 1981. Although the country has a weak tradition of representative democracy, Thomas Anderson notes that there are elements of political pluralism in Honduras that are exceptional by Central American standards: the press is freer than in most of the isthmus; the university has a measure of genuine academic freedom and moral authority; unions are more fully accepted and less subject to bloody repression; and some agrarian reform occurred in the 1970s, thus providing relief to pressures on the land.[41] In November 1989 elections were held in which power was transferred to a third successive civilian regime, this time to an opposition party. Perhaps for these reasons, then, revolutionary movements have not spread in Honduras as rapidly as in the three more repressive cases. There is some space in which the reformist center can operate, even though the military remains a powerful force behind apparent civilian rule.

Panama, as we know, was a system in decay during the late 1980s. What emerged under the reign of General Omar Torrijos from 1968 to 1980 was a sustained attempt at preemptive reformism undertaken by a military government.[42] An accommodation was reached for a while between the reformists and a military government. That accommodation unraveled when Torrijos died in a helicopter crash in 1981 and eventually was replaced by General Noriega. The military strongman who made and unmade civilian presidents, Noriega also made deals with Colombian drug dealers, Fidel Castro, the Central Intelligence Agency (CIA), Daniel Ortega, and the Nicaraguan contras.[43] The major consistency in Noriega's behavior appears to have been self-aggrandizement. By the mid-1980s all semblance of reformist content to the Panamanian military regime was gone. Domestic opposition grew as military authoritarianism, untempered by reform-oriented policy, became increasingly less attractive.

The United States, of course, had its own reasons for invading Panama in December 1989. Ostensibly intervening to reestablish democracy, Washington had waited twenty-one years and five presidencies before taking such dramatic action. One has to wonder, why the wait? Another overt justification was to bring General Noriega to justice in this country where he faced criminal indictment on drug charges—a goal attained. Other, less laudable motives have been attributed to the United States. Some argue that once allegations surfaced publicly of drug dealing by General Noriega, leaders in Washington sought to "compensate" politically for payments made by the CIA to the general starting in 1964.[44]

Whatever U.S. motivations were involved, the most notable feature of Panama's discontent is that, once blocked by electoral fraud, it ultimately was given effective expression only through external military intervention, not through domestic insurrection. A truly national revolution did not happen in Panama because 1) there was some hope that domestic opponents of Noriega, if brought to power, might prove to be the agents of progressive public policy; 2) even if General Noriega were deposed by the military, other military elements who remember the "true legacy" of General Torrijos might return Panama to the track of nationalist reformism; and 3) economic pressure or military invasion by the United States might get rid of the tyrant, thereby opening up the system to reformist impulses. The Bush administration's invasion rid Panama of a military strongman who certainly did not share the inclusionary vision of Latin American reformists. Whether the reformists will reemerge as major players in Panamanian politics remains to be seen. The 1989 U.S. intervention cost over three hundred lives, but it may have helped to avert a violent Panamanian popular insurrection in the early 1990s. Yet, prior to 1981, an indigenous tradition of military reformism also blunted the threat of revolution.

Consideration of the six major polities of the isthmus, therefore, reveals a pattern.[45] Where the reformists have been most systematically excluded from power over the longest period of time, revolutionary insurrections have advanced the furthest. The United States may impose constraints upon governments that it does not like, including revolutionary ones, but those governments come to power from a dynamic that Washington influences only indirectly.

Notes

1. Dennis Gilbert, "Nicaragua: Afloat on a Sea of Troubles," *Dialogue* (University of Virginia) 2, no. 1 (Fall 1989): 19–21; idem, *Sandinistas* (New York, 1988).

2. See, inter alia, two articles by Lindsey Gruson in the *New York Times*: "Salvador Rebels Launch Offensive: Fighting Is Fierce," November 13, 1989; and "Six Priests Killed in a Campus Raid in El Salvador," November 17, 1989.

3. Tom Barry, *Guatemala: A Country Guide* (Albuquerque, 1989). See also *New York Times*, March 7, 1990.

4. On these issues see James D. Cockcroft, *Neighbors in Turmoil: Latin America* (New York, 1989), 150–66. Recent reports indicate the recurrence of death squad activities. See "Honduras: Death Squads Reappear, Kill Unionists," *Latinamerica Press* (Lima, Peru) 21, no. 27 (July 20, 1989): 1, 8; and "Honduras: Accusations Fly as Violence Turns to the Right," *Central America Report* (Guatemala City) 16, no. 28 (July 21, 1989): 221–22.

5. On Costa Rican electoral practice see Ronald H. McDonald and J. Mark Ruhl, *Party Politics and Elections in Latin America* (Boulder, 1989), 169–82. Tom Barry, *Costa Rica: A Country Guide* (Albuquerque, 1989), offers a far more negative assessment of Costa Rica, arguing that electoral politics are not the sole basis on which to judge the country.

6. On the stolen elections see "Panama: Elections Annulled—Noriega Hangs On," *Central America Report* (May 12, 1989): 137–38. On the U.S. invasion, coverage by the *New York Times* from December 21, 1989, through January 1990 was extensive and is accessible. On Noriega's support and the emergence of confrontation in his relationship to the United States see John Weeks, "Panama: The Roots of Current Political Instability," *Third World Quarterly* 9, no. 3 (July 1987): 763–87; and Weeks and Andrew Zimbalist, "The Failure of Intervention in Panama: Humiliation in the Backyard," ibid. 11, no. 1 (January 1989): 1–27.

7. Charles W. Anderson, *Politics and Economic Change in Latin America: The Governing of Restless Nations* (New York, 1967).

8. Ibid., 163–64.

9. Specifically, DeWalt and Bidegaray discuss how the expansion of the cattle industry has served the interests of a small elite of agrarian capitalists, while impinging on the ability of a large number of peasants to subsist through traditional forms of agriculture. For a more detailed discussion of such issues see Robert G. Williams, *Export Agriculture and the Crisis in Central America* (Chapel Hill, NC, 1986).

10. One might wish to contrast the cases of El Salvador, where the traditional communal lands, or *ejidos*, were effectively stripped from the indigenous peoples in the initial coffee booms of the 1850–1880 era, with neighboring Honduras, where a semblance of these communities remained. See Tommie Sue Montgomery, *Revolution in El Salvador: Origins and Evolution*, rev. ed. (Boulder, CO, 1990); and J. Mark Ruhl, "Agrarian Structure and Political Stability in Honduras," *Journal of Interamerican Studies and World Affairs* 26 (February 1984): 33–68.

11 Anderson, *Politics and Economic Change*, 167–68 (emphasis added).

12. This typically would involve organizing the previously unorganized to make them effective participants in the political process.

13. Anderson, *Politics and Economic Change*, 177 (emphasis added).

14. The classic discussion of these tactics can be found in Albert O. Hirschman, "Models of Reform-Mongering," *Journeys toward Progress: Studies of Economic Policy-Making in Latin America* (New York, 1963), 227–97.

15. A recent survey emphasizing positive dimensions of Costa Rica's political experience is Charles Ameringer, *Costa Rican Politics* (New York, 1983). For a more critical view see Barry, *Costa Rica: A Country Guide*.

16. This evolution is chronicled in Mitchell A. Seligson, *Peasants of Costa Rica and the Development of Agrarian Capitalism* (Madison, WI, 1980).

17. Daniel Oduber, president of Costa Rica from 1974 to 1978, represents that vision.

18. See Thomas John Bossert, "Can We Return to the Regime for Comparative Policy Analysis? or The State and Health Policy in Central America," *Comparative Politics* 15, no. 4 (July 1983): 424.

19. See ibid. for Bossert's figures on gross domestic product per capita.

20. Barry, *Costa Rica: A Country Guide*, 19–21; "Costa Rica: The Dark Side of Democracy," *Central America Report* (April 28, 1989): 121–22.

21. The other major ideological fount of reformism is Christian Democracy, which heretofore has proved to be the predominant source of such ideas in El Salvador and Guatemala, perhaps because identification with the church provides a measure of protection in these two extraordinarily right-wing environments.

22. Stephen Webre, *José Napoleón Duarte and the Christian Democratic Party of El Salvador, 1960–1972* (Baton Rouge, LA, 1979), 7–8.

23. Thomas P. Anderson, *La Matanza: El Salvador's Communist Revolt of 1932* (Lincoln, NE, 1971), 134–37.

24. Webre, *José Napoleón Duarte*, 164.

25. Ibid., 157.

26. Ibid., 166.

27. *Economist*, February 26, 1972, cited in Webre, *José Napoleón Duarte*, 171.

28. Thomas P. Anderson, *Politics in Central America*, rev. ed. (New York, 1988), 94.

29. See Morris J. Blachman and Kenneth E. Sharpe, "Things Fall Apart: Trouble Ahead in El Salvador," *World Policy Journal* 6, no. 1 (Winter 1988–89): 107–39.

30. Lindsey Gruson, "Salvador Army Steps Up Raids on Strongholds of Rebel Forces," *New York Times*, November 15, 1989.

31. See Richard Morin, "Ignacio Martín-Baró: In Search of the Truth in El Salvador," *Washington Post National Weekly Edition*, December 4–10, 1989, 38; and William Bollinger, "Taking the Pulse of Social Justice in Central America: The Public Opinion Research of Ignacio Martín-Baró," paper delivered at the 1989 Annual Meeting of the Latin American Studies Association, Miami, Florida, December 4–6, 1989.

32. For introductory surveys of Guatemalan politics see T. P. Anderson, *Politics in Central America*, 19–69; and Barry, *Guatemala: A Country Guide*. For an understanding of the tragic U.S. role in bringing about the political stalemate that yields so much violence today see Stephen Schlesinger and Stephen Kinzer, *Bitter Fruit: The Untold Story of the American Coup in Guatemala* (Garden City, NY, 1982); or Richard Immerman, *The CIA in Guatemala* (Austin, TX, 1982).

33. See, for example, the report of a massacre assembled in Shelton H. Davis and Ricardo Falla, *Voices of the Survivors: The Massacre at Finca San Francisco, Guatemala* (Boston, 1983); or Amnesty International, *Guatemala: The Human Rights Record* (London, 1987); or Henry J. Frundt, *Refreshing Pauses: Coca Cola and Human Rights in Guatemala* (New York, 1987).

34. This is a pseudonym.

35. The conversations reconstructed here are not verbatim transcripts of our encounter but rather represent selected highlights of a conversation that lasted much longer. They capture the flavor of our meeting.

36. Cerezo told a similar story to others at this time. See "Guatemala: Christian Democrats Seek US Support for Election Guarantees," *Latin America Weekly Report* 20 (May 22, 1981), wherein similar figures are cited. A U.S. embassy official in Guatemala City, in charge of estimating the origins of political killings in the country, estimated that "80% are the work of government-linked death squads." Personal interview, 1981.

37. Most U.S. specialists on Guatemala today judge Cerezo harshly. My reasoning then was that, while Cerezo paid some moral costs by trying to position his party in order to profit should the military ever relinquish power (which it did), and he paid even higher costs while governing under military supervision, there are also moral costs to revolution. Once power has been seized by violence, the capacity to compromise with one's political opponents may be eroded. Since respect for other human beings is a value fundamental to democracy, the revolutionary route to power may impede the subsequent attainment of a culture of democratic compromise. The choice is not an easy one. Both reformists and revolutionaries may warrant respect.

38. Amnesty International, *Guatemala* (Washington, DC, 1987); Americas Watch, *Closing the Space: Human Rights in Guatemala* (Washington, DC, 1988), and *Persecuting Human Rights Monitors: The CERJ in Guatemala* (Washington, DC, 1989).

39. The literature on Nicaragua has mushroomed since the success of the revolution. Four particularly useful volumes are John Booth, *The End and the Beginning: The Nicaraguan Revolution*, 2d ed. (Boulder, CO, 1985); Thomas W. Walker, *Nicaragua: The First Five Years* (Boulder, CO, 1985); idem, *Reagan versus the Sandinistas: The Undeclared War on Nicaragua* (Boulder, CO, 1987); and Gilbert, *Sandinistas*.

40. Richard R. Fagen and Olga Pellicer, eds., *The Future of Central America: Policy Choices for the United States and Mexico* (Stanford, 1983), 3–4.

41. T. P. Anderson, *Politics in Central America*, 164–67; Ruhl, "The Influence of Agrarian Structure."

42. See Steve C. Ropp, *Panamanian Politics: From Guarded Nation to National Guard* (New York, 1982).

43. Frederick Kempe, *Divorcing the Dictator* (New York, 1990), excerpted in *Newsweek* (January 15, 1990): 19–24, 28.

44. See Weeks, "Panamá: The Roots"; and Weeks and Zimbalist, "The Failure of Intervention."

45. These polities exclude English-speaking Belize, which has not been fully embroiled in the political turmoil of the area.

The Catholic Church and
Central American Politics

Kathleen M. Blee

Recent events in Central America have underscored the changing role of the Roman Catholic church in the politics of the region. A church whose hierarchy traditionally has been allied with ruling classes and center/right politics now faces persecution from rightist forces allied with the agrarian elite in El Salvador. The revolutionary left, long hostile to Christian principles of faith and morality, now proclaims these as the foundation of transformation in Nicaragua. In Guatemala, a traditionally quiescent church hierarchy has begun to challenge the inequity of land ownership concentrated in the hands of a small elite.

Changes in the political allegiances of the Catholic clergy and laity in Central America have not been uniform or consistent. Long-simmering splits within the church along lines of authority, ideology, and region have erupted into the secular political realm. Priests, nuns, layworkers, and bishops cite church authority to support often conflicting political processes and goals. The Vatican itself is involved in an internally divisive and bitter public dispute with prominent Latin American theologians and clergy over "liberation theology" and the proper role of the church in class conflict and national revolutions. These contradictions among Catholics and between church and nation-state in Central America have made the church's powerful political role in the region increasingly contentious.

The political realignment of the Catholic church in Central America and the ensuing fissures within it are the product of separate but intertwined historical processes. Internal changes have reshaped the church's secular mission in the twentieth century. At the same time, changes in Central America altered the relationship of church to state. This essay examines these historical processes. First, the doctrinal and organizational changes within the global Catholic church that redefined the place of religious values in secular politics are explored. Second, attention is given to how changes in the wider church were implemented in a Latin American context. And finally, the role of the Catholic church in El Salvador and Nicaragua is compared and evaluated.

In Latin and Central America the Catholic church has long been an influential, but contradictory, actor. As a product of European colonialism, it often reflected and reinforced the interests of the colonial land-owning classes against native peoples and the peasantry. The church encouraged the poor in the virtues of patience and obedience, values based in spirituality and clericalism but with a clear message in the world of economics and politics. Yet, even during the colonial period, it played other roles in Latin American society. The church, for example, preserved aspects of indigenous cultures by incorporating them into a new religious framework and protected Indians and African slaves from the rawest excesses of the colonial system.[1] Such contradictions were not only the product of differing interests and perceptions within the hierarchy (that is, between priests and bishops) but also reflected the complex and uneven nature of colonialism in Latin America.

In the twentieth century the mission of the Latin American Catholic church changed as a result of external economic and political forces and internal pressure. The political independence and industrialization of many nations in the region undermined the viability of the agrarian sector as a primary church constituency. Agrarian elites, tied to colonial powers, increasingly faced challenges by new elites, based in manufacturing and commerce, who favored political nationalism. At the same time, rapid urban expansion eroded the peasantry and created large working classes in cities that offered insufficient employment opportunities and underdeveloped education, health, and social service systems.[2] This combination of wide disparities in living standards between elites and nonelites and a legacy of successful political movements against colonial domination left twentieth-century Latin America in crisis and increased the likelihood of class-based revolutions. Moreover, these changes coincided with movements within the church for greater ecumenical cooperation and a broader interpretation of doctrine, which further directed the church's attention toward social problems, secular political movements, and urban cultures.

In Latin America, the church became interested in economic development models and political reforms as a way to alleviate the plight of urban migrants, undermine the appeal of left-wing political movements, and retain its own influence in the political arena. This led to an array throughout the region of Christian social services, trade unions, youth organizations, universities, and radio schools, heavily financed by direct appeals from the Vatican to West European churches. In parts of Latin America the church allied itself with Christian Democratic parties as the framework for injecting its values into a program of reform and development.[3] Christian Democracy stressed collaboration between rich and poor in the pursuit of economic growth, democratic political participation, and state support for selected ventures in the private sector.[4]

Even as the Latin American Catholic church appeared to act as one body, serious political and theological disputes simmered below the surface. Priests and nuns often were critical of the Christian Democratic models of development backed by the church hierarchy, seeing these as doing little to narrow the gap between rich and poor and as blocking concerted political action to change the concentration of land and industrial ownership. Some clergy and theologians took this disillusionment with Christian Democracy further and invoked Catholic thought as a foundation for popular opposition to capitalist social systems.[5] These internal divisions began to assume an institutional form and become public as the consequence of the worldwide ecumenical council of Catholic bishops, known as Vatican II, in Rome in the 1960s.

Vatican II opened against a background of theological and doctrinal changes developed by Pope John XXIII in a series of encyclicals that declared as basic the right to a decent standard of living, to education, and to political participation. In the years of the council, changes in the church's political perspectives were accompanied by a fundamental shift in the perception of its role in twentieth-century society. Rather than viewing the church as a fixed body that transmitted dogma from one generation to the next in an unchanging form, Vatican II declared it to be a social institution based on a living and changing community.[6] Such doctrinal change opened the door to a general reinterpretation of society. If social institutions were always in flux, then they must be understood as historical entities that have possibilities for development and transformation. If social institutions, governments, and economics could develop in various ways, then the church had no interest in maintaining any particular social structure.[7] Further, acceptance of the notion of the church as a living community, together with a lessening of the doctrine of clerical obedience, meant that analysis of societies need not be taken from dogma or hierarchical proclamations alone but could be derived as well from the daily life of priests, nuns, and laity.[8]

Despite the implications of such change for the church as a whole, the initial repercussions of Vatican II were experienced largely within the North American and European churches. The primary theologians of the council were West Europeans, and the scope of their discussion was centered around church issues, although social issues had become more pressing in Latin American nations.[9] The application of the changes of Vatican II to the Latin American church awaited the 1968 meeting of its bishops, the second convention of the Latin-American Episcopal Conference (CELAM) at Medellín, Colombia.

CELAM II was a major turning point of modern church history in the region. It was held at the juncture of sweeping internal changes from Vatican II and widespread dissatisfaction over the role of the church in Latin American political life. The 1964 military coup in Brazil and disappointment over the progress of Christian Democratic reforms in Chile had provoked political strife within the church. Traditionalists remained committed to moderate reform movements while others, such as Bishop Dom Helder Camara of Brazil, pushed for the creation of a "church of the poor."[10]

The CELAM II meetings, the forum for political divisions within the hierarchy, resulted in a victory for those forces pushing for dramatic change. Documents of CELAM II reveal a broadening of the concept of sin to include an entire social system that inhibits a fully moral life, an analysis of poverty as a problem of societies rather than individuals (thus a problem amenable to political change rather than personal reform), and a sense that Latin American nations had not been well served by either capitalist or Communist models of development.[11] CELAM II backed a political process based not on the importation into Latin America of pre-existing development models but on new models of society, created through the active participation of the masses. CELAM II thus popularized a model of participation developed by Paulo Freire in Brazil, in which education and change result from a dialogue between teacher and student on the conditions of daily life and the possibilities for changing oppressive structures.[12] In the aftermath of CELAM II, this model was drawn on by priests, nuns, and layworkers throughout Latin America who fused the religious and political implications of the daily life experiences of their impoverished constituency.

Despite these changes, the documents of CELAM II might have remained a footnote in theological history except for two developments within the church that institutionalized the message of the conference. The first was the development of a theory based on the work of Latin American theologians such as Gustavo Gutierrez of Peru, which came to be known as the "theology of liberation." Liberation theology is historically specific, requiring a critical analysis of the society in which faith is exercised. Social analysis, for liberation theologians, must reflect the spiritual and cultural perspectives of the majority of people in the society. In this view, the historical experience of the majority of Latin Americans was not an experience of development and progress but rather one of injustice and repression. On this scale, neither capitalism nor colonialism could be judged successful in the region.[13]

Liberation theologians expanded ideas developed in Vatican II to argue that all history should be seen in terms of change and movement. Change does not arise from external sources; rather, people change and create themselves and their societies in every social action. The role of the church, therefore, should not be to lead people toward a predetermined economic or political goal but to ensure that they are free to determine their own course of change. The church should facilitate the movement of societies toward liberation and choice.[14] Although liberation theology is a political theory, it is not a partisan or ideological theology since its practical application has been developed not through political parties but through vehicles of popular participation known as "base communities."[15]

These were the second structure to institutionalize the doctrines of CELAM II. Although base communities differ in structure and ideology across and within countries, all share certain fundamental similarities. They tend to be relatively small, tight-knit communities of people who share similar levels of income, types of employment, and education. They are focused on adults as opposed to the usual church emphasis on youth. They discourage individualism in favor of a pooling of experience and a sense of unity and equality among members.[16] These communities, often located in rural areas or in poor neighborhoods on the outskirts of cities, have been a vehicle whereby the doctrines of CELAM II have been popularized among poorly educated and illiterate populations. Further, they have provided a structural framework through which people are encouraged to reflect on their experiences and envision possibilities for the future. In the base community movement, clergy and the impoverished laity become teachers and students of each others' experiences and knowledge. Many progressive clergy, confronted with the reality of life for the Central American poor, became committed to a politics of change. Likewise, the poor were urged to use theological understandings to create social and political alternatives for their own lives. In this way, base communities became a catalyst for local movements of agrarian and political reform throughout Latin America.[17] In El Salvador, for example, these movements in rural areas provided one of the bases of peasant mobilization for land reform in the mid-1970s. In Nicaragua, base communities were active in the anti-Somoza efforts.[18]

The base community and liberation theology movements coincided with other structural changes in the Latin American church. Over the past few decades, there has been a move away from foreign-born clergy and the training of native-born clergy in European seminaries toward indigenous development of clergy.[19] Popular religion or "folk Catholicism," based on a synthesis between Indian and African culture and Catholicism, has been rediscovered. It is expressed in the incorporation of popular images such as suns and moons into the liturgy and the use of liturgical vehicles such as baptism to express both Catholic and native-meaning systems.[20]

While the message of CELAM II was spreading throughout a portion of the base of the Latin and Central American church, there were increasing signs of discontent with its message in other sectors of the church. These discontents broke into open political battle in the late 1970s as the region's bishops prepared for their next meeting at Puebla, Mexico. By this time—ten years after CELAM II—the implications of the CELAM II documents had become clear. Conservatives as well as the hierarchy were unhappy with the church's implicit criticism of development models in Latin America.[21] Further, they were opposed to the democratization that had occurred within the church, fearing that it would undermine its unity, the basis of its moral strength.

In preparation for CELAM III, a series of documents and counterdocuments was drawn up by various competing factions. Conservative forces, led by the Colombian bishops and representatives of the Curia (the Vatican Senate), produced working papers that explicitly rejected the principles of CELAM II. These papers focused on secularization of Latin American life as a critical problem. They called for increased attention to the preservation of the tradition of faith through religious education, individual prayer, and liturgy. The mission of the church within this conservative perspective was to strengthen institutional religion in order to provide a moral foundation from which a range of political programs could be drawn. Such a mission would not forsake concern with poverty and injustice in Latin America, but neither would it propose a specific Catholic agenda to alleviate these problems.[22] In response to these papers, Brazilian bishops and liberation theologians issued counterdocuments that reaffirmed the message of CELAM II and argued that the practice of faith required recognition of social "sins" existing in secular society. Christian theology, according to this perspective, can provide a symbol of justice and a sign of hope, but only if the church positions itself on the side of the poor and oppressed masses. The substitution of secularization for poverty and injustice as the primary issue for the Latin American church, therefore, is a step away from the true mission of the Catholic faith.[23]

In the two years of preparation for the Puebla conference, the regional discussion of these documents made public the deep and multifaceted division within the Catholic church. Conflict was evident not only between conservatives and liberationists but also between the religious base and hierarchy and between the Vatican and substantial elements of the Latin American church. In recognition of the latter's serious internal problems, Pope John Paul II came to Puebla to open the conference. In his address, he argued that it is not possible to reread the Gospel from an ideological viewpoint without destroying the essence of the church's mission, a message heralded by conservatives. But he also noted, in a public address to an Indian group, that while rights to private property are essential, so, too, are rights to be free from exploitation by property. Moreover, in Mexico the pope echoed a sentiment of Latin American liberation theologians, calling for "daring innovations to overcome the grave injustices of the past"—messages welcomed by liberationists.[24]

Pope John Paul II's conflicting political messages were repeated through the conference.[25] The bishops praised popular participation but not lay leadership in the church or base communities. They gave subtle approval to the theology of liberation but denounced the influence of Marxist analysis within this theology. Liberation theology, they argued, allows the church to "live liberating evangelization in its fullest" but is overideological "when it uses as a point of reference a praxis with resource to Marxist analysis."[26] Further, the conference refused to engage in direct political actions such as a proposed denunciation of the Somoza government in Nicaragua. What the Puebla conference affirmed, and what continues today, is the message of a Catholic church split deeply along many lines.

The consequences of this split are seen in the peculiar roles that the church plays in Nicaragua and El Salvador. In El Salvador, serious conflict between the church and the government dates from the 1970s, when Archbishop Luis Chavez Gonzalez encouraged the development of base communities in rural areas. Within a few years, hundreds of these communities had been established, led by a largely native-born clergy and lay leaders who were urging peasants to become agents of change in their own lives and social world.[27] Not surprisingly, the first serious attacks on church members came around issues of agrarian reform. In the mid-1970s there was a series of kidnappings, fires on church properties, and expulsions of foreign missionaries.[28] This initial cycle of repression had a major influence on many base religious workers, who increased their attempts to organize peasants for social reform. Such organizing led to another cycle of repression, and by 1977 sectors of the church in some rural areas saw themselves to be identified targets of right-wing death squads.[29] Such perceptions were not altered by a series of rumors that targeted all Jesuit priests under the slogan, "Be a patriot, kill a priest."[30]

In this tense atmosphere Oscar Arnulfo Romero was appointed archbishop of San Salvador. Although known as a conservative at the time of his appointment, Romero, as a consequence of continual persecution of the church, moved quickly to the center, adopting a sense of the Salvadoran church as an institution under attack from the right.[31] He flew to Rome to complain to the Vatican about government repression of the church and, in doing so, provoked a further division between the church and the government as well as within the hierarchy between himself and the conservative caucus of bishops.[32] However, Romero did not ally himself with the leftist forces of El Salvador, and he alienated a segment of base community priests in 1979 by continuing to legitimate a middle ground as he insisted that a new rightist civilian-military junta should be supported.

By 1980, Archbishop Romero decided that his position in the political middle had become untenable since it was neither reuniting the church nor lessening political repression. He argued that private property and national security had become exalted concepts in his country—a politico-religious idolatry—and he wrote to President Jimmy Carter calling for an end to U.S. military and economic aid to El Salvador.[33] Moreover, seeing negotiation and compromise as largely futile in this divided society, Romero increasingly gave sanction to those who opposed the government by violent as well as nonviolent means.[34] In March 1980 he was assassinated while saying Mass.

Any hope that the split within the church could be healed was broken by Romero's assassination. At this time, many laity, pastoral workers, and clerics fled the country, while others went underground and entered antigovernment revolutionary organizations or became pastoral agents in the rebel-controlled territories of El Salvador.[35] The persecution continued, and local religious leaders held up the popular church as a symbol of resistance. In contrast, the conservative hierarchy, valuing preservation of the institution, became increasingly removed from a large portion of the base that identified with liberation theology, either as a pastoral or as a political message.[36]

Today the Salvadoran church continues to be factionalized. Romero's successor, Archbishop Arturo Rivera y Damas, has sought with little success to play a mediating role in national politics. He has called for talks with rebel forces and denounced the presence of paramilitary troops and death squads in the country and the practice of torture by government troops. Yet, the archbishop continues to recognize the existing government, thereby undermining rebel claims to legitimacy.[37] A striking example of his implicit support for the official government came in a 1987 clash with the Oscar Arnulfo Romero Committee of Mothers of the Disappeared and Political Prisoners, known as *comadres*. The archbishop attacked a hunger strike and occupation of Metropolitan Cathedral in San Salvador by fifty members of the *comadres* as intolerable in light of the nation's "incipient democracy." When the women further challenged the archbishop's progovernment stance, he threatened to have them excommunicated.[38]

At the lower levels of the hierarchy, many clerics and pastoral workers differ markedly from the politics of the archbishop. Indeed, the split between the Salvadoran Catholic hierarchy and church base has become so serious in some regions of the country that religious leaders refer to "parallel churches." Many layworkers support the insurgents' claim that the government condones, even encourages, rightist paramilitary violence against the civilian population. Such sentiment has embittered relations between segments of the church and the state. Death threats have been made against bishops, nuns, and clerics, and the Salvadoran army has charged that the national church is riddled with Communists and rebel priests.[39]

Repeated attacks on the church in El Salvador have taken their toll. Ten years later, neither the assassination of Archbishop Romero nor a rape and murder of four U.S. Maryknoll nuns and layworkers has been fully prosecuted. Indeed, former President José Napoleón Duarte's effort to prosecute rightist leader Roberto D'Aubuisson for the murder of Archbishop Romero only strengthened the alliance between opposition right-wing and military officers. The conviction of five National Guardsmen for the murder of the U.S. churchwomen also provoked a rightist backlash and an attempt to have the guardsmen covered under an amnesty law.[40]

Any possibility of reconciliation between right-wing forces within and outside the government and critical elements of the Catholic church of El Salvador became even more remote as the government responded to a serious rebel offensive in late 1989. On November 16, six Jesuit priests, together with their housekeeper and her daughter, were massacred in their residence on the campus of the Universidad

Centroamericana. Among the murdered priests were the country's most prominent intellectual leaders, including Ignacio Ellacuría, rector of the university; Ignacio Martín-Baró, vice rector and a pioneer in Salvadoran public-opinion polling; and Segundo Montes, dean of the department of social sciences. Outspoken advocates of peace talks between leftist guerrillas and the right-wing government of current president Alfredo Cristiani, the Jesuits were murdered one day after D'Aubuisson issued a threat against rebel sympathizers. In January 1990, Colonel Guillermo Benavides, commander of operations over the military zone that included the university, together with three lieutenants and five enlisted men, were indicted for the murders, based on evidence obtained from an informant. Colonel Benavides became the highest-ranking military officer indicted during El Salvador's current civil war.[41]

Less than two weeks after the murders at the university, a U.S. citizen, Jennifer Casolo, was arrested and held in jail for eighteen days on charges of stockpiling weapons for leftist rebels. A cache of 20,000 rounds of ammunition, grenades, and explosives was unearthed in Casolo's backyard, a discovery that progressive church and humanitarian workers widely dismissed as fraudulent. An employee of the U.S.-based Christian Education Seminars, Casolo organized tours of El Salvador for U.S. officials and other Americans. Under great pressure from religious and humanitarian agencies, the Salvadoran government eventually released her for lack of evidence and had her deported.[42]

The Jesuit murders and Casolo detention were only the most publicized cases of governmental repression of progressive church forces in the past year. In the three months that followed the November 1989 offensive, Salvadoran troops raided twenty-six Catholic and six Lutheran churches or schools. Eighteen Lutheran and twenty-three Episcopal churchworkers were detained by the armed forces, and forty foreign and humanitarian workers fled the country. At the end of 1989, Salvadoran air force planes dropped flyers whose message—"You have the plain and legitimate right to defend your life and property; if to do that, you have to kill terrorists or their international allies, do it"—was seen by many as a death threat against workers in church-related humanitarian agencies and international relief groups. Yet the Salvadoran government continues to deny that the church is a special target for repression. As Colonel Rene Emilio Ponce, chief of staff of the armed forces, declared, "There's no persecution of the church. There's persecution of subversive terrorists. Unfortunately, some of them hide in the skirts of the religious workers." Even the archbishop, who stated that the killings of the Jesuits "put our country in first place in terms of barbarity," opposed the rebel offensive as "useless and unjustifiable."[43]

In Nicaragua, the Catholic church has moved in a different direction. Through the 1960s there was little conflict between its hierarchy and the Somoza government. With the impetus of Vatican II and CELAM II, however, some challenge to the government was mounted by the church in the 1970s. Nicaraguan bishops in 1972 issued a pastoral letter condemning Anastasio Somoza's violation of human rights. In 1974 no Nicaraguan bishops attended his inauguration.[44] Unlike in El Salvador, though, government attacks on the church were sporadic and directed at the lower levels rather than at the hierarchy.[45]

Nevertheless, as popular dissatisfaction with Somoza grew, the church became an important vehicle for organizing the opposition. Yet, the common goal within much of the church—to end the Somoza regime—masked a variety of political positions as to the nature of a post-Somoza government.[46] The conflict in Nicaragua has not been a simple division between church and state. As in El Salvador, in Nicaragua the church itself is internally divided. Unlike in El Salvador, where much of the division is over theological questions of the role of the church in society, in Nicaragua political and partisan lines divide church members. These differences between the two countries reflect the greater repression of the church in El Salvador that has unified the church internally, the cataclysmic effect of Archbishop Romero's assassination on the Salvadoran church, differences in leadership style and personal ideology between the archbishops of Nicaragua and El Salvador, and the varying levels of incorporation of the church into guerrilla movements in El Salvador and postrevolutionary government organizations in Nicaragua.[47]

Conflicts within the Nicaraguan church began in the first months after the overthrow of the Somoza regime. Base community priests, bolstered by clergy from other Central American nations, built an infrastructure of "people's churches" allied with the revolutionary forces but strongly opposed by the Nicaraguan hierarchy.[48] Nicaragua's bishops, in fact, in their first pastoral letter after the revolution, criticized the new government for curbing legal due process and freedom of expression.[49]

The early years of the Nicaraguan revolution sharpened these lines of political division within the Catholic church. Base clerics saw the mobilization of the poor through base communities and lay minister programs as central to the implementation of wide-ranging social reforms and literacy education. These progressive forces within the church instituted formal channels of communication and joint action between churchworkers and leaders of the revolution. Some religious leaders even accepted top posts in the government. The Catholic hierarchy in

Nicaragua reacted with greater caution toward the revolutionary government. Priests and nuns considered favorable to the Sandinista government were transferred by their superiors, even over the protests of parishioners.[50] Although Archbishop (later, Cardinal) Miguel Obando y Bravo supported social reform, he labeled the massive 1980 literacy campaign as indoctrination and worried about the proliferation of mass organizations supportive of the Sandinistas.

Between 1980 and 1982 hostility between the increasingly Sandinista-dominated government and the hierarchy deepened. In 1980 the bishops ordered four priests to resign their posts in the government. When the priests refused, they were stripped of their right to perform the sacraments. Such incidents of conflict among the Sandinistas, the church hierarchy, and portions of the church base grew more serious over time.[51] In 1981 the Sandinistas insisted that television broadcasts of Sunday Mass cover not only the service of the archbishop (a foe of the government) but also services by local priests friendly to the Sandinistas. In response, the archbishop cancelled all filming.[52] In 1981 the junta refused to allow the publication in the influential newspaper *La Prensa* of a letter from Pope John Paul II that encouraged the church base to be more obedient to the hierarchy. Although this policy was later reversed, it also widened the gulf between church and state.[53] By mid-1982 tensions were public and sharp. The Nicaraguan bishops continued to stress a traditional, mystical form of religion and, together with media opposed to the government, publicized several "miracles" that were said to demonstrate God's displeasure with the direction of the revolution. In February of that year the bishops issued a statement that criticized the government for violations of the human rights of Miskito Indians when the Indians were relocated away from a zone on the Nicaraguan-Honduran border. In response, some Sandinistas verbally attacked the bishops for failing to substantiate their claims and for repeating U.S.-initiated charges against them.[54]

These tensions came to the surface once again during the 1983 visit of Pope John Paul II to Nicaragua. The pope demanded the resignation of five priests from the government as a precondition of his tour. When these demands were rejected by the priests, the demands were dropped.[55] Yet, during his visit, the pope made clear his dissatisfaction with the Sandinista government as well as with sectors of the Nicaraguan church. The pope attacked what he called the "people's church" and told the masses that they must obey their bishops lest they undermine the unity of the church: "It is absurd and dangerous . . . to imagine alongside—

not to say against—the Church built up around the bishop another Church conceived only as 'charismatic' and not institutional, 'new' and not traditional, alternative and, as lately announced, a popular church."[56]

The pope's visit to Nicaragua set a tone of hostility to the Sandinista government that carried on throughout the years that the Sandinistas held power. The Nicaraguan Episcopal Conference, representing all nine of the country's bishops, issued a pastoral letter in April 1984 urging peace talks with the rebels. Sandinista junta member Sergio Ramirez Mercado denounced it at a public meeting as "a document which is not only totally against the national interest, but which favors the United States." Junta coordinator Daniel Ortega Saavedra said that the letter was "conceived, calculated and structured by the C.I.A." and charged that "some of the bishops have received orientation at the American Embassy in Managua."

The role of Cardinal Obando y Bravo, in particular, was controversial. He characterized the Nicaraguan government as "capable of any barbarity" and was central to the movement of opposition to the Sandinistas. During the Sandinista regime, Enrique Bolanos Geyer, president of the Supreme Council of Private Enterprise, claimed that "the church is the most important source of encouragement for those of us who don't like what is happening. . . . Monsignor Obando is by far the most important leader we have."[57]

The cardinal's political role after 1986, when his chief spokesman and a close associate were expelled from Nicaragua, was increasingly antagonistic toward the Sandinista government. Traveling constantly to rural villages, he drew large crowds to hear his denunciation of the Sandinista regime and its program of compulsory military service.[58] Over time, the cardinal's message became more strident. He accused Sandinista ideology of sowing "the seeds of division and [creating] a desire for vengeance." Moreover, his support of the contra rebels, once implicit in his refusal to condemn contra atrocities against civilians and churchworkers, became more open over the years. The contras considered the cardinal a heroic symbol of the anti-Sandinista movement and circulated leaflets claiming that "Cardinal Obando is with us."[59]

A major public rupture within the Catholic church over the cardinal's support of U.S. aid to the contras occurred in 1986. Nicaraguan Foreign Minister Miguel d'Escoto Brockmann, a Catholic priest, labeled Obando as "on the side of the imperialist aggressor," echoing the charge by the Sandinista-controlled newspaper *Barricada* that the cardinal was "in favor of more death and crimes against our people." To underline his opposition to Obando's support for U.S. aid to the contra rebels, d'Escoto launched an "evangelical insurrection," including a month-long fast and a lengthy Way of the Cross for peace.[60]

Cardinal Obando, despite dissent within the hierarchy and Vatican pressure to soften his public role as government antagonist, counterattacked. He called d'Escoto a devil sent to divide Catholic believers in Nicaragua and attacked the popular church movement as a "belligerent group . . . [who] by their acts, work actively to undermine the unity of the same church."[61]

In 1987, Cardinal Obando was appointed chairman of the four-member National Reconciliation Commission to verify Nicaragua's compliance with the terms of the Central American peace accord. Later that year, Obando's adviser was allowed to reenter the country and the cardinal was named by the Sandinista government as a mediator between contra rebels and the regime, a move welcomed by contra leaders who saw him as an ally.[62] Yet, relations between the Sandinistas and the cardinal remained contentious. The government repeatedly closed, re-opened, and reclosed the Catholic radio station in Managua, accusing it of "inciting to violence, disorder and lack of respect."[63] At the same time, continued contra attacks on churchworkers increased pressure on the hierarchy to censor contra military actions.[64]

By 1988 the facade of goodwill between the cardinal and the Sandinistas was dropped entirely. The Nicaraguan government dismissed Obando as a mediator, citing his bias against the Sandinistas. The government also claimed that Obando pressured the Sandinistas to make unreasonable political concessions in an attempt to sabotage the cease-fire initiative and thereby legitimize continued U.S. aid to the contra rebels.[65] For his part, the cardinal labeled the Sandinistas intransigent and said that the government was to blame for the collapse of peace talks.[66] Even a visit to the Vatican by Nicaraguan President Daniel Ortega did little to ease the conflict. Pope John Paul II gave Ortega a chilly reception, lecturing him on the need for greater democracy and freedom in the Sandinista government.[67]

Tensions between church and state, such as those described above in Nicaragua and El Salvador, are not only a matter of national political battles within those nations. Conflict within the Catholic church also has erupted within theological circles. In March 1984 a right-wing Italian Catholic lay magazine carried an article on liberation theology by Joseph Cardinal Ratzinger, the West German who heads the influential Vatican office, Sacred Congregation for Doctrine of the Faith. The article accused several Latin American liberation theologians of flirting with Marxism and class warfare. In response to the ensuing furor the

Vatican issued a statement claiming that the document was intended as a working paper and had been published without the cardinal's consent. Nonetheless, many within the church regarded this publication as an attempt to influence a meeting in Bogotá between the Sacred Congregation and CELAM that would consider the issue of liberation theology.[68]

Ratzinger's attacks on liberation theology as "a fundamental danger for the faith of the church" resulted in the interrogation of Leonardo Boff, a Brazilian liberation theologian, by the Sacred Congregation. Boff was called to the Vatican to answer charges of doctrinal error in his book, *Church: Charisma and Power*, which analyzed the hierarchical church from a Marxist perspective.[69] In 1985 he was ordered silenced by the Vatican. Moreover, the Vatican also issued a document entitled "Instructions on Certain Aspects of the 'Theology of Liberation,' " prepared by the Sacred Congregation and issued by Pope John Paul II, which criticized liberation theology for identifying religious salvation with human liberation. By 1986, however, the Vatican softened somewhat in its opposition.[70]

The response from liberation theologians has been strong and public. In answer to Cardinal Ratzinger's initial attack, a group of prominent theologians, including Gutierrez of Peru, Edward Schillebeeckx of the Netherlands, and Hans Kung of West Germany, issued a statement defending liberation theology and attacking its critics: "There are tensions necessary to the life of the church, but today these are exacerbated by integrist and neoconservative groups. Resisting all social change and holding that religion has nothing to do with politics, they fight against movements of liberation and make choices that constitute an offense against the poor and oppressed."[71]

What is the likely scenario in Central America, based on the experiences of Nicaragua and El Salvador and internal strife in the church? Such prediction is necessarily tentative and speculative since regional and national church alignments are often the product of shifting global church politics. However, some trends do emerge from this historical analysis of Central American Catholic church history.

First, in countries where official and quasi-official repression targets significant portions of the clergy or lay leadership, the hierarchy of the church is likely to be drawn into at least verbal confrontation with the government. The pattern of El Salvador is currently being repeated in Guatemala. There, intense repression of churchworkers, especially those affiliated with the Justice and Peace Commission, the expulsion and withdrawal of foreign priests and nuns, and the murder of thirteen priests since 1974 have broken the historical alliance of church and state.[72] Under the leadership of Archbishop Prospero Penados del

Barrio, appointed in 1984, the Guatemalan church has begun to encourage democratic forces within the country. In 1988 the bishops issued a pastoral letter entitled "Clamor for Land," which called for serious agrarian reform.

The well-publicized land reform efforts of Andres Giron, a Guatemalan priest, have been an impetus to the bishops' action. Giron is a major force behind the Pro-Land Peasant Federation, a land reform organization with three hundred thousand members. Dissatisfied with the slow pace of agrarian reform under President Vinicio Cerezo Arevalo, Father Giron has threatened to invade and seize land illegally for peasant cooperatives.[73] As a consequence, tension between the military sectors of the Guatemalan government and the church remains very high.

Even in Panama and Honduras, countries with little history of Catholic church involvement in reform movements, there is beginning to be pressure on the hierarchy from those in the lower ranks to challenge the government. Yet, for the most part, the Catholic church in these two countries has remained largely apolitical.[74]

Second, although the years since Vatican II have seen the rise of a counterreform movement within the church to moderate or reverse its liberalization, this movement is not likely to succeed. The theological, liturgical, and political reforms of Vatican II were institutionalized in many forms throughout the global church. In Central America, they gave rise to theological and political movements of a Christianity from the perspective of the poor and oppressed and to structural links between secular reform movements and the church in the base communities. Despite the desire of some people within the church to move away from confrontation with right-wing governments, these reforms, once widespread and institutionalized, are not likely to be reversible within the immediate future.[75]

Third, although the Roman Catholic church continues to dominate religious life in Central America, fundamentalist and evangelical Protestant churches are quickly gaining adherents. One quarter of Guatemala's population now participates in a Protestant evangelical church, fueled by an extensive and repressive conversion program during the 1982–83 regime of General José Ríos Montt, a member of the evangelical Gospel Outreach. Evangelical Protestantism also has found converts in Nicaragua, with its anti-Sandinista, anti-"popular church" message, and in Panama. As evangelicals, with their emphasis on otherworldliness and moral conservatism, gain converts in Central America, the participation of church members in political and theological liberation movements may be reduced.[76]

Finally, the continuing struggle for, and within, the Central American Catholic church has had ramifications outside the region as well. In the United States and Western Europe, the hierarchy and laity have become politically active in Central American issues, largely in opposition to Western intervention. Church members have been the major impetus in the movement to provide sanctuary to Salvadoran and Guatemalan refugees. During the Sandinista regime, for example, the National Conference of Catholic Bishops urged an end to Washington's support of the contra war in Nicaragua, calling current U.S. policy "morally flawed."[77]

In Central America, the Catholic church fundamentally shapes the nature of political conflict and possibilities for political change. Since the colonial period, the church has been a powerful actor. This influence is not likely to be eroded substantially in the near future. Yet, political processes are not molded in a simple way by the power of the church; it is a complex and dynamic institution whose political agendas do not always correspond to secular political divisions of right and left. Thus, the Catholic hierarchy may support revolutionary movements of the left in some countries and oppose leftist governments or parties in other countries. Moreover, the Catholic church, especially in Central America, does not speak with a single voice. Internal divisions, reflecting differences of authority and political analysis, can be seen in the contradictory views that members of the hierarchy and laity espouse in secular politics. The future results of the church's influence in Central American politics will be determined not only by the relations of church and state in each country but also by the shifting balance of power within the larger institution of the Catholic church.

Notes

1. Penny Lernoux, *Cry of the People* (New York: Penguin, 1982), 18.

2. See André Gunder Frank, *Latin America: Underdevelopment or Revolution* (New York: Monthly Review Press, 1969), 3–17 for a history of the "development of underdevelopment" in Latin America. See also Phillip Berryman, *The Religious Roots of Rebellion* (Maryknoll, NY: Orbis Books, 1984), for an interpretation of the colonial "original sin" in Central America.

3. Daniel Levine, "Religion and Politics," in Levine, ed., *Churches and Politics in Latin America* (Beverly Hills: Sage, 1980), 23.

4. On the case of Christian Democracy in Chile see James Petras, *Politics and Social Forces in Chilean Development* (Berkeley: University of California Press, 1969), 197–255.

5. Cornel West, "Religion and the Left: An Introduction," *Monthly Review* 36 (July-August 1984): 13–16. The conversion of Camilo Torres, a Colombian priest, to the guerrilla movement and his subsequent death is an extreme example of this. See Maurice Zeitlin, ed., *Father Camilo Torres: Revolutionary Writings* (New York: Harper Colophon, 1969), passim. See also Blase Bonpane's reflections on the *Cursillos de Capacitacion Social*—a Catholic pastoral movement in the Guatemalan highlands that ultimately secularized and established ties with the guerrillas—in his *Guerrillas of Peace* (Boston: South End Press, 1985).

6. See Gustavo Gutierrez, *A Theology of Liberation* (Maryknoll, NY: Orbis Books, 1973), 8 for a discussion of *Gaudium et spes*, no. 1, which details Vatican II's position that the church "does not 'find itself' except when it 'loses itself,' when it lives 'the joys and the hopes, the griefs and the anxieties of men of this age.' " See also Edward L. Cleary, *Crisis and Change* (Maryknoll, NY: Orbis Books, 1985).

7. Levine, "Religion and Politics," 21.

8. The theological basis of this is found in Vatican II's *Gaudium et spes*, No. 44, discussed in Gutierrez, *A Theology of Liberation*, 8–9. See also Michael Fleet, "The Church and Revolutionary Struggle in Central America," *Social Text* (Spring-Summer 1983): 106–14; Lernoux, *Cry of the People*, 31; and Levine, "Religion and Politics," 22–23.

9. Phillip Berryman, "Basic Christian Communities and the Future of Latin America," *Monthly Review* (July-August 1984): 32.

10. Michael Dodson, "The Christian Left in Latin American Politics," 114–16, as well as Brian Smith, "Churches and Human Rights in Latin America," 156–57, 162–67, and Levine, "Religion and Politics," 23–25; all in Levine, ed., *Churches and Politics*.

11. Michael Dodson, "The Church and Political Struggle: Faith and Action in Central America," *Latin American Research Review* 23 (1988): 230–43; Levine, "Religion and Politics," 24; Lernoux, *Cry of the People*, 38.

12. Lernoux, *Cry of the People*, 40, 372–75; Berryman, "Basic Christian Communities," 29–31.

13. Jose Miguel Bonino, *Doing Theology in a Revolutionary Setting* (Philadelphia: Fortress, 1975), passim; Gutierrez, *A Theology of Liberation*, 21–42; Dodson, "The Church and Political Struggle," passim.

14. Levine, "Religion and Politics," 28–30; Tommie Sue Montgomery, "Cross and Rifle: Revolution and the Church in El Salvador and Nicaragua," *Journal of Inter-American Affairs* (Fall-Winter 1982–83): 209–21.

15. Berryman, "Basic Christian Communities," 27–40.

16. Lernoux, *Cry of the People*, 40–41.

17. Berryman, "Basic Christian Communities," 27–40; Fleet, "The Church and Revolutionary Struggle," 106–14; Smith, "Churches and Human Rights," 162–77; Dodson, "The Church and Political Struggle," 233.

18. Berryman, "Basic Christian Communities," 34–37.

19. Lernoux, *Cry of the People*, 381.

20. Ibid., 18, 382.

21. Michael Fleet, "Neo-Conservatism in Latin America," *Concilium* 161 (January 1981): passim; Cesar Jerez, *The Church in Central America* (New York: Inter-Religious Task Force in El Salvador and Central America, 1981), passim.

22. Fleet, "Neo-Conservatism," passim.

23. Phillip Berryman, "What Happened at Puebla," in Levine, ed., *Churches and Politics*, 61–62; Lernoux, *Cry of the People*, 412–25. See also *Reflections and Problems of a Church Being Born among the People: Popular Church Challenge to Puebla, Mexico Meeting* (Washington, DC: EPICA, 1978), passim.

24. Conor Cruise O'Brien, "God and Man in Nicaragua," *Atlantic Monthly* 258 (August 1986): 50–72; Lernoux, *Cry of the People*, 425–32. Such seeming contradictions in ideological perspective reflect the complex mission of the papacy, which translates dogma and tradition for contemporary issues while attempting to reconcile conflicting goals and issues within the church. Papal pronouncements, therefore, rarely can be categorized along a simple ideological spectrum. For example, see Pope John Paul II's 1983 discourses on labor and economics, published as "Work and Unemployment" and "Man and His Values: The Aim of Economics," in *The Pope Speaks: The Church Documents Quarterly* 28 (1983): 259–68.

25. Gary MacEoin and Nivita Riley, *Puebla: A Church Being Born* (New York: Paulist Press, 1980), passim.

26. "La Evangelizacion en el Presente y en el Futuro de America Latina" (Puebla, CELAM, February 13, 1979): 1–232, quoted in Lernoux, *Cry of the People*, 442.

27. Fleet, "The Church and Revolutionary Struggle," passim; Montgomery, "Cross and Rifle," passim.

28. Lernoux, *Cry of the People*, 61–80.

29. National Assembly of Women Religious, "Crucifixion and Resurrection in El Salvador," *Probe* (March 1981): passim.

30. Lernoux, *Cry of the People*, 61–80.

31. Berryman, "Basic Christian Communities," 35–36.

32. Fleet, "The Church and Revolutionary Struggle," 111–12.

33. Dodson, "The Church and Political Struggle," 237.

34. John Sobrino, "Archbishop Romero: A Powerful Prophet," *Maryknoll* 75, no. 3 (March 1981): 26–29.

35. Berryman, *The Religious Roots*, 271–72.

36. Fleet, "The Church and Revolutionary Struggle," passim.

37. "Salvador Cleric Sees Death Squad Threat," *Los Angeles Times*, November 16, 1987; Phillip Berryman, "El Salvador: From Evangelization to Insurrection," in Daniel H. Levine, ed., *Religion and Political Conflict in Latin America* (Chapel Hill: University of North Carolina Press, 1986).

38. "News in Brief—El Salvador's Roman Catholic Archbishop Threatens to Excommunicate Women," *Christian Science Monitor*, June 9, 1987; "Salvadoran Prelate Assails Rights Protest at Cathedral," *Boston Globe*, June 8, 1987. For background on *comadres* see "America Sosa Explains Why She Joined *Comadres*," *Chicago Tribune*, January 18, 1987.

39. "Salvadoran Army Says Church Is Infiltrated," *New York Times*, January 31, 1989; Peter O'Driscoll, "Letter from El Salvador," *America* 158 (April 16, 1988): 401–5.

40. "Salvadoran Judge Bars Amnesty for Killers of 4 U.S. Women," *New York Times*, January 9, 1988; "A Reminder of a Painful U.S. Role in El Salvador," ibid., December 6, 1987; "Rightists in Salvador Challenge Duarte," ibid., November 26, 1987; "Salvadoran Rightists Warn Duarte, Back d'Aubuisson," *Los Angeles Times*, November 26, 1987.

41. "Court in El Salvador Indicts 8 Soldiers in Jesuit Slayings," *New York Times*, January 20, 1990; "Cristiani Describes Colonel's Role in Killings," ibid., January 17, 1990; "6 Priests Killed in a Campus Raid in San Salvador," ibid., November 17, 1989.

42. "Salvador Judge Faults Evidence and Frees American in Arms Case," ibid., December 14, 1989; " 'People Cared,' Casolo Says of Her Release,"*Los Angeles Times*, December 15, 1989.

43. "In El Salvador, a Widening Campaign of Repression," *New York Times*, December 21, 1989; "Salvador Army Is Cracking Down on Relief and Church Agencies," ibid., December 8, 1989.

44. "The Church in Nicaragua," *El Salvador Bulletin* (October 1982): 1, 5–6.

45. Montgomery, "Cross and Rifle," 218.

46. Fleet, "The Church and Revolutionary Struggle," 112–13.

47. Montgomery, "Cross and Rifle," passim; "Church and Revolution in Nicaragua," *Central American Update* (November 1982): passim.

48. Roger N. Lancaster's research on barrios in Managua suggests that the "popular church" is strongest in lower and middle working-class neighborhoods, while evangelical Protestantism has the most appeal among the residents of marginated slums. See Lancaster, "The Church and Revolutions in Nicaragua: Popular Religion and Class Consciousness in Managua's Working-Class Barrios," paper presented at the meeting of the Latin American Studies Association, 1988.

49. "The Church in Nicaragua," 1, 5–6; Berryman, *The Religious Roots*, 221–76.

50. Berryman, *The Religious Roots*, 270.

51. Ibid.; "Are Nicaragua's Churches Free?" *Christianity and Crisis* (September 20, 1982): 250–53.

52. The history of many of these early conflicts is detailed in "Are Nicaragua's Churches Free?" 250–53; and "Church and Revolution in Nicaragua," passim.

53. "Church and Revolution in Nicaragua," 1–5.

54. Thomas W. Walker, "Nicaragua: Catholic Unity Dissolves in Revolutionary Nicaragua," *Mesoamerica* (September 1982): 8.

55. "Pope Says Taking Sides in Nicaragua Is Peril to Church," *New York Times*, March 5, 1983; "Truce between Nicaraguan Catholics and Junta Discussed," *Christian Science Monitor*, December 17, 1982.

56. Pope John Paul II, "Unity of the Church: Homily at Mass in 'July 19 Square' during Visit to Managua, Nicaragua," *The Pope Speaks: The Church Documents Quarterly* 28, no. 3 (Fall 1983): 206–10.

57. "Archbishop Denounces Sandinistas," *New York Times*, May 22, 1984.

58. "Obando: Sandinista Critic Takes Role as Mediator," *Los Angeles Times*, November 13, 1987.

59. "Obando as Peacemaker: A Stormy Path," *New York Times*, November 10, 1987.

60. Ibid.; O'Brien, "God and Man in Nicaragua," passim.

61. "Obando: Sandinista Critic Takes Role"; O'Brien, "God and Man in Nicaragua," passim.

62. "Sandinistas Name Cardinal in Talks for a Cease Fire," *New York Times*, November 7, 1987; "The World: For Bishops and Sandinistas, There's No Reconciliation," ibid., October 25, 1987; "Clergyman to Return to Managua," ibid., August 27, 1987.

63. "Nicaragua Lifts Ban on Catholic Radio Station," ibid., September 23, 1987; "Sandinistas Ban Stations' Plan for Radio News," ibid., October 20, 1987. See also *Wall Street Journal*, July 12, 1988.

64. See Edgar Rivera, "Death and Resurrection in Matiguas," *America* 157 (October 24, 1987): 261–62.

65. "Sandinistas Go on the Political Offensive," *New York Times*, March 5, 1988; "Strife Grows in Nicaragua," ibid., February 24, 1988.

66. "An Impasse Halts Nicaraguan Talks," ibid., February 20, 1988; "Sandinistas Are at Fault, Mediator Implies," *Chicago Tribune*, February 22, 1988.

67. "Pope Gives Ortega a Cool Reception," *New York Times,* January 30, 1988; "Pontiff Lectures Ortega in Chilly Vatican Meeting," *Los Angeles Times*, January 30, 1988.

68. T. M. Pasca, "Church of the Poor: A Wafer the Vatican Can't Swallow," *Nation* (June 2, 1984).

69. "Church's Activist Clerics: Rome Draws Line," *New York Times*, September 6, 1984; "Brazilian Faces a Vatican Inquiry over Support for Social Activism," ibid., August 20, 1984.

70. O'Brien, "God and Man in Nicaragua," passim; "Vatican Censures Marxist Elements in New Theology," *New York Times*, September 4, 1984.

71. "Text of Statement Issued by Catholic Theologians," *New York Times*, June 25, 1984.

72. Berryman, "El Salvador," 74–78.

73. "Guatemalan Priest Rev. Andres de Jesus Giron," *Boston Globe*, January 18, 1987; "Rev. Andres Giron Crusades," *Chicago Tribune,* May 13, 1987; "Guatemalan Peasants Find New Ally in Land Bid," *Christian Science Monitor*, May 3, 1988.

74. "Panama's Reluctant Church," *Christian Science Monitor*, April 12, 1988; "Reportedly Slain Priest's Family Sues U.S. for Papers," *Los Angeles Times*, February 5, 1988; "Leaders of Panama's Roman Catholic Church Accuse Government Troops," *Boston Globe*, June 14, 1987; "Panama Church Joins Noriega Foes," ibid., March 10, 1988; "In First Public Plea, Church Asks Noriega to Quit," ibid., March 30, 1988.

75. Fleet, "Neo-Conservatives," passim.

76. Berryman, *The Religious Roots*, 272–73; Penny Lernoux, "The Fundamentalist Surge in Latin America," *Christian Century* 105 (January 20, 1988): 51–54; Enrique Dominguez and Deborah Huntington, "The Salvation Brokers," *NACLA Report on the Americas* 18 (January-February 1984): 2–36; Deborah Huntington, "Visions of the Kingdom: The Latin American Church in Conflict," ibid. 19 (September October 1985): 27–47.

77. "Churches and U.S. Clash on Alien Sanctuary," *New York Times*, June 28, 1984.

Democracy and Revolution in Nicaragua*

Ilja A. Luciak

Nicaragua was once considered the "country in the world with the greatest opportunity to arrive at revolutionary democratic Marxism."[1] In North America, democracy and socialism generally are considered mutually exclusive, yet the reality of the Nicaraguan revolution frequently challenged conventional wisdom.

Historic Roots of Sandinista Democracy

The Sandinista vision of democracy synthesized two policy goals: popular hegemony and national unity.[2] These goals complemented and contradicted each other. Popular hegemony was supposed to transform the inherited political system to benefit the previously marginalized majority, yet success required the cooperation of the capitalist class in a framework of national unity. Thus, the Sandinistas set out to pursue a revolutionary transformation of society implying a redistribution of benefits toward the poor through an institutional framework in which the rich were to be represented.

Held out as an incentive for the bourgeoisie to join the revolution, the goal of national unity had precise limits. The interests and demands of the bourgeoisie were to be subordinated to the central objective of the revolution—transformation of the political and economic structures to benefit the impoverished workers and peasants. These "popular classes"[3] did not include the bourgeoisie, although at times agreements were to be concluded with it. Thus, popular hegemony in itself was a policy of alliance. The common denominator for all groups was support for some portion of the Sandinista vision of Nicaragua's future. By contrast, the goal of national unity permitted coalitions among opposing sectors of Nicaraguan society. The dialectic relationship between popular hegemony and national unity would be determined by the respective strengths of the popular classes and the bourgeoisie. Hence, the task facing the Sandinistas was Herculean—to transform society in ways that elicited bourgeois cooperation while presupposing its domination.

Three factors influenced Sandinista efforts to reconcile these contradictions: 1) the splitting and reunification of the Frente Sandinista de Liberación Nacional (FSLN); 2) the role of the masses in the insurrection of 1977–1979; and 3) the weakness of the worker and peasant classes. The conditions of the guerrilla struggle, especially the difficulty of communication, impeded development of a common strategy. The leaders of the FSLN could not meet between 1970 and 1975 to discuss the lessons learned since the inception of revolution in the early 1960s, and they could not resolve internal differences on the crucial questions of class alliances and strategy.[4] These disagreements developed into an open rift in 1975 when Carlos Fonseca, an eminent leader, expelled several high-ranking members. One of them, Jaime Wheelock, later became a member of the Sandinista National Directorate and minister of agriculture.[5]

Several factions emerged. One embraced Che Guevara's ideas on the importance of armed struggle.[6] The guerrilla fighters would constitute a vanguard that would lead the peasants to victory. Other Sandinistas held that the "war of the guerrilla" eventually would be eclipsed by insurrectional fighting. The latter formed the Proletarian and the Insurrectional *tendencias*, while the former became known as the Prolonged Popular War (GPP) faction. The Proletarian Tendency (TP) advocated clandestine organizing among workers, peasants, and progressive youth as a precondition for a successful insurrection. The Sandinista fighters needed to end their isolation from the proletariat and take advantage of this growing, militant sector.[7] The Insurrectional Tendency (commonly known as *Terceristas*) favored broad class alliances and believed that a progressive accumulation of different social forces would bring down Anastasio Somoza. The *Terceristas* thought that conditions for a successful uprising already existed, while the GPP faction urged mobilizing the peasantry for long-term conflict.[8]

Each group attempted to dominate the guerrilla movement, and relations between them were tense until a spontaneous September 1978 uprising led to a reassessment of strategy. The Sandinistas realized that the guerrillas would support the masses rather than the reverse. In

March 1979 increased mass participation and the growing crisis of the Somoza dictatorship reunified the Sandinista Front.[9] The leadership was flexible enough to acknowledge that the popular forces had advanced more rapidly than the vanguard. Comandante Humberto Ortega, member of the National Directorate of the FSLN and minister of defense under the FSLN (and President Violeta Chamorro), summarized the lesson:

> The uprising of the masses in the aftermath of the assassination of [publisher Pedro Joaquín] Chamorro was not led exclusively by the FSLN. It was a spontaneous reaction on the part of the masses, which, in the end, the Sandinista Front began to direct through its activists and a number of military units. *It was not a mass movement responding to the call of the Sandinistas.*[10]

This experience demonstrated the importance of a strategy of alliance. The united movement was headed by the nine-member National Directorate composed of Daniel Ortega, Humberto Ortega, and Victor Tirado of the Insurrectional Tendency; Tomás Borge, Bayardo Arce, and Henry Ruiz of the Prolonged Popular War faction; and Carlos Núñez, Luis Carrión, and Jaime Wheelock of the Proletarian Tendency. The directorate agreed on the increased importance of the *Terceristas*. The main elements of its platform were the insurrectional character of the struggle, the necessity for a flexible alliance, and a broad pragmatic program.[11]

The FSLN's evolution toward greater pragmatism was not entirely the work of the *Terceristas*. Marxist-Leninist ideology predominated until the mid-1970s, when increased resistance to the dictatorship brought in many non-Marxists.[12] In particular, many radicalized Christians joined the Sandinistas, thus making the movement less doctrinaire and broadening its ideological appeal.[13] Nicaraguan peasants and workers, who belonged to the marginalized class of society and did not constitute a political force under Somoza, also shaped the Sandinista vision. The working class, only 210,000 people, represented less than one third of the economically active population. The proletariat was strongest in the rural sector with 130,000 salaried agricultural workers, compared to 80,000 urban workers.[14] The Sandinistas realized that a revolutionary strategy based exclusively on workers and peasants would fail. Thus, they recruited nonsalaried workers, small merchants, and professionals. The weakness of the Nicaraguan worker and peasant class along with Somoza's ousting by a coalition led the revolutionary authorities to envision an order of political pluralism. The Sandinistas sought the support of all groups that had suffered under Somoza.

Representative and Participatory Concepts of Democracy

To understand Sandinista concepts it is necessary to distinguish between formal and substantive democracy. *Formal democracy* consists of rules governing the election of leaders and popular participation in decision making. *Substantive democracy* refers to the ways in which public policy reflects popular interests. Representative democracy and participatory democracy are two subcategories of formal democracy. The former emphasizes the electoral process, while the latter considers mass participation essential. Substantive democracy also has subcategories representing socialist and capitalist visions of how public policy can be presumed to reflect societal interests. These categories are not mutually exclusive, however. The form of decision making frequently can condition the substance of the decision.[15] From a formal perspective, the Sandinistas seek to combine elements of representative and participatory democracy. Their model is socialist, but it incorporates strong capitalist and even some precapitalist features. Consequently, the aspiration to attain a new model of revolutionary, democratic Marxism was not without cause. The participatory element is central to the Sandinista notion of popular hegemony, and representative features are necessary for national unity. Participation by the masses would set the priorities of a proposed socioeconomic transition according to "the logic of the majority," yet this transformation would occur within a kind of national unity that required a mixed economy and political pluralism.

In the 1980s many writers shifted to participatory democracy, and theorists across the ideological spectrum criticized representative democracy. In the North American context, Benjamin Barber argued "that an excess of liberalism had undone democratic institutions" and advocated a return to participatory politics.[16] Revolutionary movements rejected formal democracy. Elections every four years were not enough. Those held by Somoza had been meaningless exercises, mere show elections designed to legitimize the regime rather than determine the makeup of the government.[17] In this context the institutions of representative democracy were considered of little value in a social revolution.[18] In general, new regimes considered their revolutionary project more important than adherence to the rules of formal democracy. Where revolutionary governments have demonstrated their capacity to construct social and economic democracy, meaningful political participation has often been restricted.[19]

The Sandinistas began to promote participation during the insurrection. For postinsurrectional tasks they were influenced by the Cuban experience of mass mobilization. The Sandinista Front even enjoyed an advantage over the Cuban guerrillas. Mass participation was limited in the Cuban case, but the Nicaraguan insurrection involved thousands of civilians, giving the peasants and workers confidence in their ability to better their living conditions and providing the foundation for mobilizing the masses for reconstruction. Comandante Borge, member of the National Directorate and minister of the interior (1979–1990), emphasized that "the masses themselves must always—now and in the future—speak up in a loud, clear voice on their own behalf. They must develop ways of participating and taking initiatives."[20]

Participatory Democracy and Popular Hegemony

The initial political structures in revolutionary Nicaragua emphasized participatory democracy. At the national level the Council of State, a corporatist, co-legislative body, was to guarantee the participation of every major social movement. Originally, the Sandinista leadership doubted the virtue of electoral democracy, although elections had been promised. Structured according to Leninist principles of party-building, the FSLN conceived itself the vanguard of the revolution, and it was not prepared to be challenged in elections. Further, the immediate concern was to improve the conditions of the poor, not to provide a political forum for the bourgeoisie.[21]

Nicaragua's history played an important role in Sandinista thinking. When General Augusto Sandino secured the withdrawal of U.S. Marines in 1932, his forces disarmed, believing their task accomplished. After Sandino's assassination, however, the oligarchy resumed control, and the possibility of restructuring society was lost.[22] Thus, the Sandinistas did not want to squander their opportunity. Finally, electoral democracy had been thoroughly discredited by the fraudulent elections held by the Somoza dynasty.

Some FSLN radicals argued that electoral structures were irrelevant to the institutionalization of a participatory model. In 1980, Julio López, the FSLN's secretary for propaganda and political education, argued that "the purpose of elections is not to determine who will have power in Nicaragua. This question has been determined by history and the people affirm this fact on a daily basis."[23]

The bourgeois opposition vehemently rejected this view.[24] While they advocated the institutionalization of representative features that would have benefited them, the Sandinistas initially implemented participatory democracy.[25] According to Humberto Ortega, power was to be "exercised by Sandinismo, which means the people, through a higher form of organization and their own form of mass organization; here other sectors that are not Sandinistas subsist, but they do so inasmuch as this power permits them to and inasmuch as they really do not affect the revolutionary project."[26] This statement indicates the leadership's intent to establish hegemony over opposing sectors of Nicaraguan society. The official view of democracy was outlined by the National Directorate of the FSLN in 1980:

> For the Frente Sandinista democracy is not measured solely in the political sphere, and cannot be reduced only to the participation of the people in elections. Democracy is not simply elections. It is something more, much more . . . it means participation by the people in political, social and cultural affairs. The more people participate in such matters, the more democratic they will be . . . democracy neither begins nor ends with elections. It is a myth to want to reduce democracy to that status. Democracy begins in the economic order, when social inequalities begin to diminish, when the workers and peasants improve their standard of living. That is when true democracy begins, not before. . . . In a more advanced phase, democracy means the participation of the workers in the running of factories, farms, cooperatives and cultural centers. To sum up, democracy is the intervention of the masses in all aspects of social life.[27]

Sandinista democracy thus incorporated representative features, but it emphasized the participatory element. Popular democracy began in the economic order, and direct participation by the people in all sectors of life was crucial. Although the leadership did not reject electoral democracy, elections were not important. From a pluralist perspective, the problem with this view of democracy was the limited importance given to representative features: The ruling elite determines whether there is democracy and judges whether policies serve the poor. Without elections, how are workers and peasants to express their opinion and change the government? Further, it does not necessarily follow that if more people participate in the political system it will be more democratic. The Fascist experience in Europe in the 1930s demonstrated that mass participation cannot be equated with increased democracy. Indeed, mass participation is not by itself sufficient. Quality of participation is the issue.

Formal State Power and Participatory Structures

Formal political power in the early days of the revolution was invested in the Governing Junta, established in exile in Costa Rica several weeks before the successful insurrection, and the Council of State, inaugurated in May 1980.[28] The first junta, composed of the broad forces that overthrew Somoza, included Daniel Ortega, a member, as we know, of the National Directorate of the FSLN; Sergio Ramírez of the Group of Twelve; Moisés Hassan of the United People's Movement (MPU); Violeta Barrios de Chamorro, widow of Pedro Joaquín Chamorro and co-owner of the newspaper *La Prensa*; and Alfonso Robelo, a businessman and head of the Nicaraguan Democratic Movement (MDN).

Although the junta was nominally the highest decision-making authority, real power was vested in the Sandinista party and its National Directorate. The ideological preferences of the junta members ensured Sandinista hegemony, since Ortega, Ramírez, and Hassan were all part of the FSLN.[29] The authority of the FSLN as the arbiter of all major decisions was officially recognized in September 1980.[30] Within the party, in turn, the nine-member directorate's supremacy was uncontested. It not only determined major policies but also frequently intervened in their execution.[31] The authority of the FSLN and its directorate was based on its role as the revolutionary vanguard and on its control over the army and police.

The composition of the junta changed between 1979 and 1981. In April 1980, Chamorro resigned for "personal" reasons, although she later criticized the Sandinista agenda.[32] A few days later, Robelo resigned over the changed membership of the Council of State. The FSLN immediately replaced them with two other representatives of the bourgeoisie, Rafael Cordova Rivas and Arturo Cruz. By 1981 the junta consisted of only three members; Cruz had left to become ambassador to the United States, and Hassan had joined the cabinet.[33]

During the first year of the revolution, in the absence of a national legislature, the Governing Junta had legislative authority. Thus, from a formal democratic perspective, the new political system had important limitations. There were no representative political structures and even a participatory framework emerged slowly. Popular participation was limited to the role of the emerging Sandinista mass organizations in representing their constituents' interests.

This improved with the inauguration of the Council of State, Nicaragua's corporatist co-legislative assembly, in May 1980. It consisted of forty-seven delegates from twenty-nine political, professional, and grass-roots organizations and shared legislative functions with the Governing Junta. Originally, it was composed of thirty-three members, only twelve of whom represented the Sandinistas.[34] The composition of the council reflected the importance of the bourgeoisie in the anti-Somoza coalition in early 1979. Predominant on the battlefield, the FSLN could not establish hegemony in the coalition without losing bourgeois support. Thus, participation by the bourgeoisie in the insurrection and the policy of national unity led to its strong representation in the original government.

The balance of forces shifted rapidly when the revolutionary coalition took power. In October 1979 the Sandinistas postponed the constitution of the Council of State until May 1980. Changing its original plans, the FSLN added delegates from fourteen new groups to the proposed council, altering the voting in favor of the peasant and worker classes and establishing popular hegemony. Twelve of the fourteen new organizations supported the FSLN, which had an obvious interest in adding them to the council. The bourgeois opposition argued that this violated an agreement concluded prior to Somoza's fall,[35] but the Sandinistas held that the original composition of the council did not take into account important changes in society since 1979. For example, not a single grass-roots movement was included. Several of these organizations had demonstrated explosive growth and demanded representation. The Association of Rural Workers (ATC), for example, had organized more than one hundred thousand rural workers and agricultural producers by mid-1980, and some of the council's original organizations, such as the Group of Twelve, had been dissolved.[36] The mass organizations, together with the FSLN and the armed forces, controlled twenty-four of the forty-seven seats in the assembly. The absolute majority held by the popular forces and the FSLN made clear the latter's determination to ensure popular hegemony and the limits of national unity. The importance of the grass-roots movements in the legislature further confirmed the Sandinista emphasis on participatory democracy.

Over its four years, the Council of State's composition changed several times. Membership was expanded to fifty-one in the assembly's second session. Most significantly, the newly founded National Union of Farmers and Ranchers (UNAG) obtained two seats in 1981.[37] The final change took place on August 6, 1984, when the Marxist-Leninists (MAP-ML) and their labor union, the Workers' Front (FO), entered the council. These ultraleft sectors had been excluded in 1980 because the Sandinistas considered their radical criticism counterrevolutionary.[38] The private sector, represented by the Superior Council of Private

Enterprise (COSEP) and several right-wing parties, left the council in November 1980 when COSEP's vice president, Jorge Salazar, was killed by Sandinista police. The bourgeoisie's representatives returned, however, in May 1983.

From the perspective of Sandinista democracy, the Council of State was the first attempt to create a representative structure with a strong participatory component, thus embodying two central features of the revolutionary project. By 1981 the six main Sandinista mass organizations controlled eighteen seats, compared with thirteen for all parties represented, including the FSLN. The popular, corporatist character of the council was to give all sectors of society participation in national decision making. The grass-roots organizations ensured that the poor majority finally had political representation. The Council of State enabled the grass-roots movements to participate in decision making and to voice their concerns. They introduced several important laws.[39] Nevertheless, considering their significant role in Sandinista democracy, their participation in the council was limited. Comandante Núñez, president of the Council of State, several times criticized them for not representing their constituents' interests more forcefully.[40]

The grass-roots movements constituted central features in the Sandinistas' attempt to strengthen participatory democracy. The six main organizations were the Sandinista Workers' Federation, the ATC, the UNAG, the Luisa Amanda Espinosa Association of Nicaraguan Women, the Sandinista Defense Committees, and the July 19th Sandinista Youth.[41]

When the Sandinistas took power in 1979, Nicaragua had only 138 unions, with fewer than 30,000 members.[42] During the revolution, several organizations representing the urban proletariat united into the Sandinista Workers' Federation (CST). By 1989 this group had six hundred affiliated unions with 150,000 members. It promoted economic policies based on raising productivity and expanding social services rather than on increasing salaries. This created problems for the CST, which had to compete with right-wing and ultraleft organizations whose demands for immediate improvements, although more in tune with working-class wishes, were impossible to satisfy.[43] Once government programs for the workers started to improve living conditions, the CST began to gain the trust of the working class.[44] Following the 1990 elections, the Sandinista labor movement integrated in the National Workers' Front (FNT) has become more belligerent, demanding salary increases and job security. This new militancy translated into strikes during May and June 1990, presenting the Chamorro government with its first significant challenge.

The Association of Rural Workers (ATC) was formed in March 1978 as the result of efforts by the Catholic church and the Sandinistas to organize committees of agricultural workers to protest the exploitation of the peasantry.[45] Initially, the ATC organized both agricultural workers and small and medium producers. The organization grew rapidly, numbering 105,000 by 1981. The movement could not accommodate the conflicting demands of its diverse membership, thus causing the exodus of the agricultural producers and a substantial loss for the rural workers' movement. In 1989 it represented about 50,000 permanent and 70,000 seasonal agricultural workers, with the majority employed on state farms.[46]

The National Union of Farmers and Ranchers (UNAG) was established on April 25, 1981, and is the youngest of the organizations. It was created by farmers and ranchers who felt inadequately represented by the ATC and the established producers' organizations.[47] It has evolved into the most important organization in the countryside, representing 124,000 agricultural producers in 1989. Its significance is attested through its recognition by the International Labor Organization (ILO) as the agricultural representative of Nicaragua's private sector. Both the ATC and UNAG have made substantial contributions to the development of the countryside.

In the 1970s the Association of Women Confronting the National Problematic (AMPRONAC) promoted the participation of women in the insurrection and spoke out against human rights abuses by the Somoza regime. After taking over, the movement honored one of its martyrs by renaming itself the Luisa Amanda Espinosa Association of Nicaraguan Women (AMNLAE), and it started to organize women from all social sectors. Its "Plan of Struggle" sought to integrate women into society on equal terms and to overcome injustices and inequalities.[48] Membership totaled eighty-five thousand in 1984.[49] In 1987, AMNLAE decided to concentrate on strengthening the women's sections in the other grass-roots movements instead of its own growth. Although AMNLAE has been instrumental in passing new legislation to improve the legal status of women, it has not changed the predominant culture of machismo.

The Sandinista Defense Committees (CDS) grew out of neighborhood organizations that provided logistical support for the FSLN during the insurrection. Loosely modeled on the Cuban Committees for the Defense of the Revolution, these groups had more than five hundred thousand members throughout the country by 1984.[50] Although open to all citizens over the age of fourteen, they sought to mobilize people behind the revolution and to assist the state to implement various health, education, and food-distribution programs. Participation in the CDS declined precipitously after the mid-1980s. They were partially revived in 1988 and changed into nonpartisan community organizations under Omar Cabezas, a charismatic Sandinista leader.[51]

The July 19th Sandinista Youth (JS-19) originated in the student movement, which played an important part in the insurrection. Comandante Núñez considers it the youth organization of the party rather than an independent mass organization.[52] Although the JS-19 is not as selective as the FSLN in choosing members and purports to represent all Nicaraguan young people, its close association with the Sandinista Front distinguishes it from other mass organizations. Its greatest accomplishments were the mobilization of tens of thousands of young people in the literacy campaign of 1980, the coffee and cotton harvest brigades, and most significantly the war against the counter-revolution.

According to Núñez, the mass organizations are to "guard and . . . strengthen the political project of the Revolution . . . and . . . be true instruments for expressing, channeling, and receiving the most urgent demands of the masses."[53] These organizations were formed to facilitate participation by the people in all areas of their lives. The involvement of the grass-roots movements in improving basic needs is an essential goal of Sandinista democracy, which advocates "the intervention of the masses in all aspects of social life."[54] The grass-roots movements were particularly active in the literacy and health campaigns. According to Sergio Ramírez, no revolutionary program could have been accomplished without them.[55] At their height, they incorporated more than one half of the adult population and facilitated base democracy.[56]

Whereas the Sandinista party represented a vanguard of the most dedicated revolutionaries, the mass organizations were to mobilize broad popular sectors around their own interests.[57] The close relationship between the masses and the FSLN started to develop only two years before the insurrection.[58] Although the Sandinista Front obviously sought hegemony in these organizations, moderate Sandinista leaders also encouraged pluralism and favored their autonomy. These high-ranking officials opposed FSLN groups that wanted the mass organizations to evolve into important political movements only if they remained under the party's strict control. This position is expressed by radical Sandinista leaders such as Bayardo Arce.[59] While the radicals supported grass-roots movements because they facilitated mobilization of the masses, they feared a threat to their hegemony by independent mass movements and showed little interest in allowing unfettered popular participation.

All these mass organizations recognized the FSLN as their legitimate vanguard, but they demonstrated various degrees of independence from the party. The autonomy of the grass-roots movements was of central importance to Sandinista democracy. Only militant, independent organizations could participate in the development of a democratic political system, represent the interests of their constituents, and ensure the democratic practice of Sandinista hegemony. The Sandinistas conceived of the party, the state, and the mass organizations as three pillars of the revolutionary project, tied together by a common goal but enjoying relative autonomy.[60] The degree of autonomy of any mass organization ultimately depended on its strength and its willingness to challenge the government.

The FSLN and the mass organizations have fought publicly. In particular, the farmers' movement demonstrated its militancy in 1988 when UNAG, over government opposition, obtained debt relief for cattle producers.[61] On other occasions the organizations have changed the government's position and enlarged their own autonomy. The movements range from the JS-19, which had little autonomy, to UNAG, which successfully pursued its interests. Both groups may exhibit autonomy in a post-FSLN era.

Another problem in the development of strong mass organizations is their lack of democracy. As of 1989 these organizations had yet to institutionalize elections at all levels. In general, elections were held only at the base level, while regional and national leaders were appointed by the national leadership upon consultation with the Sandinista Front. Recent elections in the agricultural workers' organization illustrate this point. According to Comandante Arce, in the case of the ATC the FSLN presented thirty candidates for national leadership positions from which the ATC delegates chose ten.[62] This made it difficult to hold leaders accountable. Nevertheless, efforts to strengthen the internal democracy of the grass-roots movements were evident and some leaders were removed by base pressure. The CDS, in particular, experienced abuses by local leaders and a general lack of internal democracy.[63] After a critical reevaluation in 1985, elections were held at every level of the neighborhood committees. At times, the Sandinistas sought to strengthen the grass-roots movements by imposing new leadership. In 1988 two high-ranking Sandinista officials, Lea Guido and Cabezas, were named to head the AMNLAE and CDS, respectively. While Cabezas had some success in restructuring the neighborhood committees, such top-down measures are counterproductive to autonomous, democratic organizational growth.

The dialectic between the grass-roots movements and the FSLN has been described as follows: "at times led by, at times ahead of and autonomous from the leadership of the FSLN, in general without a neat definition of the relationship between the revolutionary party and the mass organizations."[64] The necessity of organizing the masses while ensuring the autonomy of their organizations posed a crucial dilemma for the FSLN and the grass-roots movements. The character of this dialectic would be determined by the future of the revolutionary process.[65] The mass organizations could play an effective part in transforming society only if they capably represented their members' interests, and autonomy was essential for this. The popular movements seemed to grow in autonomy during the Sandinista era of governance (1979–1990), but this did not lead to gratitude at the polls, with the FSLN losing the 1990 elections. Strong grass-roots movements are now essential for the Sandinistas to protect the achievements of the revolution. After its electoral defeat, the Front began a process of self-evaluation. The Sandinistas seem to realize that, to strengthen base democracy, they must abandon the vertical tradition which characterized their relations with the grass-roots movements.[66]

Institutionalization of the Revolutionary Project

Despite their initial doubts about electoral democracy, pragmatists such as President Daniel Ortega, Vice President Ramírez, and National Assembly President Núñez soon recognized its importance.[67] The pragmatic Insurrectional Tendency once again seems to have modified an ideologically based position. As noted, during the insurrection the *Terceristas* convinced the two other Sandinista factions to create a broad-based alliance, which became a cornerstone of the policy of national unity. Similarly, the pragmatists argued that representative features would strengthen rather than weaken the regime. Revolutionary legitimacy would be transformed and further strengthened by electoral legitimacy. Moreover, the FSLN was under pressure from internal opponents and West European governments. Sectors of the middle class and the business community had demanded elections since 1979, and the attainment of national unity required meeting these demands. Also, support by West European governments would be strengthened by assurances that the revolution was following European social democracy. As a result the government began to emphasize representative elements such as the election of a president and legislature with popular participation.[68]

The first sign that the leadership was prepared to institutionalize representative features was the election of 1984. When the Front came to power in 1979, it promised to hold elections. These were not new to Sandinista ideology; they had been contemplated in the 1977 FSLN program and the June 1979 Governing Junta of National Reconstruction program.[69] Nevertheless, many observers doubted that the government would permit them. These doubts were put to rest on February 21, 1984, when the FSLN set elections for November 4. A new law determined that the electorate would comprise all Nicaraguans age sixteen and older. Voting was voluntary and the elections were for president, vice president, and the National Assembly of ninety members. The president and the legislators were elected to six-year terms, the presidency going to the candidate with a plurality.[70] To ensure pluralism in the National Assembly, the electoral system provided for proportional representation, and losing presidential candidates were assured a seat.

The counterrevolutionary forces, or contras, operating in several regions of Nicaragua threatened and at times disrupted the electoral process. More than 100 voter registration centers could not be opened in their zones.[71] Nonetheless, 93 percent of the estimated voting-age population was registered.[72] Despite Sandinista efforts to ensure a favorable climate for the campaign (the state of emergency was lifted), the bourgeoisie regarded the process with ambivalence. Having insisted on elections since 1979, it denounced the decision to set the date for November 4 as too soon and threatened to abstain.[73]

The opposition candidate who received the most attention was Arturo Cruz, a former member of the government and presidential candidate of the Democratic Coordinator (CD). The CD represented a broad spectrum of the opposition, including the MDN, the Social Christian Party (PSC), the Liberal Constitutionalist Party (PLC), the Social Democratic Party (PSD), five private-sector groups integrated into COSEP, and two unions: the Nicaraguan Workers' Confederation (CTN) and the Council for Labor Unification (CUS). The CD announced a set of conditions, including separation of party and state, autonomy of judicial power, and inclusion of contra leaders in a national dialogue, which had to be met by the government before the opposition would permit its candidate to participate.[74] The CD opted not to register by the deadline, using the government's refusal to talk with the contras as a pretext.[75] The government and the CD continued to negotiate, with several leaders of the Socialist International serving as mediators. The negotiations broke down in mid-October, as each side charged bad faith. Thus, Cruz did not participate. It has since become known that the main forces in the opposition alliance never intended to take part, fearing that they would help legitimize the revolutionary process.[76]

The Reagan administration sought to discredit the electoral process and advised the opposition to abstain. U.S. diplomats urged the presidential candidates of several conservative opposition parties to pull out, and Virgilio Godoy, minister of labor until 1984 and head of the Independent Liberal party, did so.[77] Despite the administration's attempt to disrupt the electoral process and discredit the FSLN victory, U.S. and international observers confirmed that the elections were the freest and cleanest in Nicaragua's history.[78]

In light of the difficult economic conditions and counterrevolutionary aggression, the margin of Sandinista victory was impressive. Daniel Ortega received 63 percent of the presidential vote, and FSLN candidates won sixty-one of the ninety-six seats in the National Assembly.[79] Had the Sandinistas favored the U.S. system of majority vote, the FSLN would have carried every seat.[80] The three parties to the left got only their presidential candidates into the legislature, while the three to the right obtained twenty-nine mandates. From a pluralist perspective, 40 percent of the FSLN's slate were not members of the party. The Sandinistas believed that the delegates' influence among the populace was more important than their membership in the FSLN.[81]

Members of the Sandinista Front vigorously debated the meaning of the elections in the context of Nicaragua's model of popular democracy. The majority of the National Directorate recognized the importance of institutionalizing the revolution through elections. The moderates prevailed over the radical Marxist perspective of Comandante Arce.[82] During the campaign, Arce secretly explained to the political committee of the Nicaraguan Socialist party that elections were being held to satisfy the demands of the bourgeois opposition and international opinion rather than to decide who would govern. Since the Sandinistas were under attack from left and right, Arce's speech was interpreted by some observers as an FSLN tactic of adapting its position to the audience. Yet, an analysis of Sandinista statements reveals important differences among the leadership.

Whatever the internal deliberations of the National Directorate, the outcome is evident—elections were held and the moderates prevailed. According to Comandante Núñez, the directorate discussed the possibility of strengthening participatory democracy through direct representation of the mass organizations in one chamber of a two-chamber assembly.[83] Such a design would have emphasized the priority Sandinista thought assigns to participatory structures, yet this proposal was not approved.

The elections were held, although the government was the victim of military aggression and ideological attack by counterrevolutionary forces and an economic boycott by the United States. That the FSLN submitted to a popular referendum under such conditions seems further evidence of its commitment to combining social revolution and democracy. The large voter turnout and the substantial majority of ballots cast for the FSLN added legitimacy and deepened the commitment of many West European and Latin American governments and solidarity movements to aiding the government.[84] Yet the elections failed to end U.S. efforts to destroy the revolution. Washington's hostility finally ended with the 1990 elections, but the price for the Sandinistas was relinquishing power.

In 1985, Comandante Arce, a member of the National Directorate, outlined the main characteristics of the Sandinista project: participatory democracy, mixed economy, political pluralism, and nonalignment.[85] Participatory democracy guaranteed that the priorities of transformation were determined by "the logic of the majority." National unity required a strong commitment to political pluralism and a mixed economy, consisting of a private sector, a socialized sector of state property, and various forms of cooperative association. Political pluralism was to be based on this economic structure. Nonalignment expressed the FSLN's determination to follow its own path in the world and secure international support.[86]

When Sandinista Nicaragua celebrated its tenth anniversary, it was a state seeking to institutionalize a form of revolutionary democratic Marxism based on a combination of more direct elements of participatory democracy, the mass organizations, and representative democracy through elections. Sandinista democracy was distinct from the "popular democracy" of the former one-party states of Eastern Europe since it allowed political pluralism. Or, to note another contrasting case, the Cuban Communist party's one-party system and monopoly of power restricted Cuba's democracy.[87] The representation of seven parties in Nicaragua's National Assembly from 1984 through 1990 contrasts with Cuba, where, in the early 1980s, 96.7 percent of the 441 delegates were affiliated with the Communist party.[88]

The contribution of the Sandinistas to socialist governance consists of the realization that to assure political democracy, representative structures must allow for pluralist elections that hold programs accountable and encourage consideration of alternate political and social visions. The goal was to overcome the limits of representative democracy and integrate it into a much more profound structure that would allow participation by the previously marginalized majority. The institutionalization of Sandinista democracy through elections was not a concession but a fundamental feature of the revolution, and it became central to the definition of the revolutionary project after 1979. Some analysts have attributed the Front's commitment to pluralism and an electoral process to pressure by the domestic opposition and international opinion. In fact, elections were part of the FSLN's original program. Further, the elections of 1984 and 1990 make clear that the Sandinistas took their commitment seriously, despite the misgivings of some members of the National Directorate. In the words of Vice President Sergio Ramírez: "Pluralism is . . . essential to the revolution, maintained not merely by the recognition of certain right-wing parties so that they can function within the country, but also to make possible the political and democratic participation of different sectors of the population that never before in our history had access to that participation."[89]

Thus, political pluralism is a precondition for authentic political life, a real confrontation of views, which allows the masses decision-making power. Political pluralism in today's Nicaragua would not exist without being ensured by the Sandinista leadership. Important sectors in the Front agreed with Rosa Luxemburg that socialism could not be introduced without the widest possible democracy and freedom: "Freedom only for the supporters of the government, only for the members of one party—however numerous they may be—is not freedom at all. Freedom is always and exclusively freedom for the one who thinks differently."[90]

National Unity: The Bourgeoisie, the Left, and the Sandinistas

One of the most important aspects of Sandinista democracy was the inclusion of the bourgeoisie.[91] This resulted from the policy of national unity, based on the FSLN's commitment to political pluralism and a mixed economy. Although the Sandinistas controlled Nicaragua from 1979 to 1990, the power structure was far from monolithic. The business community, the church, and political opposition groups were also important contenders. This analysis of the role of the opposition focuses on the private sector and the left-wing opposition, which illustrate the dialectic in Sandinista national unity.

From July to December 1979, when initial readjustments of the new political structures took place, the bourgeoisie's share of important political positions was astonishing. Only two members of the FSLN's National Directorate occupied cabinet positions, while the bourgeoisie held important ministries and a majority on the Council of State. The private sector felt particularly reassured of the Sandinista commitment to a mixed economy, since central positions in the revolutionary government (Planning, Finance, and the Central Bank) were held by individuals with excellent reputations in the domestic and international business community.[92] A drastic reorganization of the government in December 1979, however, increased the power of the Sandinistas, displaced several bourgeois members, and reduced the power of the bourgeoisie considerably. It felt betrayed. Relations with the FSLN were bound to deteriorate because of fundamentally different conceptions of the future development of Nicaraguan society. Cordial relations ended when the bourgeoisie realized that implementation of the Sandinista design would threaten its privileged position.

Those bourgeois who opposed the Sandinistas, therefore, organized into the Democratic Coordinator (CD), an alliance of political parties, labor unions, and private sector organizations. The five groups constituting the Superior Council of Private Enterprise (COSEP) were most important because of their economic power. Opposition political parties were weak, several having lost legitimacy because of their previous collaboration with Somoza.[93] COSEP was considered the most effective representative of bourgeois interests. Thus, the FSLN directed its dialogue with the opposition toward the business community represented by COSEP, rather than toward the political parties.[94]

The Sandinista Front realized from the outset that cooperation from the business community was essential to reconstruction, and the policy of national unity was an incentive for the bourgeoisie to cooperate. While the political power of the bourgeoisie was restricted under this policy, the business community retained substantial economic power. The mixed economy was established as a consequence of the social compromise implied by the policy of national unity, yet the advance of Sandinista hegemony over the political system was accompanied eventually by the consolidation of economic power. The economic base centered around business enterprises confiscated from Somoza and his associates. These holdings, mostly agricultural, were integrated into the sector of People's Property (APP) and managed by the state. The Sandinistas soon gained control over other key areas of the economy. Indeed, Article 99 of the 1987 Nicaraguan constitution affirmed that "the state directs and plans the national economy . . . to guarantee and defend the interests of the majority and to guide it in accordance with the goals of socio-economic progress. The Central Bank, the National Financial System, Insurances and Reinsurances and External Trade, which are [all] instruments to direct the economy, are irrevocably a part of the state sector."[95]

Since the state's control over key sectors of the economy is embodied in the 1987 constitution, it will be difficult if not impossible for the National Opposition Union (UNO) government to change the economy. Following the 1990 elections, the UNO commanded neither the 60 percent of the votes required for partial changes in the constitution nor the two-thirds majority needed for approving a new one.[96]

Comandante Wheelock affirms that

> The hegemony of the economic development process is in the new relations of production created by the revolution. It is a hegemony achieved by the nationalization of foreign commerce, of natural resources and of strategic industrial sectors, and with the nationalization of banks. With these measures we have created a system of production and of management which predominates, which is hegemonic, which coexists with forms one could call capitalist to an appreciable degree, and with others that are backward or precapitalist.[97]

In the eyes of the business community, the bourgeoisie had lost economic power. COSEP complained that the government had eliminated the private sector's ability to make important decisions.[98] Despite this weakened position, the business community retained substantial power and forced the Sandinistas to cooperate. This was difficult, since the revolutionary authorities needed to control the destructive efforts of some right-wing members of the private sector without losing the trust of the bourgeoisie. They also had to restrain some zealots who considered all capitalists enemies and could not see the need to consolidate the revolution slowly.

The expanding state sector and continuing invasions of private property during the first months of the revolution provoked dissent in the business community. Anxiety in the private sector increased dramatically when private property seemed to be threatened by a March 1980 law.[99] This "decapitalization" act was directed against members of the business community whose distrust of Sandinista policies and insecurity about their economic future led them to halt further investments and allow their plants to run down. The capitalists showed imagination in undermining the economy: refusing to cultivate land, reducing the productive capacity of factories, transporting machinery out of the country, refusing to reinvest profits, and depleting Nicaragua's foreign currency reserves.[100] These responses contributed to the country's economic problems and strengthened popular pressure to take action against the private sector. The Sandinistas responded by seeking to increase the control of the work force over management by instituting regular assemblies of workers and administrators to discuss the production process of each enterprise.[101] At the same time, the FSLN responded to the private sector's insecurity by legitimizing private ownership of the means of production and by promising to end invasions of private properties by mass organizations.

After a short truce, business and government were at odds again. COSEP withdrew from the Council of State in November to protest, among other things, the postponement of the elections. Relations deteriorated sharply when Jorge Salazar, head of the Union of Nicaraguan Agricultural Producers (UPANIC) and vice president of COSEP, was killed by Sandinista police. According to government accounts, Salazar was part of a conspiracy to overthrow the Sandinistas.[102] Many in the business community, however, believed him a victim of government entrapment.[103] This incident considerably damaged relations between the private sector and the government, and the business community continued its decapitalization. Rhetorical attacks from both sides increased.

The Sandinistas repeatedly stressed the class character of the revolution and referred to the bourgeoisie as "our internal class enemies."[104] In this climate, COSEP wrote a letter to Daniel Ortega in October 1981, charging the Sandinista Front with betraying the original program of the revolution. It made clear that it would "in no way support the project to transform this revolution into a new Marxist-Leninist adventure which will only bring more blood and suffering for our own people."[105] It also accused the Sandinistas of attacking the mixed economy, which was being "set back under the advance of the nationalization of property, signaling a project drawn up behind the backs of the people."[106] Perceiving the letter as part of a coordinated initiative to destroy the revolution,[107] the government sentenced the authors to several months in prison. Ramiro Gúrdian, one of the six signers, escaped to Venezuela. Under intense external pressure and with the mediation of President José López Portillo of Mexico, the COSEP leaders were released in February 1982 and Gúrdian returned from exile.[108]

The war contributed to the tense political climate. One of the fundamental problems between the private sector and the Sandinista Front was the conviction by important groups in COSEP that the government would be overthrown by the U.S.-sponsored counterrevolutionary forces. Thus, the bourgeoisie had no incentive to cooperate.

In 1988, after the contras ceased to constitute a military threat, the bourgeoisie continued to resist politically. The Nandaime incident of July 10, 1988—an antigovernment demonstration that provoked clashes between police and demonstrators and led to the arrest of several business leaders—indicated the private sector's intent to create a climate of popular unrest to bring down the government. In the same month, the private-sector opposition, led by COSEP and with the participation of U.S. Ambassador Richard Melton, formed a "government of national salvation" and demanded the dissolution of the government.[109] These measures sought "to provoke a government crackdown, create martyrs, isolate Nicaragua internationally and derail the Esquipulas peace process."[110] The Sandinistas responded by expropriating the most important private enterprise, a sugar refinery owned by the Pellas family.

Challenges to FSLN hegemony were not limited to the bourgeoisie. The Sandinistas also had to contend with opposition from the left, in particular the ultraleft Marxist-Leninist Movement (MAP-ML) and its affiliated union, the Workers' Front. Antagonism between the Sandinistas and the Workers' Front dates to 1972 when a group of Sandinista guerrillas was accused of planning to assassinate the entire Sandinista leadership.[111] These dissidents formed the Workers' Front and participated in the insurrection through their military organization, the Popular Anti-Somocista Militia (MILPAS), which enjoyed substantial working-class support. Its contribution to the overthrow of Somoza was recognized by a seat on the original Council of State. Early on, the Marxist-Leninists were considered a challenge to the Sandinista project. A secret 1979 FSLN document describes the movement as an "enemy of the revolution" and affirms that it must "be destroyed."[112]

Contrary to popular belief, the Marxist-Leninists, not the bourgeoisie, claim the dubious honor as the first jailed opponents of the Sandinistas. Also, the radical left joined the bourgeoisie in having its political representation restricted. The Sandinistas eliminated the seat of the Workers' Front when they changed the makeup of the Council of State. The Marxist-Leninists were not allowed to participate in this co-legislative body until mid-1984.[113] The Sandinistas repressed the Marxist-Leninists, apparently threatened by their ultraleft-wing critique of the revolution. The MAP-ML denounced the policy of national unity as a capitulation to the bourgeoisie and demanded a dictatorship of the proletariat and the nationalization of all means of production.[114] Further, members of the Workers' Front tried to obtain support among their own class by demanding immediate substantial pay increases and the confiscation of factories when the Sandinistas told the workers that the reconstruction of the country took priority over demands for higher salaries. This populist rhetoric challenged the more pragmatic FSLN. The government was in the unenviable position of being attacked simultaneously from left and right. This opposition was evidently strong enough for Communists and socialists to unite in 1989 with right-wing parties into the UNO.

During the first years of the revolution, the FSLN overreacted to challenges, but in time it matured. The Nicaraguan voters endorsed the pragmatism of the Front in the 1984 elections. Sandinista candidates gained more than 60 percent of the vote, while the radical Marxist-Leninists obtained only 1 percent and the COSEP affiliates abstained. Nevertheless, the policy of national unity proved only partially successful in gaining bourgeois cooperation for reconstructing the economy. While the so-called patriotic producers—sectors of the rural bourgeoisie who joined the Sandinistas in reconstruction—demonstrated the feasibility of a revolutionary aspiration to national unity, the majority of the capitalist class was not prepared to contribute in the economic arena without sharing political power. In the eyes of leading industrialists, the policy of national unity, if it ever existed, ended six months into the revolution when most representatives of the private sector left the government.[115]

At this juncture the revolutionary leadership firmly established the hegemony of the popular classes. The bourgeoisie was not prepared to subordinate its class interest to a development strategy to benefit the impoverished majority. The Sandinistas, while attempting to incorporate the opposition into reconstruction, were always clear on the limits of national unity. According to President Ortega:

> Our socialism is a socialism that defends, in the first place, the workers and the peasants as the fundamental forces of the nation. Our socialism also provides all economic and social sectors which exist in Nicaragua with the opportunity to produce and to contribute to the progress of the country. . . . Thus, our socialism defends the institution of a mixed economy and defends political pluralism but within the institutional and constitutional framework, not to deny the power of the people but to work with the government and to work with popular power.[116]

The bourgeoisie had little incentive to participate under Sandinista hegemony as long as it had a chance to overthrow the government. In this regard, the policies of the Reagan administration impeded economic recovery and contributed decisively to the Sandinista defeat in 1990.

Governing from Below: From Hegemony to Opposition

The hegemonic project of the Sandinistas was based on the reality that the coalition of popular forces that overthrew Somoza was not confined to workers and peasants. Thus, the establishment of a "dictatorship of the proletariat" would have imposed a narrow class vision on a broad coalition. Instead of following orthodox Marxism, the Sandinistas relied on their own political understanding that was closer to the tradition of Antonio Gramsci, whose theory of hegemony "accepts social complexity as the very condition of political struggle and . . . sets the basis for a democratic practice of politics, compatible with a plurality of historical subjects."[117] The Sandinista strategy attempted to enlist all sectors for the revolution. Indeed, the Sandinista project provides an interesting example of a revolutionary society's effort to combine representative and participatory forms of democracy while seeking to benefit the impoverished majority. However, serious questions must be raised as to the "popular" content of the Sandinista experiment and its democratic or authoritarian practice.

One of the central problems of Sandinista democracy is the concept of popular hegemony. The Sandinistas favor a participatory, direct model of democracy based on grass-roots movements. Yet, with the exception of the National Union of Farmers and Ranchers, the mass organizations could not assume their intended role. Without strong and independent mass organizations to guarantee popular hegemony, the Front became the guarantor of the "revolutionary" substance of the experience. This raises the question of whether the content of the hegemonic project was actually popular or merely Sandinista. Hegemony was guaranteed through the FSLN's control over the armed forces and the police. All significant lines of power converged on the nine-member National Directorate of the FSLN, which controlled the presidency, the National Assembly, and all important ministries.

Popular hegemony thus was mediated by the FSLN's control of power. This constitutes a problem since the Sandinista Front does not necessarily represent the interests of the poor majority. Indeed, the leadership became increasingly detached from the popular classes, which contributed to its electoral defeat.[118] The self-conception of the FSLN as representing the vanguard is part of this dilemma.[119] The Sandinista party was instrumental in overthrowing Somoza and constituted the vanguard during the insurrection. For one sector of the FSLN, however, the conception of vanguard implies that the Sandinista leadership knows best the interests of the people.[120] This view perpetuates in power an elite that becomes detached from the people. The Leninist principles, according to which the Sandinista movement was built, proved very effective during the insurrection. While they were essential for the survival of a clandestine movement, however, they were detrimental to the building of revolutionary democratic Marxism in Nicaragua. Rosa Luxemburg's criticism of V. I. Lenin and the Russian revolution provides an important lesson for the Sandinista leadership.

This Sandinista conception of vanguard, together with the lack of internal democracy, deserves further scrutiny. The FSLN is a vanguard party that had only 12,000 members in 1985.[121] Since the leadership is not elected, the nine-member National Directorate has absolute control over its policies. In the opinion of Moisés Hassan, a member of Nicaragua's original Governing Junta, the Front cannot be considered a traditional party.[122] The FSLN maintains its military structure from the days of the insurrection and has yet to implement the principles of democratic centralism, envisioned by Lenin as the path to follow upon taking power.

The lack of internal democracy is evident in the case of the Sandinista Assembly, the highest decision-making body below the National Directorate. Its one hundred members, appointed by the directorate, have no decision-making power but serve as a ratifying body for decisions taken by the directorate.[123] Thus, the National Directorate decided the course of the revolution. Its predominance is bound to change following the Sandinista Front's electoral defeat. In May 1990, during critical self-evaluation to find the proper strategy to defend revolutionary achievements and prepare for regaining power, Tomás Borge, former minister of the interior and member of the directorate, argued: "There are no longer, nor can there be, vertical lines and silent assent that, in practice, asphyxiate criticism. . . . It is so crucial to regroup forces without sectarianism but with agreement on basic criteria. This requires . . . a redefinition . . . of the content of our Sandinista revolutionary project. Keeping the essence intact, we must look with a critical spirit at our program."[124] "To emerge victorious," Borge continued, it is necessary "to regroup and consolidate our forces through democratic discussion and within the framework of party discipline. To initiate an open democratization of the organization through which the base can elect zonal, regional and national leaders directly, secretly and by making use of constructive criticism of their leaders."[125] The Sandinistas thus recognize the need to democratize their movement and regain popular support.

The revolutionary government's defeat in the 1990 elections stunned friends and foes alike. In light of the overwhelming majority of polls predicting a Sandinista victory, the fourteen-point defeat by the UNO coalition led by Violeta Chamorro was a humiliating upset. In addition to gaining the presidency, the UNO alliance secured fifty-one seats in the National Assembly, while the Sandinistas obtained thirty-eight and one went to the Social Christian party.[126] Considering the economic crisis at the time, the Sandinista loss at the polls should have been expected. A harsh austerity program had brought inflation down from 33,000 percent in 1988 to 1,700 percent in 1989, but unemployment was rampant and the loss in buying power (real wages were less than 10 percent of 1980) had drastically reduced popular consumption.[127] If one adds the threat of continued U.S. aggression in case of a FSLN victory, it is rather astonishing that 40 percent of the electorate voted for the Sandinistas.

Although the UNO controlled an absolute majority in the Nicaraguan legislature, it fell short of the 60 percent of votes needed to implement partial changes in the constitution. This left the Sandinistas in a position of considerable influence. The Chamorro regime could govern effectively only if they would play the role of loyal opposition.

Ironically, the bourgeoisie needed to continue the Sandinista policy of national unity, albeit the roles had been reversed. The Front declared its willingness to cooperate with the new government while establishing clear boundaries. It would "support the government's positive steps without intransigent opposition at all times and under all circumstances, without impairing a firm and unwavering opposition to any measure intended to destroy [revolutionary] achievements and all that affects popular interests."[128] The Sandinistas demonstrated their commitment to defend popular interests during the summer of 1990, mobilizing the grass-roots movements to oppose the government. Several major strikes brought the country to a halt and exposed the government's weakness. This was "governing from below," anticipated in a speech by Daniel Ortega two days after the election.

In defeat, the Sandinistas proved wrong those critics who maintained that they would not relinquish power. They were rightly proud of having institutionalized democracy in Nicaragua. Most observers agreed with Ortega that "the big victor, the big winner of these elections is the Sandinista Front, which brought democracy to Nicaragua."[129] Yet there were also voices of dissent. Leftist critics argued that the innovative model of Sandinista democracy had been stripped of its participatory content, leaving it a traditional representative Western-style political system. Many wondered whether the future would prove the Front's prediction that "the change of government in no way means the end of the revolution."[130] The fate of the revolution would be determined by the Nicaraguan people and depended on one factor: Did ten years of revolution irrevocably change the consciousness of the popular classes or were they prepared to return to the ideas of the past?

Notes

*Excerpts in this article were reprinted from "Popular Democracy in the New Nicaragua: The Case of a Rural Mass Organization," *Comparative Politics* 20, no. 1 (October 1987): 35–55. Copyright 1987 by *Comparative Politics*. Reprinted by permission.

1. Such a concept would be totally alien to U.S. policymakers, but it represents a vision that scholars have never fully rejected. See, for example, Alfred Stepan, "Paths toward Redemocratization: Theoretical and Comparative Considerations," in Guillermo O'Donnell et al., eds., *Transitions from Authoritarian Rule: Comparative Perspectives* (Baltimore: Johns Hopkins University Press, 1986), 84.

2. One of the first discussions of the policies of popular hegemony and national unity can be found in Carlos Vilas, *The Sandinista Revolution* (New York: Monthly Review Press, 1986); this section is informed by his analysis.

3. Vilas, *The Sandinista Revolution*, 175.

4. Gabriele Invernizzi, Francis Pisani, and Jesús Ceberio, *Sandinistas: Entrevistas a Humberto Ortega Saavedra, Jaime Wheelock Román y Bayardo Arce Castaño* (Managua: Editorial Vanguardia, 1986), 50.

5. Interview with a Sandinista source, Managua, January 1986.

6. Che Guevara, *Guerrilla Warfare* (Lincoln: University of Nebraska Press, 1985).

7. Gary Ruchwarger, *People in Power: Forging a Grassroots Democracy in Nicaragua* (South Hadley: Bergin & Garvey, 1987), 19.

8. Martha Harnecker, *Nicaragua: El Papel de La Vanguardia: Entrevista al Comandante de la Revolución Jaime Wheelock sobre la Historia del Frente Sandinista* (Panamá: Centro de Capacitación Social, 1986), 84–88.

9. Invernizzi et al., *Sandinistas*, 52–53.

10. Quoted in Bruce Marcus, ed., *Sandinistas Speak: Speeches, Writings, and Interviews with the Leaders of Nicaragua's Revolution* (New York: Pathfinder Press, 1982), 63. Emphasis added.

11. Pablo González Casanova, *El Poder al Pueblo* (México, D.F.: Ediciones Océano, 1988), 44. See also Tendencias Guerra Popular Prolongada, Proletaria, Insurrecional, *Del FSLN a los Pueblos del Mundo: Informe sobre la Coyuntura* (Barcelona: Ediciones Conosur, 1979).

12. John Booth, *The End and the Beginning: The Nicaraguan Revolution* (Boulder: Westview Press, 1985), 146.

13. For an excellent discussion of the ideological roots of the Sandinista movement see Donald C. Hodges, *Intellectual Foundations of the Nicaraguan Revolution* (Austin: University of Texas Press, 1986).

14. Ruchwarger, *People in Power*, 246.

15. Mats Hårsmar, "Centralamerikanska Demokratiuppfattningar: En analys av demokratisynen hos PLN i Costa Rica, FSLN i Nicaragua och Nicaraguas väpnande opposition," Uppsala University (Sweden), 1988, unpublished manuscript, 4.

16. Benjamin Barber, *Strong Democracy: Participatory Politics for a New Age* (Berkeley: University of California Press, 1984), xi.

17. Edward S. Herman and Frank Brodhead, *Demonstration Elections: U.S.-Staged Elections in the Dominican Republic, Vietnam, and El Salvador* (Boston: South End Press, 1984).

18. Richard Harris and Carlos Vilas, eds., *Nicaragua: A Revolution under Siege* (London: Zed Books, 1985), 231.

19. Ibid.

20. Quoted in Marcus, ed., *Sandinistas Speak*, 130.

21. I am indebted to Michael Fruehling, first secretary of the Swedish embassy in Nicaragua until 1987 and now an analyst at the Latin American desk of the Swedish foreign ministry, for sharing his views on this subject.

22. Hårsmar, "Centralamerikanska Demokratiuppfattningar," 26.

23. Quoted in Henri Weber, *Nicaragua: Den Sandinistiska Revolutionen* (Stockholm: Bokförlaget Röda Rummet, 1983), 145.

24. For a discussion of the role of the bourgeoisie during the period of the consolidation of Sandinista power see Dennis Gilbert, *Sandinistas: The Party and the Revolution* (New York: Basil Blackwell, 1988), chap. 5.

25. Booth, *The End and the Beginning*, 186.

26. Quoted in Vilas, *The Sandinista Revolution*, 45. One must be struck by the irony that Humberto Ortega later served as minister of defense in the cabinet of Violeta Chamorro, whose election decidedly affected the revolutionary project of the Sandinistas.

27. FSLN, "Declaración del FSLN Sobre la Democracia," *Barricada*, August 24, 1980. See the translation of this text in George Black, *Triumph of the People: The Sandinista Revolution in Nicaragua* (London: Zed Press, 1981), 255–56.

28. The section on formal state power draws on Black, *Triumph of the People*, 223–63; Booth, *The End and the Beginning*, 185–202; and Gilbert, *Sandinistas: The Party and the Revolution*, 108–14.

29. Interview with Moisés Hassan, member of Nicaragua's first Governing Junta in 1979, Managua, August 15, 1988. Hassan renounced his membership in the FSLN in 1988, formed his own party (claiming to represent the authentic Sandinista revolution), and, along with Daniel Ortega, obtained a seat in the National Assembly in the elections of 1990 as a losing presidential candidate. The new constitution affords seats in the National Assembly to duly registered but losing presidential candidates if they obtain at least 1 percent of the popular vote.

30. Gilbert, *Sandinistas: The Party and the Revolution*, 42.

31. Interview with Moisés Hassan.

32. Booth, *The End and the Beginning*, 187.

33. Ibid., 188.

34. Ibid., 191.

35. Interview with Ramiro Gúrdian, president of the Union of Nicaraguan Agricultural Producers (UPANIC) and vice president of the Superior Council of Private Enterprise (COSEP), Managua, June 28, 1985. See also Black, *Triumph of the People*, 245.

36. Black, *Triumph of the People*, 245.

37. One of the seats obtained by UNAG previously belonged to the Association of Rural Workers (ATC).

38. Black, *Triumph of the People*, 245.

39. Luis Serra, "The Grass-Roots Organizations," in Thomas W. Walker, ed., *Nicaragua: The First Five Years* (New York: Praeger, 1985), 76.

40. Interview with Comandante Carlos Núñez, president of the National Assembly and member of the FSLN's National Directorate, Managua, February 18, 1986.

41. This section on the grass-roots movements is based on interviews with officials of these movements and draws on two chapters by Luis Serra, "The Sandinista Mass Organizations," in Walker, ed., *Nicaragua in Revolution*, 95–113; and "The Grass-Roots Organizations," in Walker, ed., *Nicaragua: The First Five Years*, 65–89.

42. Ruchwarger, *People in Power*, 246.

43. Serra in Walker, ed., *Nicaragua: The First Five Years*, 66.

44. Interview with Lúcio Jiménez, secretary general of the Sandinista Workers' Federation (CST), Managua, August 3, 1989.

45. For a discussion of the evolution of the rural grass-roots movements see Ilja A. Luciak, "Democracy in the Nicaraguan Countryside: A Comparative Analysis of Sandinista Grassroots Movements," *Latin American Perspectives* 17, no. 3 (Summer 1990): 55–75.

46. Interviews with Edgardo García, secretary general of the Association of Rural Workers (ATC), Managua, July 5, 1985, and July 27, 1989.

47. Interview with Daniel Núñez, president of the National Union of Farmers and Ranchers (UNAG), Managua, November 14, 1989.

48. Asociación de Mujeres Nicaraguenses Luisa Amanda Espinosa (AMNLAE), *Plan de Lucha* (Managua: AMNLAE, 1984).

49. Maxine Molyneux, "Women," in Walker, ed., *Nicaragua: The First Five Years*, 152.

50. Serra in Walker, ed., *Nicaragua: The First Five Years*, 66.

51. Interview with Omar Cabezas, coordinator of the Sandinista Defense Committees (CDS), Managua, July 27, 1989.

52. Interview with Comandante Carlos Núñez.

53. Carlos Núñez, *El Papel de las Organizaciones de Masas en el Proceso Revolucionario* (Managua: Secretaría Nacional de Propaganda y Educación Política, 1980), 20–21.

54. FSLN, "Declaración del FSLN Sobre la Democracia."

55. Marifeli Pérez-Stable. "Pluralism and Popular Power: An Interview with Sergio Ramírez Mercado," in Marlene Dixon, ed., *Nicaragua under Siege* (San Francisco: Synthesis Publications, 1985), 170.

56. Walker, ed., *Nicaragua: The First Five Years*, 27.

57. Michael Lowy, "La Democracia no es un Lujo," *Pensamiento Própio* 18 (1984): 12.

58. José Luis Coraggio, *Nicaragua: Revolución y Democracia* (México: Editorial Linea, 1985), 75.

59. See interview with Comandante Bayardo Arce in Invernizzi et al., *Sandinistas*, 63–78.

60. Serra in Walker, ed., *Nicaragua: The First Five Years*, 76.

61. Luciak, "Democracy in the Nicaraguan Countryside," 67.

62. Invernizzi et al., *Sandinistas*, 69.

63. Equipo de Sectores Populares (SPU), Lourdes Aguilar et al., "Orígenes y Situación Actual de los CDS," classified report, Instituto Nacional de Investigaciones Económicas y Sociales (INIES), Managua, 1985.

64. Coraggio, *Nicaragua: Revolución y Democracia*, 78.

65. Ibid., 109.

66. Instituto Histórico Centroamericano, *Envío* 9, no. 107 (1990): 44.

67. Interviews with Sergio Ramírez, vice president of the Sandinista government, Managua, July 24, 1989; and with Comandante Carlos Núñez.

68. Coraggio, *Nicaragua: Revolución y Democracia*, 19.

69. Lucrecia Lozano, *De Sandino al Triunfo de la Revolución* (México: Siglo XXI, 1985), 322.

70. *"Ley Electoral"* in *Cuadernos de Pensamiento Própio*, no. 7 (May 1984): 69–91.

71. Instituto Histórico Centroamericano, *Envío* 4, no. 38 (1984): 5a.

72. Ibid.

73. Harris and Vilas, eds., *Nicaragua: A Revolution under Siege*, 231. See also Latin American Studies Association (LASA), "Report of the Latin American Studies Association Delegation to Observe the Nicaragua General Election of November 4, 1984," *LASA Forum* 15, no. 4 (Winter 1985).

74. Instituto Histórico Centroamericano, *Envío* 4, no. 38 (1984): 6a.

75. Booth, *The End and the Beginning*, 216.

76. Gilbert, *Sandinistas: The Party and the Revolution*, 122.

77. Booth, *The End and the Beginning*, 217. Godoy was subsequently to be elected vice president in 1990 as a running mate of Violeta Chamorro.

78. LASA, "Report of the LASA Delegation."

79. Even though only ninety candidates were elected, the National Assembly consists of ninety-six members, since all presidential candidates of the losing six parties were guaranteed a seat.

80. I am grateful to José Luis Coraggio for pointing this out to me.

81. Carlos Núñez, "Un parlamento nuevo que sea reflejo del poder del pueblo," *Barricada*, October 27, 1984.

82. See "Comandante Bayardo Arce's Secret Speech before the Nicaraguan Socialist Party (PSN)," U.S. Department of State Publication 9422 (1985).

83. Interview with Comandante Carlos Núñez.

84. This analysis was offered by senior diplomats from Western Europe and Latin America in conversations held in Managua from 1984 to 1986.

85. Bayardo Arce, "En Nicaragua se Juega el Destino de America Latina," speech by Comandante Bayardo Arce delivered at the First Anti-Imperialist Congress, February 20, 1985. In *Pensamiento Própio* 21 (1985): 8.

86. Waltraud Morales Queiser and Harry E. Vanden, "Relations with the Non-aligned Movement," in Walker, ed., *Nicaragua: The First Five Years*, 481–82.

87. Michael Lowy, "Las Organizaciones de Masas, El Partido y El Estado: La Democracia en la Transición al Socialismo," paper presented at seminar on "Los Problemas de la Transición en Pequeñas Economías Periféricas," Managua, September 1984.

88. Martha Harnecker, *Cuba: Dictadura o Democracia* (México: Siglo XXI, 1984), 376.

89. Quoted in Pérez-Stable, "Pluralism and Popular Power: An Interview with Sergio Ramírez Mercado," in Dixon, ed., *Nicaragua under Siege*, 169

90. Rosa Luxemburg, *The Russian Revolution and Leninism or Marxism?* (Ann Arbor: University of Michigan Press, 1982), 23.

91. The analysis of the relationship between the Sandinista government and the bourgeoisie draws on Gilbert, *Sandinistas: The Party and the Revolution*, 105–27.

92. Ibid., 109.

93. Ibid., 122.

94. Black, *Triumph of the People*, 64.
95. *Constitución política de Nicaragua* (Managua: Editorial El Amanecer, 1987),
33.
96. Ibid., 59–60.
97. Quoted in Vilas, *The Sandinista Revolution*, 157.
98. Interview with Ramiro Gúrdian, Managua, July 27, 1988.
99. Gilbert, *Sandinistas: The Party and the Revolution*, 111–12.
100. Ruchwarger, *People in Power*, 261.
101. Ibid., 265.
102. Gilbert, *Sandinistas: The Party and the Revolution*, 113.
103. Interview with Ramiro Gúrdian, Managua, July 27, 1988.
104. Gilbert in Walker, ed., *Nicaragua: The First Five Years*, 174. The discussion of this incident is based on the account in Gilbert, COSEP documents, and interviews with COSEP leaders.
105. Superior Council of Private Enterprise (COSEP), Carta a Daniel Ortega, Coordinador de la Junta de Gobierno de Reconstrucción Nacional, October 19, 1981, mimeograph.
106. Ibid.
107. Gilbert in Walker, ed., *Nicaragua: The First Five Years*, 174.
108. Interview with Ramiro Gúrdian, Managua, July 27, 1988.
109. Instituto Histórico Centroamericano, *Envío* 8, no. 92 (1989): 7. Ambassador Melton held meetings with the private sector throughout Nicaragua in an effort to convince opposition leaders of the viability and necessity of this latest anti-Sandinista strategy.
110. Ibid.
111. Black, *Triumph of the People*, 335. This section also is based on discussions with Marvin Ortega, a former leader of the MAP-ML, who was imprisoned for several months in 1979. Ortega is now the director of ITZTANI, an independent research organization.
112. Frente Sandinista de Liberación Nacional (FSLN), "Analisis de la Coyuntura y Tareas de la Revolución Popular Sandinista (Documento de las 72 Horas)," in Octavio y Elvyra Sanabria, *Nicaragua: Diagnostico De Una Traición* (Barcelona: Plaza & Janes Editores, 1986), 231.
113. Interview with Fernando Maletin, secretary general of the Workers' Front, Managua, July 5, 1985.
114. Interview with Carlos Cuadra, vice president of the MAP-ML, Managua, July 10, 1985.
115. Interview with Ramiro Gúrdian, Managua, July 27, 1988.
116. *Barricada*, July 20, 1988.
117. Ernesto Laclau and Chantal Mouffe, *Hegemony & Socialist Struggle: Towards a Radical Democratic Politics* (London: Thetford Press, 1985), 71.
118. For an analysis of this problem see Kenneth M. Coleman, John Speer, and Charles L. Davis, "The Urban Informal Economy in Nicaragua: Preliminary Observations," paper presented for delivery at the 1989 World Congress of the Latin American Studies Association, Miami, Florida, December 4–6, 1989.
119. See interview with Comandante Bayardo Arce in Invernizzi et al., *Sandinistas*, 63–78.
120. Daniel and Humberto Ortega held a different view, indicated by their efforts to implement the will of the electorate following the Sandinista defeat at the polls.
121. Ibid., 66. For an excellent discussion of the structure of the Sandinista party see Gilbert, *Sandinistas: The Party and the Revolution*, 41–58.

122. Interview with Moisés Hassan.

123. Ibid.

124. Instituto Histórico Centroamericano, *Envío* 9, no. 107 (1990): 44.

125. Ibid., 48.

126. In addition to the ninety regular members, any losing presidential candidate who receives over 1 percent of the vote gets a seat. Under this provision Daniel Ortega and Moisés Hassan joined the legislature, bringing the total membership to ninety-two.

127. Carlos M. Vilas, "What Went Wrong," *NACLA* 24, no. 1 (June 1990): 12.

128. Instituto Histórico Centroamericano, *Envío* 9, no. 107 (1990): 48.

129. Ibid., 9, no. 104 (1990): 40.

130. Ibid.

U.S. INTERVENTION IN
CENTRAL AMERICA

After the Battle of San Salvador*

William M. LeoGrande

"The stated purposes of the general uprising have failed," President Lyndon B. Johnson said a few days after the National Liberation Front of South Vietnam launched the Tet offensive in 1968. "Communist leaders counted on popular support in the cities for their effort; they found little or none."[1] Johnson was right; Tet was a military defeat for the Vietnamese guerrillas. But it was a political victory. The stunning scope and intensity of the offensive—especially the attack on the capital city of Saigon—demonstrated that the war in Vietnam was not gradually being won, as Johnson had been assuring the American public. After Tet, Vietnam looked like a war without end.

The Bush administration's public reaction to the November 1989 offensive in El Salvador by the Farabundo Martí National Liberation Front (FMLN) was reminiscent of the hollow optimism voiced after Tet. "The FMLN failed totally in this offensive," Assistant Secretary of State for Inter-American Affairs Bernard Aronson said with assurance. "They lost between 15 and 20 percent of their forces."[2] But here, too, the narrow military assessment of the battle was misleading. The principal effect of the attack was not to alter the military balance, but to shatter conventional wisdom in Washington about the course of the war.

Since 1984, U.S. policy toward El Salvador and the bipartisan congressional consensus behind it have rested on two key assumptions. The first was that the Salvadoran armed forces, bolstered by U.S. military aid, were gradually winning the war. The second was that the Salvadorans were building a democracy to replace their nation's traditional military dictatorship. The strength and tenacity of the November 1989 guerrilla offensive shattered the first illusion, while the army's response to the offensive shattered the second.

* This article was originally published in *World Policy Journal* 7 (Spring 1990): 331–56. Reprinted with permission of the journal and the author.

The FMLN attacks began on November 11, when guerrillas occupied six poor neighborhoods along the northern rim of San Salvador. Simultaneously, other FMLN units launched assaults in seven more of the nation's fourteen provinces. At first, the armed forces advanced cautiously against guerrilla positions in the capital, and government officials denied that air power would be used in such densely populated areas. But when the army was unable to dislodge the guerrillas by ground assault, the high command began to worry that it was losing control of the situation. The air force then unleashed its full firepower, producing over one thousand civilian casualties and leaving thousands homeless. The guerrillas dug in, fought the army house to house in some neighborhoods, and after two weeks withdrew in an orderly fashion to their strongholds in the north.

The FMLN's offensive shocked Washington and thrust El Salvador back into the headlines, derailing the Bush administration's yearlong effort to keep it on the back burner. The fighting touched off a vigorous policy debate between congressional Democrats and the administration. It remains an open question, however, as to whether the trauma of the offensive will indeed provoke a serious reassessment of U.S. policy toward El Salvador—or whether, after the initial shock, the American position will remain fundamentally unchanged.

The Origins of Consensus

Both Jimmy Carter and Ronald Reagan had tried during their presidencies to build a stable, reformist regime in San Salvador based on the moderate political center—the Christian Democrats. As with President John F. Kennedy's Alliance for Progress, reform was to be the long-term antidote for revolution, while U.S. military assistance would eliminate any revolutionaries who might spring up in the meantime. Both Carter and Reagan resisted efforts by the extreme right, especially the Nationalist Republican Alliance (ARENA), to turn back the clock to the authoritarian past when politics were dominated by a partnership between oligarchs and officers. Carter believed the old order was inherently unstable and would simply pave the way for a guerrilla victory. Reagan was more skeptical of reform and more tolerant of what the former U.S. ambassador to the United Nations, Jeane Kirkpatrick, referred to euphemistically as "moderately authoritarian regimes." But Reagan was forced to embrace reform in El Salvador as a condition for continued congressional funding of the war.

By 1984 both the White House and Congress believed that the United States had turned the corner in El Salvador. Christian Democrat José Napoleón Duarte was elected president that year on a platform pledging to improve human rights, raise the living standard of the poor, and negotiate an end to the civil war. Despite his role in the 1980–82 civil-military junta, which presided over the worst bloodletting since the *matanza* (slaughter) of 1932, Duarte nevertheless enjoyed great popularity in Washington.[3] His Christian Democrats had led the fight for reform in El Salvador in the 1960s, and Duarte would have won the 1972 presidential election if only the army had not stolen the ballot boxes. The oligarchy's visceral hatred of Duarte seemed to validate his credentials as a democrat, and his inauguration as president in 1984 seemed to offer hope for a more peaceful future.

Duarte's election was the most visible symbol of change in 1984, but it was not the only one. The number of death squad killings declined significantly that year, largely as a result of the demarche that Vice President George Bush delivered to the Salvadoran military in December 1983. Bush was blunt: if the army expected to receive enough military aid from the United States to win the war, then the death squads, most of which were run by intelligence units of the armed forces, had to be reined in. Although no military officers were ever punished for the forty thousand noncombatant civilians murdered over the previous five years, the armed forces did curtail death squad operations and reassign some of the officers implicated in them.

In addition, the military situation in 1984 looked much brighter for the government than ever before. The hundreds of millions of dollars worth of military training and equipment delivered to El Salvador by the United States in the early 1980s had finally begun to have a noticeable effect. The FMLN's annual offensives in 1981, 1982, and 1983 hurt the armed forces badly, leading some U.S. military analysts to worry that the guerrillas were near victory. In early 1984, Washington took the precaution of drawing up contingency plans for U.S. air strikes if the Salvadoran army began to crack during the expected FMLN offensive of 1984. But the 1984 offensive never materialized. The improved mobility of the government's U.S.-trained troops and the heavy firepower of its rapidly expanding air force kept the FMLN off balance and prevented it from launching a sustained offensive. Adjusting to the army's new capabilities, the guerrillas returned to small unit hit-and-run tactics.

Although the shift in FMLN strategy was effective, allowing the guerrillas to continue a war of attrition without exposing themselves to the government's superior firepower, it also made the war less visible.

At a distance (that is, from Washington), it appeared that the tide of battle had shifted in the government's favor. This assessment seemed to be confirmed with each passing year as the guerrillas mounted no major offensives.[4]

With Duarte committed to reform and negotiations, death squad killings on the decline, and the FMLN losing the initiative on the battlefield, Washington's policy in El Salvador looked like a qualified success. No one doubted that there was still a long way to go, but few congressional Democrats were still willing to argue that the direction of Reagan's policy was fundamentally flawed. After 1984 the Reagan administration faced no significant congressional opposition to its massive aid program, which eventually poured $4.5 billion into El Salvador during the 1980s. Indeed, Congress did not even hold a serious debate about El Salvador for the next five years.

In early 1988, however, the bipartisan consensus began to show signs of strain. In March, Duarte's Christian Democrats (PDC) suffered a stunning defeat in the National Assembly elections. Plagued by inefficiency and corruption, the PDC lost its legislative majority to ARENA, the far-right party founded by Maj. Roberto D'Aubuisson and long linked to the death squads of the paramilitary right. A year later, ARENA's presidential candidate, U.S.-educated businessman Alfredo Cristiani, swept to a first-ballot victory against the Christian Democrats and a small leftist coalition, the Democratic Convergence.[5]

The Christian Democrats lost their populist social base among the urban and rural poor because they failed to live up to the "social pact" they had made in 1984. Reneging on the social reforms he had promised, Duarte imposed an austerity program whose costs fell mainly on his own constituents. Instead of a negotiated peace, Duarte continued the war. Some disgruntled PDC supporters switched to ARENA, which in 1989 ran on a platform that echoed the 1984 program of the Christian Democrats—Cristiani made promises for an economic recovery and a quick end to the war. But most of the voters who deserted the PDC dropped out of the electoral system entirely. In the 1982 election, turnout was over 80 percent; by 1989 it had fallen to barely 50 percent.

Poorly organized, underfunded, and running a distant third, the Democratic Convergence was unable to capitalize on the erosion of the PDC's support. Closely identified with the FMLN, it suffered from unpopular guerrilla actions such as the assassination of mayors in contested areas and the detonation of car bombs in the capital. But the Convergence also failed to attract many guerrilla sympathizers after the FMLN called for a boycott of the election.

In the wake of Cristiani's victory, Congress once again began to debate U.S. policy toward El Salvador. On the face of it, the triumph of ARENA seemed to mark the collapse of a decade of U.S. strategy. Even though Cristiani was said to represent a more moderate, less violent faction of ARENA than D'Aubuisson, the victors were still unquestionably the political representatives of the Salvadoran upper class. Once in power, ARENA was not likely to undertake economic and social policies that would address the deeper grievances that gave rise to the Salvadoran insurgency in the first place.

Moreover, officials in Congress and the executive branch worried that an ARENA government might lift the constraints imposed on the death squads in the mid-1980s. Political killings had never stopped entirely, and the harassment and persecution of trade unionists and other civic leaders continued throughout Duarte's presidency. But the wholesale slaughter that characterized El Salvador in the early 1980s did subside enough to allow a revival of the popular organizations that had been crushed during the 1980–83 *matanza*. In late 1987, Guillermo Ungo and Rubén Zamora, the top two officials of the Revolutionary Democratic Front (FDR), a coalition of civilian organizations allied with the FMLN, felt secure enough to return from exile and openly engage in political organizing.

Hard-line army officers were antagonistic to the tolerant attitude that the government displayed toward resurgent union activities and toward Ungo and Zamora, both of whom had refused to break their ties with the guerrillas. There was real concern in Washington that extremists in the army or in ARENA itself would see Cristiani's electoral triumph as a mandate for repression. Indeed, ARENA's victory in the 1988 legislative elections was followed by the first increase in death squad killings since the early 1980s. Fearful that a surge in political killings would break the bipartisan consensus on El Salvador, President Bush dispatched Vice President Dan Quayle to San Salvador in June 1989 on a mission reminiscent of Bush's 1983 trip. Quayle warned the government and the army that Washington's continued support depended on the new government's preventing any backsliding on human rights.

In the summer of 1989 growing congressional concern led to the first full debates on El Salvador since 1984. Liberal Democrats proposed making military aid conditional on the government's human rights performance and on its willingness to seek a negotiated end to the war. President Bush opposed any conditionality, arguing that Cristiani had won a free election and therefore deserved unqualified support. The administration prevailed in the House by the relatively close vote of 233 to 185.

In the Senate, Christopher Dodd (D-CT), an early critic of Reagan's policy in El Salvador, surprised his colleagues by arguing the administration's case. Having met Cristiani, Dodd was convinced that the new president sincerely wanted to find a political solution to the war. He should be given a chance to make good on his pledge to reopen talks with the guerrillas, Dodd argued. As a result, the effort to condition aid was soundly defeated in the Senate by a vote of 68 to 32. The consensus on El Salvador had wobbled a bit, but in the end it held up— at least until November when the FMLN launched its offensive.

Why an Offensive?

The FMLN's decision to launch its first major offensive in five years was motivated by a deadlock on the political front.[6] Ever since the failure of their "final offensive" in 1981, the guerrillas had been calling for a negotiated settlement of the civil war. To be sure, some factions of the FMLN, in particular the Popular Forces of Liberation, at times saw negotiations mainly as a tactical ploy aimed at setting the stage for an eventual military triumph. But others, such as the Armed Forces of National Resistance and the People's Revolutionary Army led by FMLN military commander Joaquín Villalobos, doubted that victory was attainable so long as Washington was prepared to match every improvement in the FMLN's military fortunes with an escalation of aid for the armed forces. For those FMLN leaders, negotiations were "strategic" rather than "tactical"; a negotiated solution to the war was an acceptable outcome if it guaranteed for the left a significant, secure role in politics.[7]

In 1984, Duarte opened a dialogue with the FDR and FMLN, meeting them at the Salvadoran towns of La Palma and Ayagualo. Almost immediately, the talks were deadlocked because neither side would accept any significant modification of its initial negotiating position. The FDR and FMLN demanded that an interim government that included their representatives be established prior to new elections, that the armed forces be "cleansed" of officers responsible for human rights abuses, and that the guerrilla army then be merged with the military. The government demanded that the guerrillas simply lay down their arms and join the existing political process. With neither side willing to countenance the other's proposal, the talks collapsed.

A new flurry of diplomatic activity followed the August 1987 signing of the Esquipulas agreement by the presidents of the five Central American countries. The presidents pledged to establish pluralist democratic political systems with free elections and respect for human rights. They also pledged to strive for a cease-fire and national reconciliation through political dialogue in those countries that had armed insurgencies. In the spirit of Esquipulas, Duarte agreed to resume talks with the FDR and FMLN. Two meetings were held and no progress was made before the rebels withdrew to protest the assassination in October 1987 of Herbert Anaya, president of the Salvadoran Human Rights Commission.

At first, the FMLN thought that the Esquipulas agreement might signal a new flexibility on the part of the government. Even when the post-Esquipulas discussions collapsed, FMLN officials nevertheless hoped that public opinion, led by the growing popular movement of trade unionists and civil groups in San Salvador, would pressure the government to return to the bargaining table. An opinion poll taken in January 1989 found that 68 percent of the public favored a negotiated end to the war.[8] The whole purpose of the Democratic Convergence's participation in the 1989 presidential election was to capitalize on this sentiment by using the campaign as a forum for demanding serious negotiations.

The FMLN had a parallel strategy. In January 1989, at the height of the presidential campaign, it unveiled a new peace proposal. For the first time, the guerrillas agreed to participate in elections conducted under the auspices of the existing government and constitution and to cease their armed struggle regardless of the result. The key condition attached to the offer was that the election be postponed for six months to allow the FMLN to mobilize its supporters for a campaign. With Cristiani widely predicted to win the balloting in March, ARENA had no desire to postpone the election. But since the popular desire for peace was so strong, both ARENA and the PDC felt compelled to react positively to the FMLN's proposal and to open talks with the guerrillas about it. In the end, however, neither ARENA nor the army was willing to postpone the vote. Defense Minister Eugenio Vides Casanova went so far as to warn that the armed forces would overthrow the government if the constitution was abrogated by changing the electoral schedule. That settled the issue.

Although Cristiani was elected on the first ballot and the Democratic Convergence was embarrassed by its poor showing in the election (only 3.8 percent of the vote), the FMLN nevertheless seemed to believe, naively perhaps, that the prospects for a negotiated settlement were auspicious. During the campaign Cristiani had pledged to resume talks with the guerrillas if he won, a promise he reiterated on the evening he was elected. Some FMLN officials reasoned that Cristiani would be more willing and able to negotiate seriously than Duarte had been, precisely because ARENA represented the oligarchy. The FMLN regarded the Christian Democrats as little more than a creation of Washington that faithfully reflected U.S. opposition to a negotiated settlement. ARENA, on the other hand, represented a real social base— a wealthy constituency historically less dependent on the United States and less willing to take orders from the U.S. embassy. And business-men, after all, were paying a heavy price as the ongoing war devastated the economy. Finally, the FMLN also calculated that Reagan's departure from the White House would mark the beginning of a less ideological policy in Washington and of a greater willingness to let Salvadorans find a negotiated solution among themselves.[9]

The FMLN had miscalculated what Cristiani was capable of offer-ing at the bargaining table, however. No matter how well intentioned, he could offer no concessions without the assent of the armed forces. The army, in turn, had never favored any sort of talks with the guerrillas and was not likely to change unless Washington pressed forcefully for a genuine dialogue. Washington, in turn, was not disposed to change policies because it was convinced that the military was gradually winning the war. The FMLN's seeming inability to launch a single major offensive in five years suggested that the guerrillas no longer had the capacity to seriously endanger the regime. Time, therefore, was on the side of the army. Thus, there was no need to make any significant concessions to achieve a negotiated peace.

Politically, the FMLN seemed to be in retreat as well. Despite FMLN opposition and sporadic efforts at disruption, Cristiani's election marked the sixth successful balloting since 1982. Moreover, the civil-ian politicians of the FDR had finally decided to participate in the 1989 election, thereby giving the process broader legitimacy. Their decisive loss undercut the FDR and FMLN's claims to represent a significant sector of the population, since the Democratic Convergence was widely regarded as a surrogate for the insurgent coalition. Finally, the election itself crystallized the growing division between the politicians of the FDR and the combatants of the FMLN, when the Democratic Conver-gence decided to stay in the election even after the FMLN's peace proposal was rejected and the guerrillas had responded by calling on their supporters to boycott the vote.

With both military and political events apparently moving in its favor, the Salvadoran government was unwilling to make any conces-sions in the months following the election. When government and FMLN negotiators met for talks in September and October 1989, it was like a replay of the 1984 dialogue. The government position had not changed and was not negotiable; if there was to be a diplomatic settlement, it would have to be on the government's terms.

The FMLN, therefore, faced a difficult dilemma. On the one hand, an outright military victory remained out of reach, but a diplomatic solution was equally unattainable so long as the armed forces and the United States believed that the army was winning the war. To create conditions conducive to fruitful negotiation, the FMLN needed to demonstrate that it retained formidable military and political strength and that the only alternative to a negotiated compromise was a perpetual bloody stalemate. "A lasting political solution will become possible only when the insurgents are convinced they cannot win through force," Henry Kissinger said of El Salvador in 1984.[10] This logic held equally well for the government in 1989.

Despite its apparent quiescence on the battlefield, the FMLN had not been idle since halting major offensive operations in 1984. While continuing small-scale attacks in the countryside, the guerrillas had set about rebuilding their political and military apparatus in the cities. During the late 1970s much of the FMLN's organized base of support was in San Salvador's popular organizations that could mobilize over one hundred thousand people for street demonstrations. These organizations were wiped out in the early 1980s by the armed forces. Cadres who managed to elude the death squads fled to the mountains and took up arms. But without any effective urban apparatus to mount a popular uprising, the guerrillas' "final offensive" of 1981 fizzled.

Thereafter, FMLN officials spoke often of the need to rebuild their urban base, but little was done before 1984. This was so because the terror of the death squads continued unabated, and because the FMLN's general command was preoccupied with building a professional army capable of meeting the armed forces of El Salvador in the field and defeating them. Duarte's 1984 victory opened up some space for renewed political activity in the cities just as the FMLN's chances for a battlefield victory began to fade.

The result was a new emphasis by the FMLN on urban organizing. The guerrillas had concluded that the revolutionary movement in the cities had failed in the late 1970s due to the absence of an effective military arm to respond to state repression. Conversely, the failure of the revolutionary army in the 1980s was due to the absence of an effective urban movement that could spark a popular insurrection to tie down government troops in the cities. The FMLN's strategy for the late 1980s, therefore, was to husband the strength of combatants in the countryside while rebuilding the urban movement.

The new popular organizations that grew up in the late 1980s were not mere tools of the FMLN. They developed spontaneously and had their own agendas based on the interests of their members. But neither were they totally independent. The FMLN operated clandestinely within many of them, trying to influence their activities in ways that promoted its political agenda. The revival of popular organizations on the left coincided with the alienation of pro-Christian Democratic trade unions from the Duarte government because of its economic policy. By 1989 the Christian Democratic unions were joining with their former rivals on the left in a united front against ongoing state repression and in favor of a negotiated end to the war.

At the same time, the FMLN established urban commando units capable of launching hit-and-run attacks against virtually any target, from general staff headquarters to the homes and families of high government officials. Actions such as the kidnapping of Duarte's daughter, the killing of four U.S. Marines in the Zona Rosa, and the assassination of several ARENA party officials just after Cristiani's election opened the FMLN to charges of terrorism. Guerrilla leaders defended the attacks as a way of making the Salvadoran elite feel the pain of the war, just as the poor had been feeling it for over a decade. The attacks also carried a more subtle message for hard-liners in the army and government. If they thought they could once again decimate the urban movement with a new *matanza*, then the FMLN's attacks put them on notice that this time the bloodshed would not be one-sided. "An eye for an eye" was how FMLN Commander Villalobos described the new policy.[11]

In need of a dramatic show of strength to shock the government out of its intransigent position at the bargaining table, the FMLN decided to test its urban apparatus. It calculated that a major offensive centered on the capital could not be ignored, even in faraway Washington. "We had to come to the heart of the enemy, because one block taken in the capital is worth 10 kilometers in the countryside," explained an FMLN commander during the offensive.[12]

While the deadlock at the bargaining table was the principal cause of the FMLN's offensive, increased repression against the popular organizations was the catalyst. Shortly after Cristiani's inauguration, he proposed an antiterrorism law that criminalized virtually all forms of political dissent, including the provision of information to international human rights groups. Death squads that had not been heard from since 1984 reappeared. The climate of violence escalated as the FMLN attacked urban military posts and assassinated ARENA party and government officials. Such attacks were invariably followed by mass arrests of activists, some of whom disappeared or were tortured. In June the armed forces accused the Catholic church and its human rights office of being a front for the guerrillas. A few weeks later someone bombed the print shop at the Universidad Centroamericana, one of the first attacks on the UCA in several years. In September the armed forces began arresting and deporting foreign missionaries engaged in refugee relief, accusing them of aiding the guerrillas.

By October the level of violence prompted Archbishop Arturo Rivera y Damas to protest the "marked deterioration of the human rights situation" since Cristiani's inauguration. After an FMLN rocket attack on the general staff headquarters, the homes of two leading members of the Democratic Convergence were bombed. On October 30, a death squad kidnapped and murdered three leaders of Zamora's Popular Social Christian Movement in Sonsonate—the first activists of the party to be killed since the early 1980s.

The catalytic event, however, was the October 31 bombing of the headquarters of the National Federation of Salvadoran Workers (FENASTRAS), a leftist trade-union federation. The blast killed ten people, including General Secretary Febe Elizabeth Velasquez, and wounded twenty-nine others. On the same day another bomb went off at the offices of the Committee of Mothers of the Disappeared, injuring four people. These attacks were so reminiscent of the murderous campaign against the popular organizations in the early 1980s that the FMLN could not allow them to go unavenged.

The Battle of San Salvador

The FMLN's offensive clearly demonstrated that the guerrillas were a long way from being defeated. Indeed, they seemed stronger than ever. Never before had they launched sustained attacks simultaneously on all the country's major cities. Although they failed to capture any of them, the military was only able to regain control of occupied neighborhoods by virtue of its overwhelming firepower and its willingness to strafe and bomb guerrilla positions regardless of civilian casualties. Even then, the FMLN was neither routed nor overrun but fell back in an organized withdrawal, preserving its capacity to launch such an offensive again in the future.

This demonstration of military prowess did not come cheaply. In San Salvador, much of the urban infrastructure painstakingly built up by the FMLN over the preceding few years was exposed when clandestine cadres took up arms. Government reports that over 2,000 guerrillas were killed and many more wounded were widely regarded as exaggerations, but the guerrillas themselves admitted that 401 of their combatants had died in the offensive. The highest toll, however, was among the inexperienced "revolutionary militia" rather than the seasoned guerrillas who had infiltrated the capital from rebel strongholds in the countryside.[13]

The battle of San Salvador also revealed a greater degree of political support for the FMLN than many observers thought they had, but less than the guerrillas themselves expected. The offensive did not spark a massive popular insurrection among the war-weary populace; the instinct of most civilians was to flee the combat zone any way they could. But the FMLN did manage secretly to move hundreds of combatants and tons of arms into the city and conceal them until the offensive was launched—operations that could not have been carried out without significant civilian collaboration. During the initial days of the offensive, people in some of the poor barrios were unmistakably supporting the guerrillas.

The offensive also demolished the facade of democracy so laboriously constructed over the past decade. The military's brutal disregard for civilian casualties and its tolerance for death squad killings demonstrated that not much had really changed since 1980. The cold-blooded murder of six Jesuit priests, their housekeeper, and her teenage daughter at the Universidad Centroamericana evoked memories of the murders of the four U.S. churchwomen, the FDR national leadership, the AFL-CIO land reform advisers, and Archbishop Oscar Romero in 1980 and 1981.

Two days after the six Jesuit priests were murdered, Cristiani's attorney general, Mauricio Colorado, who was responsible for investigating the slayings, called on the pope to withdraw some of the Catholic bishops from El Salvador because they were preaching the "questionable ideology" of liberation theology. Otherwise, Colorado warned, the bishops might be in personal danger.[14] Over the next few weeks government security forces raided churches and refugee relief offices of all denominations, ransacking files and arresting dozens of staff members (including foreign missionaries) on the grounds that the churches were outposts of guerrilla activity.

The murder of the Jesuits and the wave of persecution against the religious community demonstrated that the human rights improvements made in El Salvador after 1984 were largely instrumental and therefore ephemeral. The armed forces had gone through no change of heart, no revelation regarding the value of democracy and free expression. They had simply reduced the killing because that was what they had to do in order to get more military aid from the United States. Nor had they surrendered real power to civilian parties; they had simply adorned the regime with a civilian facade because Washington had insisted on it. Amid the crisis of the FMLN offensive, the armed forces made a mockery of any notion of pluralism or democracy; they went back to killing "subversives" and arresting dissidents wholesale.

Washington's Reaction

The Bush administration's instinctive reaction to the FMLN offensive was to denigrate it as a "desperation move" and to proclaim that the armed forces had everything under control.[15] "I think [the guerrillas] are on the brink of both a military and political defeat," said U.S. Ambassador William Walker a few days after the offensive began.[16] The self-assurance faded a bit as the offensive wore on far longer than U.S. officials had predicted, but the basic theme remained the same: the attacks were not serious, the army was coping with them, and the government was still winning the war. Administration officials would not criticize Cristiani's government for the air attacks against rebel-held neighborhoods. Instead, they accused the FMLN of using the civilians as a "shield" and blamed the guerrillas for the heavy civilian casualties. It remained to be seen whether the population would blame the guerrillas for bringing the war to the cities or the armed forces for bombing them.

The killings of the Jesuits brought forth an immediate condemnation from the State Department and demands for a full investigation. But even then, the administration denied that the murders revealed any fundamental flaw in the Salvadoran regime. At first the White House implied that the priests might have been killed by the guerrillas, but that was untenable. The murders occurred during a dawn-to-dusk curfew in a neighborhood controlled by government troops who had ransacked the Jesuit residence two days earlier. The priests were killed by high-powered rifles of the sort used by the army, and at least one witness saw twenty to thirty armed, uniformed men enter the residence just before the killings. U.S. intelligence sources later identified "rogue elements" of the armed forces as the killers, and Ambassador Walker acknowledged that the Cristiani government had a "management control problem" with the military.[17] In early January, Cristiani himself admitted that the killings were the work of the army.

As in the early 1980s the administration stuck doggedly to the claim that such atrocities were not the government's responsibility but were committed by "extremists" on the right, some of whom happened to be in the armed forces. President Bush absolutely rejected any suggestion that military aid to El Salvador be reduced or subjected to conditions because of the Jesuit killings and the ferocity of the aerial attacks on poor neighborhoods. On the contrary, when Cristiani requested emergency military aid to replenish depleted stocks, the administration pledged its support and announced it would speed up weapons deliveries.

If the administration evinced relatively little public concern over the implications of the offensive, the same was not true for Congress. Legislators were stunned by the intensity of the FMLN's attacks. Some began to wonder whether the picture of political and military success painted by the State Department since 1984 was anything more than a Potemkin village. The fear that El Salvador might deteriorate into another Vietnam was suddenly resurrected.

Congress was especially horrified by the murder of the Jesuits. Sen. Alan Cranston (D-CA) was so disgusted at the military's actions that he called for the United States simply to withdraw and leave the Salvadorans to fight it out among themselves. "The war in El Salvador has been reduced to the level of street thugs butchering each other," Cranston charged. "There is no U.S. national security interest in using taxpayer dollars to bankroll such a conflict."[18] Even Republicans who opposed placing any conditions or limits on aid to the Cristiani government demanded a full and rapid investigation of the murders.

Although many members of Congress raised their voices in bitter protest over the slayings and over the deadly air attacks, neither the House nor the Senate was willing to take any immediate punitive action. Legislators were too angry at the guerrillas for launching the attacks and too fearful that the army might be tottering. As the offensive was winding down in late November, the House narrowly refused (by a vote of 215 to 194) to even consider a proposal for temporarily withholding 30 percent of the $85 million in military aid approved for El Salvador in fiscal 1990. A similar move to withhold aid pending an investigation of the murders also failed in the Senate.

Nevertheless, congressional Democrats were no longer willing to meekly accept the status quo. When Congress returned in January, leading liberals immediately took up the El Salvador issue again. Democratic Senators Edward Kennedy and John Kerry of Massachusetts introduced a bill to cut off military aid entirely—an "end the war" bill, Kennedy called it.[19] Senator Dodd, repentant for his earlier opposition to making aid conditional on the government's human rights record and its willingness to negotiate, introduced a rival bill designed to bring both sides to the bargaining table.

Dodd proposed to withhold 50 percent of El Salvador's military aid if the FMLN agreed to negotiations, and to withhold the other 50 percent as well if the government refused to enter such talks. Full aid would be restored only if the FMLN launched another major offensive that threatened the government's survival. All aid would be cut off if Cristiani was overthrown by the army or if the government failed to move forward on a number of human rights issues, foremost among them the investigation and prosecution of the Jesuit case. By making the level of military aid dependent upon the behavior of both parties, Dodd's proposal was regarded as more evenhanded than the usual congressional human rights requirements, which in most cases made demands solely of the government. Although the bill had little chance of passing in an undiluted form, it quickly became the focal point of the debate.

The Jesuit Case

Within Congress, the Jesuit case immediately took on enormous symbolic importance, much like the case of the four U.S. churchwomen killed by the National Guard in 1980. The longer it took Cristiani to deliver the perpetrators to justice, the greater the danger that his aid program would fall victim to a congressional revolt. Consequently, the Bush administration pushed the Salvadorans hard, through both civilian and military channels, for a real investigation.

The guerrilla offensive and the subsequent pressure from Washington over the Jesuit killings crystallized divisions within the government and the armed forces between the moderate right, led by Cristiani and Chief of Staff Col. Emilio Ponce, and the extreme right, led by D'Aubuisson and former air force commander Gen. Juan Rafael Bustillo.[20] Since the early 1980s the officer corps has been divided between those who accepted Washington's counterinsurgency strategy of "low intensity conflict" with its emphasis on winning hearts and minds, and those who resented Washington's meddling, especially with regard to human rights. This latter group, long associated with D'Aubuisson and ARENA, advocated a strategy of "total war," an all-out military campaign against not only the FMLN but also against peasants and urban activists suspected of supporting the guerrillas—that is, anyone demanding social reform and an end to human rights abuses. Even if one hundred thousand people had to be killed, the hard-liners reasoned, at least the war would be over quickly. Less fanatical officers, on the other hand, recognized that the carnage of "total war" would likely provoke a cutoff of U.S. military aid, without which the armed forces could not sustain their operations.

At first the intensity of the guerrilla offensive seemed to strengthen the hand of the hard-liners. General Bustillo and the air force operated autonomously from Cristiani during the worst of the fighting, and perhaps autonomously from the general staff as well. On December 4, the air force dropped leaflets urging "Salvadoran patriots" to kill "FMLN terrorists and their internationalist allies" in order to defend the homeland. But the international revulsion prompted by the murder of the Jesuits weakened the far right and halted the surge in death squad operations. In January, Cristiani and Ponce won a key victory against the far right, forcing Bustillo into diplomatic exile as a military attaché in Israel. A few days later, Cristiani ordered the arrest of five enlisted men and four officers—including Col. Guillermo Alfredo Benavides—for the murder of the Jesuits.[21]

Winning convictions in the case is another matter. Many members of the officer corps believe that the Jesuits were the spiritual fathers of the insurgency and hence deserved to die. When the killings were reported to a meeting of senior intelligence officers a few hours after they occurred, the assembled group let out a spontaneous cheer. There is such bitterness among Salvadoran officers over the arrests that relations with U.S. military advisers are severely strained. (After his arrest, Benavides was "detained" in a luxury apartment at police headquarters and was permitted to travel freely around the country.)[22] The Salvadorans blame Washington for coercing Cristiani and Ponce into ordering the detentions.[23]

Without the threat of an aid cutoff, there probably would not have been any arrests—not because Cristiani is evil-minded, but because even moderate officers such as Ponce would not have been willing or able to surrender one of their own to civil justice. Solidarity is too high within the Salvadoran officers' caste to allow the sacrifice of a brother officer except under severe duress. And thus far, even the threatened loss of aid has not been enough to push the investigation beyond the men already arrested, even though circumstantial evidence suggests that Colonel Benavides would not have undertaken such an operation on his own authority.[24]

The U.S. pressure will have to be intense and sustained to achieve justice in the Jesuit case. Despite the expressions of outrage heard in the halls of Congress, and the warnings that aid will be cut off unless the priests' killers are brought to justice, the Salvadorans have little reason to take such threats seriously. Similar speeches were made before— after the murders of the churchwomen in 1980; the AFL-CIO advisers in 1981; and the Salvadoran peasants at Las Hojas in 1983, at Los Llanitos in 1984, and at San Francisco in 1988. There was always a fresh atrocity for Washington to be outraged about, yet U.S. military aid kept flowing. None of these cases was fully investigated and none of the military officers involved was ever punished. Over the years, the Salvadorans have learned that Washington is easily mollified by the imprisonment of a few enlisted men or the temporary reassignment of guilty officers to "gilded exile" in a foreign diplomatic post. They have no reason to think that the case of the Jesuits will be any different.

Washington's past tolerance for political murder in El Salvador thus weakened its ability to press for military reform. If the threats of sanctions were really empty, then the killers had no reason to desist and their fellow officers had no incentive to rupture the canons of the corps by holding the killers accountable.

Why Is the United States in El Salvador?

In 1981, Ronald Reagan invoked national security as the rationale for committing the United States to El Salvador, arguing that the indigenous civil conflict there had been transformed by Cuba and the Soviet Union into a case of "indirect communist aggression." Washington had an overriding security interest in preventing a guerrilla victory, Reagan continued, regardless of El Salvador's far-from-perfect human rights record. If the guerrillas won, they would establish a Communist regime, ally themselves with Nicaragua, Cuba, and the Soviet Union, and export violence to their neighbors. Dominoes would topple north toward Mexico and south toward the Panama Canal, Reagan warned, and the United States itself was "the last domino." Liberals regarded the president's apocalyptic rhetoric about the consequences of a guerrilla victory as hyperbole. They simply did not believe his refurbished domino theory. Reagan spoke as if the stakes in El Salvador were so high that Washington should pay any price in order to prevail. The liberals regarded the stakes as limited and thought the commitment should be, too.

As the debate over El Salvador resumes, the Bush administration is having an even harder time convincing Congress that U.S. national security justifies its commitment. El Salvador is now remote from Soviet concerns. Guided by President Mikhail Gorbachev's "new thinking," the Soviets have been disengaging from Third World commitments as fast as they can. They refused to finance a Nicaraguan experiment with socialism, and Gorbachev has called for "stability" in Central America—not very auspicious signs for guerrilla movements.

At the Malta summit, Bush complained that Central America was the "single most disruptive factor" in the superpower relationship. But he blamed the Cubans and the Nicaraguans rather than the Soviets, and he urged Gorbachev to rein in his wayward allies. The Kremlin's response was positive. "The Soviet Union has told us they are leaning on Nicaragua and Cuba not to send weapons to the FMLN, but that has not worked, so we are encouraging them to lean even harder," said Secretary of State James A. Baker after the summit.[25] It was a far cry from the not-so-distant past when our main complaint against Havana and Managua was that they were Soviet pawns. If the Soviet Union is no longer exploiting instability in Central America, then it is hard to imagine how events in El Salvador, regardless of their outcome, could endanger the national security interests of the United States.

Of course, national security has not been the only rationale for Washington's commitment. Early in the Reagan administration, Assistant Secretary of State for Inter-American Affairs Thomas O. Enders recognized that anticommunism was inadequate for rallying domestic support for the policy. The United States needed to be *for* something, and Enders argued it should be for democracy. Beginning with the 1982 Constituent Assembly elections, the theme of supporting incipient democracy in El Salvador received equal billing with national security as a justification for U.S. policy. After Duarte's election as president in 1984, democracy became the dominant theme and the cornerstone of the bipartisan consensus. It remains the principal rationale for U.S. policy. "I will not accept, as president, a cutoff of aid to El Salvador," Bush flatly declared during the November offensive. "We are supporting El Salvador because it had certifiably free elections. President Cristiani is trying to do a job for democracy."[26]

But is it really democracy that we have been building in El Salvador over the past decade? Or have we merely erected electoral institutions on the swampy foundation of a political culture and social system that remain as intolerant and repressive as ever? Over the past year the "democracy" that Washington constructed in San Salvador has rapidly decayed to the point that even the most basic human rights and political liberties are no longer safeguarded. The antiterrorism law proposed by Cristiani mimics, almost exactly, the infamous Law for the Defense and Guarantee of Public Order imposed by the dictatorship of Gen. Humberto Romero in 1979—a law that was a license for state-sponsored repression and a prelude to the collapse of public order inaugurating the civil war.

American foreign policy has always had an element of missionary zeal. Pride in our democratic institutions has often manifested itself in efforts to propagate those institutions in other lands. At the turn of the century, when the United States sent the marines to occupy half a dozen countries in the Caribbean Basin, we invariably tried to build democracies before withdrawing. We invariably failed. In Haiti, Cuba, Nicaragua, Panama, and the Dominican Republic, the professional, nonpartisan armies we created as bulwarks of democracy metamorphosed into instruments of brutal military dictatorship. Not coincidentally, these same countries have been among the most unstable in subsequent decades.

Under the Alliance for Progress in the 1960s, we tried to promote progressive social change and democratic political reform in Latin America. But by arming existing regimes to enable them to defeat guerrilla insurgencies, Washington ended up strengthening the very elites who were the major obstacles to change. Once armed, incumbents had little incentive to accept even modest reforms. The 1960s proved to be a decade not of democracy but of military coups.

The democratic institutions that developed naturally out of the social and political history of the United States cannot be so easily transplanted to very different societies in the Caribbean and Central America. Salvadorans are as capable of building democracy as anyone, but effective democratic institutions cannot be rooted in a social order and political culture that favor authoritarianism. The Salvadoran military treats peasants as subhuman because the social order treats them that way—paying them starvation wages, leaving them uneducated and without adequate housing or health care. When daily life conveys the message that the lives of the poor have little value, it should come as no surprise that soldiers kill poor people without compunction or remorse.

Since 1982 the Salvadoran elite, under pressure from Washington, has held elections that have shuffled civilian seats in government back and forth between the Christian Democratic center and the reactionary right. But the fear of revolution has discouraged the United States from trying to tear out the roots of authoritarianism in El Salvador. These roots are deeply embedded in the political domination of the armed forces and the economic domination of a small land-owning elite whose wealth depends on a docile labor force. To fight the war, Washington built the Salvadoran armed forces up from twelve thousand to fifty-five thousand men armed with modern weaponry and schooled in civic action and counterinsurgency. Is it any wonder that the military's political power has not diminished?

Washington has opposed any negotiated settlement that would give the left a significant share of political power. Instead, U.S. policy has aimed at stabilizing a truncated political system encompassing only the center (the PDC) and the right wing (ARENA) of the ideological spectrum. Is it any wonder that such a system is incapable of producing significant social reforms?

A negotiated settlement of the war will not end El Salvador's problems or turn it into a democracy overnight, but it is the necessary first step. Only when the war is ended and the undemocratic habits of the armed forces broken will it be possible for Salvadorans with political preferences to the left of the Christian Democratic party to organize freely to contend for political power at the ballot box. Only when the security of the democratic arena is guaranteed will it be possible for Salvadorans to choose between the supply-side free-market program of the right and the social reform program of the left.

What Next?

The FMLN's offensive demonstrated that the war remains stalemated. There will be no military solution in the foreseeable future unless Washington undertakes a massive escalation of its commitments—an option that even the Bush administration has not suggested. A negotiated settlement, therefore, is all the more urgent. Cristiani and the moderate right may be seriously interested in reaching such a settlement. They represent a "modernized" segment of the private sector that, unlike the traditional oligarchy, believes that its economic interests can be safeguarded in a democratic system. ARENA's resounding victories in the past two elections seem to have proven them right. But the consolidation of ARENA's electoral majority requires, first and foremost, reactivation of the economy. That is impossible without peace. If Cristiani could manage to both end the war and begin economic recovery, then ARENA's political fortunes would be bright indeed. If the war goes on, then ARENA risks the same fate as Duarte's Christian Democrats: continued economic crisis and eventual defeat at the polls.

Cristiani's allies in the officer corps are less sanguine about negotiations, however. Thus far, they have stood by him because the continuation of U.S. aid depends on the maintenance of civilian rule and on the government's willingness to at least begin talking again with the guerrillas. But there is no major faction within the military that actively favors negotiating an end to the war, and there is a powerful group on the far right that vehemently opposes it.

Although the FMLN has made major concessions in its bargaining position over the past year, it continues to insist on major changes in the armed forces. The FMLN demands a reduction in the size of the military from fifty-five thousand to twelve thousand men, its original size. A cutback of that dimension would require the retirement of a large number of officers. It demands separating the security forces (the Treasury police, National Guard, and national police) from the military and placing them under civilian control.

This would deprive the armed forces of primary responsibility for internal security and also take away the instruments often used in the past for the violent repression of dissent. And, most important, the FMLN demands that the armed forces "cleanse" themselves of officers guilty of human rights abuses and place them on trial. Then, and only then, are the guerrillas willing to lay down their arms.[27] These demands, especially the last one, are unacceptable to the vast majority of Salvadoran officers.[28] If Cristiani were foolish enough to agree to them in negotiations, he would almost certainly provoke a coup d'état. He faced a near revolt in the military simply for arresting a senior officer in the Jesuit case.

In the wake of the Nicaraguan elections, Cristiani was under heavy pressure from the far right not to resume negotiations at all. He quibbled over whether UN Secretary General Javier Pérez de Cuéllar would be a mediator or simply the convener of talks, and, as a precondition, he insisted that the FMLN halt attacks affecting the civilian population. In mid-March the FMLN offered to stop attacks on most nonmilitary targets, but it was doubtful that the guerrillas would agree to Cristiani's demand for what amounted to a unilateral cease-fire.

Ironically, the FMLN's demands for military reform do not conflict fundamentally with stated U.S. policy aims. On the contrary, if civilian democracy is what Washington truly wants in El Salvador, these reforms are essential to achieving it. In addition, Washington has a vested interest in reducing the size of the military once the war is over, since the United States has to foot the bill for it. The idea of reorganizing the security forces and removing them from military control actually originated in Washington back in 1982 as a way to reduce human rights abuses and thereby quiet congressional objections to military aid. And the removal of officers guilty of human rights abuses also has been a recurring theme in U.S. policy, at least since Bush's visit to San Salvador in 1983.

The problem, of course, is that the armed forces have bitterly resisted such reforms. In the midst of the war, Washington has never been willing to precipitate a major internal struggle within the officer corps by forcing the issue. The army would be demoralized by it, so the argument went; the command structure might even collapse, thus paving the way for a guerrilla victory. But if the changes in the armed forces demanded by the FMLN were the only obstacle to a negotiated peace, then Washington would have no logical reason to resist them.

With the ending of the Cold War, El Salvador no longer has much geopolitical importance. Winning a decisive victory there against the rising tide of international communism does not have the symbolic value it had for Reagan. Washington could easily settle for a negotiated peace without fear of damaging the credibility of its global foreign policy. In fact, the continuing war in El Salvador has become an albatross for the United States. Each year it consumes several hundred million dollars in foreign aid that is desperately needed elsewhere. It diverts the attention of policymakers from hemispheric issues of greater consequence. It remains a sore point in relations between the administration and Congress, frustrating efforts to build a bipartisan foreign policy. And it shows no prospect of ending.

If victory is beyond reach, and a perennial stalemate too costly to endure, then a negotiated settlement of the war in El Salvador is Washington's best hope for disposing of the issue. Behind the public facade of confidence displayed by administration officials at the time of the November offensive, some seemed shaken enough by events to seriously contemplate negotiations as a way out. In February, Gen. Maxwell R. Thurmond, head of the U.S. Southern Command, told the Senate Armed Services Committee that the Salvadoran army would not be able to achieve a military victory over the FMLN. It was a significant admission, coming from the architect of the invasion of Panama.[29]

At the same time, the State Department began voicing support for a resumption of negotiations between the Cristiani government and the FMLN through the offices of Secretary General Pérez de Cuéllar.[30] Although the United States has officially favored talks between the two sides ever since Duarte proposed them in 1984, the Reagan administration actively discouraged Duarte from making any significant concessions to the guerrillas.

Since the offensive, however, the Bush administration seems more open to the possibility of a settlement that is not merely a disguised FMLN surrender. "El Salvador needs peace, and the only path to peace is at the negotiating table," Assistant Secretary of State Aronson told the House Subcommittee on Western Hemisphere Affairs in January. "Let both sides commit to come to the bargaining table . . . and to stay and negotiate in good faith until the war is over."[31] But Washington's declaration of support for negotiations will not be enough to actually produce a settlement. The United States will have to exert real pressure on the military to accept concessions that are not in its institutional interest.

A policy of actively forcing reform on the Salvadoran military is not one that is likely to emanate spontaneously from the cautious Bush administration. Although some officials seem to recognize the need for a negotiated end to the war, the administration as a whole remains unwilling to make the hard decisions necessary to actually bring one about. The Republican right, most strongly represented in the National Security Council staff and the office of the vice president, refuses to believe that the November offensive was a significant setback to the policy that Washington has followed for the past decade. It remains confident that the armed forces are winning the war and that persistence is all that is required for victory. Consequently, the right in the United States sees no pressing need for negotiations, other than to pacify a meddlesome Congress. It is likely to block any internal initiative to alter administration policy.

Congress, however, can break the deadlock. To begin, it should impose strict conditions on any further military assistance. Unless the government demonstrates a willingness to negotiate seriously and to punish military officers guilty of human rights abuses—not just in the Jesuit case but across the board—no further aid should be forthcoming. But that alone is not enough. In the past, such conditionality proved ineffective because it was largely a bluff. The Reagan administration had no intention of cutting aid, regardless of whether or not the Salvadoran government lived up to the conditions, and the officer corps knew it. Because the threat to cut aid was never credible, $4 billion bought very little leverage.

Therefore, the first step of a new policy toward El Salvador should be to make the threat credible by cutting military aid significantly at the outset. Senator Dodd's proposal to reduce aid by 50 percent is a good beginning. Perhaps the Salvadoran armed forces will prefer to fight on alone rather than accede to the kinds of democratizing reforms that the FMLN is demanding—and that Washington ought to support. If the military is impervious to basic change, then we should follow the advice of the conservative London *Economist* and cut off aid entirely.[32] There are more pressing and more productive places for us to spend our scarce foreign-aid dollars.

After five years of passive consensus on El Salvador, is Congress now ready to spring to life, forcing the Bush administration into a more activist role than it wants to assume? At first glance, it seems unlikely. House Speaker Thomas Foley and Senate Majority Leader George Mitchell are cautious men who abhor issues such as El Salvador that divide Democrats along ideological lines (southern conservatives versus northern liberals). Both were quick to applaud the invasion of Panama, and both were happy to sign a bipartisan agreement with Bush back in 1989 in order to dispose of the bitterly divisive issue of Nicaragua. The defeat of the Sandinistas in the February elections has probably reinforced their inclination to let the executive branch take the initiative in Central America. Without the support of their leadership, liberal Democrats in the House and Senate will have difficulty in mustering the votes to impose any major restrictions on aid to El Salvador.

Nevertheless, discontent with the status quo is growing on Capitol Hill and could soon reach such proportions that the reluctant leaders can no longer ignore it. The real lesson to be drawn from the Nicaraguan experience is not that congressional passivity produces sound policy. On the contrary, Washington finally embraced the Central American peace process, which in turn led to the February elections in Nicaragua, because Congress refused to acquiesce in the Reagan administration's strategy of seeking military victory through proxy war.

When Congress cut off military aid to the contras, thereby eliminating the military option, conservative Republicans yelped that the Democrats were tying the hands of the president and fatally damaging U.S. interests. Without the contras, they insisted, Nicaragua would disappear into the black hole of totalitarianism, never to emerge. We should recall how mistaken the Republicans were about Nicaragua when they repeat the same arguments in opposing limits on military aid to El Salvador. Sometimes the most sensible policy is a product not of consensus but of conflict between Congress and the executive—conflict that the framers of the Constitution intentionally built into our structure of government precisely for that reason.

The Tet offensive was a turning point in the Vietnam War because it forced U.S. decision makers to rethink the basic premises of their policy. If the battle of San Salvador, bloody and militarily pointless though it was, has a similar effect, then it will have had some redeeming value. If hardline conservatives in the Bush administration continue to insist that nothing fundamental has changed and block other efforts in the executive branch to reassess U.S. policy and draft a new approach, Congress will then have to supply the impetus for a new course.

No legitimate U.S. interest is served by continuing the current policy. Our national security is not at risk and Salvadoran "democracy" is not worthy of the name. Washington has been financing the war in El Salvador partly out of hubris—a belief that we have the right and the power to preserve a dominant position in "our own backyard"—and partly out of inertia. It is foolish to expend billions of dollars on such a policy; it is unconscionable to expend thousands of Salvadoran lives. If the Soviet Union can repudiate the Brezhnev Doctrine that prescribed limited sovereignty for Eastern Europe, surely the United States can do the same for Central America.

On March 10, 1991, elections were held for El Salvador's unicameral legislative body. The results announced on March 23 indicated that the ruling ARENA party received 44 percent of the valid vote, while 28 percent went to the Christian Democrats and 12 percent to the Democratic Convergence, a coalition headed by Rubén Zamora, former spokesman for the guerrilla left. Another 16 percent of the votes were distributed among minor parties.[33] These results indicate the continuing polarization of the Salvadoran electorate, with ARENA's 44 percent reflecting an anti-change orientation, while the 40 percent combined vote total of the (reformist) Christian Democrats and the (revolutionary) Democratic Convergence represent a pro-change orientation. The 12 percent of the votes received by the Democratic Convergence was a threefold increase over the performance of this electoral *tendencia* in the 1989 election. The Democratic Convergence will have eight of eighty-four seats in the legislative body (and one seat will go to a Marxist party further to the left). ARENA will hold thirty-nine seats, and the Christian Democrats will hold twenty-six.

The military stalemate described by William LeoGrande in the preceding article may now be matched by a political stalemate. Much will depend on how the respective political forces choose to cooperate or compete with each other in the legislative body. LeoGrande's recommendation for a hands-off policy by the United States would seem to be even more compelling after the 1991 election results. The relatively even balance of forces gives Salvadorans an opportunity to learn to live together with fellow citizens of differing political views. [Editors' note]

Notes

1. *Public Papers of the Presidents of the United States: Lyndon B. Johnson, 1968–1969* (Washington, DC: Government Printing Office, 1970), 155.

2. ABC World News Tonight, November 22, 1989.

3. Estimates are that ten thousand to thirty thousand peasants were killed by the armed forces in 1932. The Catholic church reported over twenty thousand non-combatant civilians killed by government security forces and paramilitary death squads in 1980 and 1981.

4. The FMLN continued to launch spectacular assaults on individual garrisons every six months or so by quickly massing several hundred combatants, attacking, and then dispersing before the air force could respond. But there were no broad, sustained offensives of that sort that had rocked the army in previous years.

5. The Democratic Convergence was made up of the newly organized Social Democratic Party, the National Revolutionary Movement (affiliated with the Socialist International), and the Popular Social Christian Movement. The last two were also members of the Revolutionary Democratic Front (FDR), the civilian allies of the FMLN.

6. See "The General Situation in El Salvador: An Assessment," *Spotlight: International MNR Bulletin* 8, no. 5 (September–December 1989): 1–28.

7. Documents captured from the guerrillas in early 1988 suggested that the FMLN was still dubious about the viability of a negotiated solution, but by 1989 the guerrillas had reportedly concluded that military victory was unlikely. The captured documents are described by James LeMoyne in "El Salvador's Forgotten War," *Foreign Affairs* (Summer 1989): 105–25. The shift in FMLN thinking is reported in Douglas Farah, "Salvadoran Rebels Apologize for Civilian Deaths," *Washington Post*, May 25, 1989; and Frank Smyth, "El Salvador's Revised Revolution," *In These Times*, February 28–March 13, 1990.

8. Terry Karl, "El Salvador: Negotiations or Total War: An Interview with Salvador Samayoa," *World Policy Journal* (Spring 1989): 321–55.

9. See the interview with Joaquín Villalobos in Marjorie Miller, "Rebels Start New Offensive: Diplomacy," *Los Angeles Times*, November 17, 1988.

10. Joanne Omang, "Latin Unit Asks $8 Billion Aid Tied to Rights," *Washington Post*, January 12, 1984.

11. Douglas Farah, "El Salvador's Rebels Vow to Escalate Their Attacks," ibid., March 30, 1988.

12. Idem, "Guerrilla Gamble Proving Costly," ibid., November 20, 1989.

13. Chris Norton, "Salvador Rebels: Defeated or Just Bruised?" *Christian Science Monitor*, January 5, 1990. The armed forces admitted to 1,000 casualties of their own, in a ratio of 3 to 1 of wounded to killed. Mark A. Uhlig, "Salvadoran Security Forces Raid Episcopal Church, Arresting Seventeen," *New York Times*, November 21, 1989.

14. Douglas Farah, "Salvadoran Guerrillas Withdraw under Fire," *Washington Post*, November 19, 1989.

15. Secretary of Defense Richard B. Cheney, quoted in Douglas Farah, "127 Deaths in Salvadoran Rebel Drive," *Washington Post*, November 13, 1989.

16. Lee Hockstader, "Air Attacks Counter Salvadoran Rebels," ibid., November 16, 1989.

17. Douglas Farah, "San Salvador Revives: Another Church Raided," ibid., November 21, 1989; NBC Nightly News, November 20, 1989.

18. Robert Pear, "U.S. Official Links Salvadoran Right to Priests' Deaths," *New York Times*, November 18, 1989.

19. *Congressional Record*, February 6, 1990, S895–S897.

20. Douglas Farah, "Salvadoran President Comes to U.S. Bearing Heavy Domestic Burden," *Washington Post*, January 30, 1990.

21. The far right has hardly been beaten, however. On January 12, as if in response to the detention of soldiers in the Jesuit killings, a rightist death squad in Guatemala kidnapped and murdered Hector Oqueli, the number-two official of the Salvadoran social democratic National Revolutionary Movement (MNR). Oqueli was one of the MNR's most effective spokesmen and a respected official of the Socialist International. His murder attracted little attention in the United States, where he was not well known, but it was just as destructive to the prospects for peace as the killing of the Jesuits.

22. Douglas Farah, "Colonel Charged in Jesuit Killing Lives in Luxury," *Washington Post*, February 22, 1990.

23. Ana Arana, "Salvador Officers Met Just Before Jesuit Massacre," *Baltimore Sun*, February 4, 1990; Douglas Farah, "U.S. Pressure in Jesuit Probe Said to Alienate Salvadoran Officers," *Washington Post*, February 6, 1990.

24. Brook Larmer, "New Evidence Points to Coverup," *Christian Science Monitor*, February 7, 1990. Washington's ability to determine whether or not there was a wider conspiracy to kill the Jesuits was severely damaged when one of its better intelligence sources in the officer corps, Col. Carlos Armando Aviles, was "burned" by the U.S. embassy. It was Aviles who tipped off the embassy that the Jesuits had been killed by the army's Atlacatl battalion. The embassy then passed this information along to Chief of Staff Ponce and inexplicably told him that Aviles was the source. Aviles was then arrested. James A. Goldston and Anne Manuel, "Are We Shielding the Killers of Salvador's Priests?" *New York Times*, January 21, 1990.

25. David Hoffman, "Bush and Gorbachev Hail New Cooperation," *Washington Post*, December 4, 1989.

26. Robert Pear, "House Rejects Curb on Salvador Aid," *New York Times*, November 21, 1989.

27. "Position of the FMLN toward the New ARENA Government and Proposal to Achieve a Real Democracy, Peace and a New Society," April 6, 1989 (mimeograph, 1989). Other demands are listed in this negotiating position, but the three regarding military reform are the most politically sensitive. Slightly modified versions of these proposals were put forward by FMLN representatives in their meetings with

government officials in September and October 1989. For these see "FMLN Proposals for Negotiating a Just and Lasting Peace in El Salvador," *Envío* (Managua, Nicaragua) 9, no. 102 (January 1990): 8–12.

28.   Frank Smyth, "El Salvador's Revised Revolution," *In These Times*, February 28–March 13, 1990, reports that Cristiani and Ponce have told visiting delegations from the United States that the military reforms demanded by the FMLN are negotiable, but moderates in the government do not have a very good record of being able to force such changes on the military right.

29.   Michael R. Gordon, "General Says Salvador Can't Defeat Guerrillas," *New York Times*, February 9, 1990.

30.   A role for the United Nations was first urged by the five Central American presidents at their summit meeting in Costa Rica on December 12, 1989. "U.S. Supports U.N. Effort to Arrange Salvadoran Peace Talks," *Washington Post*, February 3, 1990.

31.   Testimony of Bernard W. Aronson, Assistant Secretary of State, Bureau of Inter-American Affairs, to the Subcommittee on Western Hemisphere Affairs, Committee on Foreign Affairs, United States House of Representatives, January 24, 1990 (mimeograph, 1990), 5.

32.   "Sad Salvador," *Economist* (London), November 25, 1989.

33.   "Ruling Salvadoran Party Wins Vote: Rightists Lose Their Majority in the National Assembly," *New York Times*, March 24, 1991.

The Aftermath of Intervention: Panama, 1990*

Richard L. Millett

It was hardly surprising that the December 1989 U.S. intervention in Panama received strong public support. General Manuel Antonio Noriega had replaced Muammar al-Qaddafi and the late Ayatollah Ruhollah Khomeini as the foreign leader the U.S. public most loved to hate. In addition, the Bush administration was quickly able to proclaim its intervention in Panama a virtually unqualified success, confidently asserting that the stated goals of protecting U.S. lives, capturing General Noriega and sending him to the United States for trial, defending the Panama Canal treaties, and "restoring democracy" to Panama had all been met.[1] The U.S. military is involved in helping form the new Panama Public Force (PPF) to replace General Noriega's Panama Defense Forces (PDF), and U.S. advisers are working to rebuild the economy. In Washington, the process of getting a special package of financial assistance through Congress has begun. In Panama, a new government has begun trying to deal with the massive economic, political, and social problems facing that nation. Public opinion in both nations seems strongly to support U.S. actions. In the United States, the president's popularity climbed in the wake of the invasion, and he may have permanently shed the wimp image which his opponents had long sought to cultivate. On the surface, at least, the administration seems to have good cause for feeling pleased with the result of its actions.

In this case, however, surface indications may be deceiving. As Yogi Berra once observed, "it ain't over till it's over," and the problems which produced the intervention and which resulted from it are still far from over. The final results of this intervention will not be clear until

* This article was originally published in the *Journal of Inter-American Studies and World Affairs* 32 (Spring 1990): 1–15. Reprinted with the permission of the journal and the author.

well into the next century, but it is already apparent that, as has so often been the case in the past, it is much easier to use force to remove a government than it is to install a stable and democratic successor.

The December invasion represented the culmination of over two and one-half years of acute political crisis within Panama and twenty-two months of high-level U.S. efforts to remove General Noriega from power. In the process, Panama's economy was devastated, long-existing class and racial divisions in its society were exacerbated, and traditional norms of political behavior, which had made Panama a relatively nonviolent nation by regional standards, were destroyed. The prolonged crisis created an atmosphere of fear, suspicion, and hatred and inflicted economic damage which may require decades to repair.

Despite political rhetoric, the invasion represented the failure, not the success, of U.S. policy in Panama. This failure has numerous dimensions. There was the failure of years of U.S. efforts—beginning with the Carter administration—to promote a peaceful transition from military to civilian rule. What seemed for a time to be limited progress in that direction proved illusory, and, by 1989, Panama was more clearly a military dictatorship than it had been a dozen years earlier.

There was a marked failure of efforts to create a professional, nonpolitical military. U.S. training and support made the PDF stronger and technically more efficient, but neither lessened the institution's propensity for corruption nor altered its fundamental hostility toward most politicians. If anything, such assistance enhanced the PDF's ability to control the political agenda.

The intervention underscored the limitations and frustrations of efforts to deal with the narcotics traffic. Official letters of praise from the Drug Enforcement Administration (DEA), which Noriega loved to display, underlined the contradictions inherent in this effort. It was money from U.S. consumers of narcotics which accelerated the corruption of the PDF and which helped sustain Noriega's power during the prolonged period of U.S. economic sanctions.

The nearly two-year effort to oust Noriega through economic, political, and diplomatic pressures, or through promoting an internal coup by the PDF, was simply the latest in a long line of such failures. Similar efforts failed to remove Anastasio Somoza from power before he was overthrown by the Sandinistas and have conspicuously failed to bring either democracy or stability to Haiti. Economic sanctions, in particular, have proved a difficult, and usually ineffective, tactic in such situations. Panama exemplified the problem of targeting such sanctions. The sanctions had their worst impact upon the business community, which formed the heart of the opposition to Noriega. Finally, the impact of such sanctions lasts long after the purpose for their employment has disappeared.

On a wider scale, the intervention symbolized the failures of U.S. policy throughout Central America. One reason the situation deteriorated so far in Panama before there was any high-level recognition of its gravity was that, for years, the Reagan administration found it convenient to ignore, or dismiss, the evolving political situation within Panama in order to cultivate PDF support for U.S. operations in El Salvador and Nicaragua. The obsession with the Sandinistas, and the effort to deal with them by developing the contras, played a particularly significant role in this scenario. However, the net result has been an ongoing insurgency in El Salvador, the virtual collapse of the contra effort in Nicaragua, and a major policy crisis in Panama. The intervention also underlined the limitations of Washington's efforts to promote civilian government and limit military abuses of power. While Panama was the most obvious example of this dilemma, the problem persists in Guatemala, Honduras, and El Salvador.

Any resort to military force in international relations symbolizes policy failure, since the objective of any rational policy is to protect and advance national interests without resorting to force. The United States could have intervened and ousted Noriega in early 1988 without undergoing nearly two years of frustration and humiliation and without devastating Panama's economy. Resort to force was the final option, the most costly and least desirable, to be employed only when all else failed.

The intervention symbolized not only the failure of U.S. policy but also the failure of efforts by the internal opposition and by the international community to promote peaceful political change in Panama. For the opposition, whose efforts were hampered as much by the nature of Panamanian society and the relatively pacific traditions of Panamanian politics as by the repressive measures of the Noriega regime, coming to power through U.S. military force, rather than through their own efforts, is—and will remain—an embarrassing, even humiliating, burden which their opponents can always use against them.

For the nations of the Americas, and for the Organization of American States (OAS), the intervention underscored their continuing inability to resolve crises of this nature. Caught between desires to promote more democratic government and avoid U.S. intervention on the one hand, and their traditional commitment to noninterference in a nation's internal affairs on the other, the efforts of the Latin American community to resolve cases such as that of Panama usually result in frustrating failure. This dilemma was summed up by Venezuelan President Carlos Andrés Pérez, who noted:

> We have witnessed a new and unfortunate humiliation inflicted on our people with the invasion of Panama. I have the authority to say this because I have been a firm critic of the shameless Panamanian regime and have eagerly sought a Latin American consensus to find a peaceful and democratic solution in Panama. Unfortunately, Latin American mechanisms have been weakened by differences over the principle of nonintervention. Its mechanisms have long clung to archaic 19th-century concepts that predate the UN, OAS conventions and declarations . . . , thereby anchoring our countries' decisions to inaction and inefficiency and thereby proving them incapable of paving the way for a solution to the crisis. Meanwhile the United States has resorted to the ancient and objectionable practice of military intervention.[2]

While the decision to intervene represents the failure of policy, primary responsibility for this failure rests not with the Bush administration but with its predecessors. Most of the elements which produced a situation where unilateral intervention could appear to be the least awful option remaining were in place before President George Bush took office. Economic sanctions were mandated by law, and the United States was committed to recognizing Eric Arturo Del Valle, an individual with little credibility and even less popular support, as Panama's president. Constant rhetorical escalation by both the Reagan administration and Congress created a popular image of General Noriega as a virtual devil incarnate: poisoning U.S. children with drugs, threatening the security of the Panama Canal, and constantly thumbing his nose at U.S. efforts to remove him from power. The image of a drug kingpin made serious negotiations with the Noriega regime a political impossibility. Nevertheless, up till mid-1989 there was a general consensus within the government that using military force would boost the cost well above the level of any benefits provided. Instead, the United States sought cheap solutions: using economic sanctions, promoting coups within the PDF, and employing threats and bluffs. But the sanctions hurt Noriega opponents more than they did the general and his supporters, and the threats and bluffs only made the dictator more intractable and more confident of his ability to withstand U.S. pressures. The means chosen to advance U.S. policy in Panama were totally inadequate to the task of achieving the publicly proclaimed objectives of that policy. Declaring that Noriega constituted a major menace to national security, while being unwilling or unable to utilize the means necessary to respond to such a threat, set the United States up for a series of defeats and humiliations.

President Bush tried to lower the rhetoric on Panama, but pressure from the press coupled with rumors of earlier dealings between himself and the dictator made this an almost impossible task. Hopes that the 1989 elections might provide a way out of the impasse proved illusory when Noriega used force and intimidation to annul the results of those elections. The effort to have the OAS mediate the conflict also failed. Finally, the unsuccessful attempt at a coup (October 1989) gave Noriega an opportunity to arrest or discharge most of the officers with whom the United States had any contacts, reducing the chances that any future coup would produce a PDF leadership acceptable either to Washington or to the Panamanian opposition. The administration was left looking weak, indecisive, and ineffective.

There is evidence that, even before October, the United States was giving serious consideration to using military force in Panama. The removal of General Fred Woerner, who had consistently opposed such action, from his post as head of the U.S. Southern Command (SOUTHCOM) at the end of September, and the failure of the coup attempt in October, made intervention a much more likely prospect. The events of December—including Noriega's open assumption of political power in Panama, his government's so-called declaration of war on the United States, and the murder of a U.S. officer—may have sped up the timetable, but these actions were not responsible for the actual decision.[3] Rightly or wrongly, the Bush administration had concluded: 1) that the situation would only get worse; and 2) that pressures for intervention would ultimately become irresistible. Under such a scenario, acting sooner, rather than later, was a defensible position.

Once begun, the invasion accomplished most of its objectives relatively rapidly. Despite numerous shortcomings (such as the destruction of homes near Noriega's headquarters, the failure to silence pro-Noriega radio stations for almost a day, the massive looting of Panama City's commercial district, and the inexplicable failure to secure the Marriott Hotel), the military side of the operation was generally satisfactory. It was soon clear that in Panama, as in Grenada, the majority of the population supported the intervention, if only because it promised an end to the nation's precipitous economic decline and to the increasingly intolerable political tension under which Panamanians had been forced to live.

The intervention had some positive results for Panama. It removed an unpopular, repressive, and increasingly isolated regime from power and made possible the installation of those who had actually won the May 1989 elections. It led to a lifting of U.S. economic sanctions. It also made possible a purging of the PDF officer corps and a reorganization of its entire structure, something which would have been much more difficult had the officers themselves ousted Noriega. For the Bush administration, it produced an upsurge in popularity, gave greater credibility to U.S. pressure for changes in the region, and made it much more difficult for the Democrats to make a popular issue out of U.S. policy failures in Panama.

Alongside these advantages, however, must be placed a larger list of present and future problems for both nations. The immediate price of the invasion has been very high in human, economic, and diplomatic costs. Twenty-three U.S. servicemen and over 650 Panamanians died in the invasion.[4] Hundreds of others were wounded, left homeless, or lost their jobs as a result of the invasion and the subsequent widespread looting. All this produced a potential reservoir of anger and resentment directed against both the United States and Panama's new government. Should efforts to promote economic recovery and provide new jobs and housing falter, these emotions could become much stronger and more widespread.

Rebuilding the economy is a massive, formidable task. Estimates of the decline in Panama's GDP per capita over the past two and one-half years range from 20 to 40 percent. To keep his government afloat, Noriega plunged Panama ever deeper into debt. Total debt is now in excess of $5.5 billion and the nation owes accrued interest payments of $700 million. The invasion produced additional losses in property destroyed and looted, with estimates of the total value of such losses ranging up to $2 billion, most of which will not be covered by insurance. This damage, in turn, cost thousands of Panamanians their jobs, pushing the unemployment rate to over 25 percent.[5] The nation lost over two years of foreign and domestic investment, the international banking sector suffered irreparable damage, the number of merchant vessels registered in Panama declined, and hundreds of businesses were forced into bankruptcy. Systematic looting of the economy by Noriega and his cronies exacerbated the situation. At the end of 1989, Panama's cash reserves were only $70 million.[6]

The release of Panamanian government assets previously frozen by the United States, and of canal payments withheld from the Noriega regime, will provide some relief. In addition, the U.S. Congress will almost certainly provide emergency economic assistance, perhaps up to

$200 million, for Panama. That country's leaders, however, have requested $1.5 billion.[7] Domestic budget pressures mean that congressional support for aid to Panama is likely to decrease, rather than increase, with the passage of time, and the temptation to reduce—or even terminate—assistance will grow. This, in turn, could undermine public support for the Endara government and further damage the already shaky credibility of U.S. commitments in the hemisphere.

International financial institutions may fill some of this gap, but they are reluctant to resume large-scale lending to Panama until progress is made on dealing with the arrears of interest on previous loans. The amount of aid ultimately made available will leave many Panamanians disappointed and will make it difficult to restore effective economic growth. Panama is unlikely to regain its economic level of mid-1987 by the end of this century. Should a major recession occur in the United States, recovery will be even slower.

Restructuring Panama's military and police provides a formidable challenge. The PDF combined police and military functions into a single force. At its peak, shortly before the invasion, its total strength exceeded fourteen thousand. The new government neither needs nor wants so large and powerful a force, fearing that it might someday return the nation to the situation where Panama was "not a country with an army but an army with a country."[8] Many have suggested that Panama does not need an army at all; that, instead, it should emulate Costa Rica and create a small, civilian-controlled, national police force. Others seem willing to go along with the U.S. position that Panama needs some military capacity to deal with potential guerilla activities, terrorism, and to ensure the defense of the canal beyond the year 2000. There is also no consensus on just how much of the old PDF officer corps and enlisted personnel should be incorporated into the new force.[9]

There are no easy answers to any of these problems. Too small a force risks the security of the nation and the government and raises the specter of a renewed and/or prolonged U.S. military presence. A larger force is more likely, ultimately, to pose a serious threat to civil liberties and civilian, democratic government. Incorporating officers and men from the PDF into the PPF inevitably means that much of the corruption and political attitudes which characterized Noriega's army will survive long after his demise. Even officers involved in efforts to topple Noriega shared traditional PDF attitudes of independence from, and superiority to, civilians. However, significantly reducing the size of the force and largely purging it of PDF veterans would discharge into the population thousands of angry, unemployed individuals, trained in the use of weapons and accustomed to getting what they want. Lacking jobs and blaming the United States and the new government for their situation, they could contribute to an explosion in the crime rate and provide potential recruits for an armed opposition.

Even the long-accepted idea that Panama's military and police forces should be separated now seems in danger of being lost in the current debate over the size and nature of the new PPF. In this century the United States helped create combined police and military forces in five Latin American nations: Panama, Cuba, Haiti, the Dominican Republic, and Nicaragua. In every case, the results were disastrous. Combining the forces not only failed to clean up the police but also contributed significantly to corrupting the military. In El Salvador, where police, army, and security forces are technically separate but operate with a common officer corps under the Defense Ministry, results have also been overwhelmingly negative. Failure to proceed with the formal separation of police and army in Panama would be a major mistake.

The training of the PPF will present ongoing problems. Close U.S. tutelage is likely to produce resentment among PDF veterans and will hamper the efforts of the Endara government to create for itself an image of independence from the United States. At the same time, the intervention has made it much more difficult to secure needed training from other sources, such as Spain or Venezuela. Although Panama has long needed its own military academy to train future officers, creating an academy could produce rivalries among graduating classes, a phenomenon common throughout the region, which often creates serious divisions within the officer corps. It is also disconcerting to picture the instruction these officers will receive on the history of Panama's military. The PDF and its predecessor, the National Guard, fought only two real battles: one against itself during the October coup attempt and, on a much larger scale, one against the United States in December. Armies give high value to tradition and glorify those who have died in previous conflicts. In these cases such glorification would not bode well for future relations between the PPF and the United States.

The political heritage of the intervention offers some major problems. The new government is made up of an uneasy coalition of parties and personalities united only by their common opposition to General Noriega and the military domination of Panama. President Guillermo Endara is neither as charismatic nor as articulate as his two vice presidents, Ricardo Arias Calderon of the Christian Democratic party and Guillermo Ford of MOLIRENA. In addition, his party is a remnant of the Authentic Panamenista party, the personal political vehicle of

Arnulfo Arias, who dominated Panamanian politics from the late 1930s until his death in 1988. Without Arias's charismatic leadership, this party is in danger of collapse; it won no legislative seats in the May 1989 elections. The Christian Democrats took thirty seats, MOLIRENA won fourteen, and the Authentic Liberal party, another member of the anti-Noriega coalition, gained eleven. Only nine seats went to parties which had supported Noriega, and new elections are supposed to be held in three other districts.[10]

The situation in the congress is nearly matched by that in the cabinet. Most key posts are held by Christian Democrats, members of MOLIRENA, and the Authentic Liberal party. The two vice presidents occupy important cabinet posts. Panama's constitution—written by the government of General Omar Torrijos in 1972 and revised under military tutelage in 1983—limits presidential power in many areas, giving much of it to the cabinet and to the Congress instead. While it prohibits the president from seeking immediate re-election, it does not bar the vice presidents from running for that office.[11]

Such circumstances seem ready-made for conflicts within the new administration. Early on, the president and vice presidents recognized these political realities and tried to deal with them. One of their first acts was to issue a "Statute on Constitutional Order," which provided for a virtual triumvirate in which all three would share much of the executive power.[12] For the moment, President Endara and his vice presidents are striving to avoid the public perception of conflict, but it will be extremely difficult to maintain this image. If the history of previous coalition governments in Latin America is any guide, then conflict—if not open division—is a likely prospect.

Creating anything that resembles a loyal opposition will prove a difficult task. The bitterness engendered by years of military dominance plus the intimate identification of the largest opposition party, the Democratic Revolutionary party (PRD), with the military presents a major obstacle. To this must be added the bitterness of many supporters of the old regime over their treatment. Accusations that government supporters, with the help of the U.S. military, are engaged in a witch hunt are common and probably not without some substance.[13] The problem is further complicated by government seizure of much of the media which supported the previous regime. The major exception to this is the newspaper *La Estrella de Panama*, edited by Tomás Gabriel Altamirano Duque. He and his paper have been the subject of attacks by other newspapers. The ability of *La Estrella* to publish with relative freedom will be a major test of the government's willingness to allow political space for its opposition.

On the other hand, the PRD and its allies have never had to play the role of opposition and may well have difficulty adjusting to the turn of events. In the past, they responded to threats to their power by appealing to class and racial divisions, emphasizing nationalism (and, thus, anti-Americanism, almost by definition) and engaging in ad hominem attacks with little regard for actual facts. Such tactics will be tempting in the future, although pursuing them will make the government more likely to restrict opposition activities.

In addition to pressing economic needs and the problems created by the need to restructure the military and form a new government as well, Panama has several other major tasks awaiting it. The nation badly needs national reconciliation, some healing of the deep wounds inflicted over the past several years. This task is complicated by the problem of how to deal with thousands of government employees, most of whom owe their jobs to ties to the old regime. The government needs their experience, and they need their jobs. In addition, thousands of government supporters believe that they are entitled to such jobs. Nevertheless, budget pressures, combined with the fact that many of those on the old payroll did little or no real work, make it likely that the Endara government will try to reduce the number of its employees. How this dilemma is resolved will have a major influence on the success of efforts at reconciliation in Panama.

The government needs to distance itself from the United States. This is essential for its credibility both at home and abroad. But it also needs U.S. financial and technical assistance. Resolving this contradiction will be a formidable task. In the short run, the best thing both governments can do is reaffirm U.S. commitments to the existing canal treaties and state publicly that the Bush administration will make no effort to negotiate an extension of U.S. military base rights in Panama. On the contrary, it would be useful to begin withdrawal of some U.S. military presence from Panama as soon as possible, most notably the SOUTHCOM headquarters.

Finally, Panama needs a new constitution. The current document reflects past military domination in that there are no real mechanisms for civilian control over the military. There should be major revisions of certain provisions, such as the complex relationship between the president and his cabinet, the nature and authority of local government, and the composition and power of the Electoral Tribunal.[14] However, a constituent assembly could upset the delicate balance existing within the current government. It could shorten or extend the current presidential term and/or convert itself into the national legislature. In any case, organizing an election at this time would be both difficult and expensive.

While the need for overhauling the constitution is urgent, such factors may put the task off until late in President Endara's term of office, or even until his successor takes power.

If Panama's new government will find it difficult to establish its credibility, then the United States faces an almost equivalent task in repairing the damage done to its relations with Latin America by the intervention. Once again, the specter of gunboat diplomacy has been raised, an issue which touches one of the most tender nerves in the Latin body politic. The problem has been made worse by many of the actions of the U.S. military in Panama, notably what appeared to be an almost contemptuous disregard for diplomatic immunity and the right of asylum. In the OAS only El Salvador supported the U.S. invasion (Honduras abstained). Even Costa Rica's President Oscar Arias, a bitter foe of Noriega, has described the U.S. presence in Panama as an occupation and indicated that formal recognition of the new government must wait until U.S. forces are withdrawn.[15] Colombia's strongly negative response to administration plans to dispatch the U.S. Navy to Colombian waters to aid in drug interdiction was a reaction, in part, to events in Panama. The reactions of such nations as Mexico, Peru, and Brazil have been even more negative, with Peru going so far as to recall its ambassador from Washington. Plans to send Vice President Dan Quayle to Latin America were widely rebuffed, leaving Quayle with only a trip to Central America for the inauguration of the new Honduran president, followed by a visit to Jamaica.

It is counterproductive continually to suggest that the reactions of Latin American governments to the Panama intervention are largely political theater, designed to mollify domestic leftists while the leaders privately applaud the U.S. action. The great majority of governments in the hemisphere were glad to see Noriega go, and many shared with President Andrés Pérez of Venezuela a realization that Latin America's inability to resolve the problem contributed to the U.S. decision to intervene. Nevertheless, this does not make any less sincere their commitment to the principle of nonintervention, nor does it negate their suspicions and fears that Washington may be about to embark on a renewed era of gunboat diplomacy. The damage done by the invasion to U.S.-Latin American relations cannot be undone and must not be ignored. It can be minimized by patience, understanding of Latin sensitivity and values, rapid withdrawal from Panama, careful abstention from similar conduct in other areas, and—perhaps more importantly—by renewed serious attention to the region's economic problems.

Perhaps the most important issue facing the United States and the other nations of this hemisphere in the wake of the Panama invasion is how to avoid such intervention in the future. Once again, the world has proved unable to protect small, weak states from a tyrannical, well-armed minority, especially when such a minority can count on external support. In the era of *glasnost*, such support from the superpowers is less likely, but private groups, such as the narcotics cartel, have both the means and the motivation to play such a role.

Unilateral intervention by an outside power is no solution. India has discovered this in Sri Lanka. The experiences of Tanzania in Uganda and Vietnam in Cambodia, when these nations intervened to oust brutal, hated regimes, has been largely negative. In neither case was the intervening power able to restore stability and economic growth or secure world support of, and credibility for, the government it installed. While the parallels with the U.S. role in Panama are far from exact, they are close enough to underscore the serious problems which confront both the United States and the Endara government.

It is in the interest of both world and regional powers, and of the small nations victimized by the Idi Amins, Pol Pots, and Manuel Antonio Noriegas of this world, to find an effective way to deal with such situations other than resorting to unilateral intervention. Part of the solution may require strengthening regional and international organizations such as the OAS and United Nations. Part may lie in dealing with the international narcotics problem. Part may require long-term changes in national armed forces and in the training and support such forces receive from abroad. Of all the tasks and problems arising from the intervention in Panama, resolving this one may be the most important. Unfortunately, if history is any guide, it is also the least likely to be effectively addressed.

Notes

1. *Christian Science Monitor*, January 5, 1990.
2. "President Pérez Gives Year-end Speech," Caracas Venezuela de Televisión Canal 8, December 30, 1989, Foreign Broadcast Information Service–Latin America (hereafter cited as FBIS-LAT) 90-001, January 2, 1990: 67.
3. J. Pichirallo and P. Tyler, "Countdown to Invasion,' " in *Washington Post National Weekly Edition*, January 22–28, 1990, 31–32.
4. "Torrijists to Resist 'U.S. Occupation,' " Paris AFP, January 16, in FBIS-LAT-90-010, January 16, 1990: 38.

5.   Economic Commission for Latin America and the Caribbean (ECLAC), *Preliminary Overview of the Economy of Latin America and the Caribbean, 1989* (Santiago, Chile: United Nations ECLAC, 1990), 10, 25; "A Special Relationship," London *Economist*, January 20, 1990; *St. Louis Post-Dispatch*, January 10, 1990.

6.   "Financial Situation, Letter to Bush Reported," Panama City ACAN, January 9, in FBIS-LAT-90-006, January 9, 1990: 34.

7.   C. Grimes, "Panamanians Suggesting $1.5 Billion in Aid," *St. Louis Post-Dispatch*, January 9, 1990.

8.   "Panama after Noriega," *Economist*, January 9, 1990.

9.   MacNeil-Lehrer News Report, Public Broadcasting System, January 16, 1990; "Arias Calderon Views Making of Public Force," Panama City ACAN, January 4, in FBIS-LAT-90-004, January 5, 1990: 38–39. Also, "Arias Calderon Discusses New Public Force," Paris AFP, January 9; "Arias Discusses Major Issues in Interview," Vienna *Die Presse*, January 8; "Goals of New Public Force Termed 'Huge Task,' " Panama City *La Estrella de Panama*, January 6; all in FBIS-LAT-90-006, January 9, 1990: 35–37, 42–43. Also, "Endara Discusses Public Force, Troops Leaving," Panama City Circuits RPC, January 9; "Arias Discusses Public Force Organization," ibid.; both in FBIS-LAT-90-007, January 10, 1990: 29; C. Grimes, "Security Smurfs," *St. Louis Post-Dispatch*, January 14, 1990; "Panama Forges Police Force from Members of Noriega Military," *Christian Science Monitor*, December 28, 1989.

10.   "ADOC Gets 55, Opposition 9 New Assembly Seats," Paris AFP, January 3, in FBIS-LAT-90-003, January 4, 1990: 36.

11.   *Constitución Política de la República de Panama de 1972: Reformada por los Actos Reformatorios de 1978 y por el Acto Constitucional de 1983.*

12.   "Text of 21 Dec Statute on Constitutional Order," Panama City *Critica Libre*, January 10, in FBIS-LAT-90-009, January 12, 1990: 31.

13.   "Diverse Sectors of Society Fear 'Witch Hunt,' " Panama City ACAN, December 28, in FBIS-LAT-89-249, December 29, 1989: 23; "Panama Uses U.S. Troops in 'Witchhunt,' Reports Say," *Belleville News-Democrat*, January 22, 1990.

14.   *Constitución Política de la República de Panama de 1972*; F. Woerner and W. Ratliff, "What's to Be Done in Panama?" *Miami Herald*, December 24, 1989.

15.   C. Grimes, "Yankee Go Home," *St. Louis Post-Dispatch*, January 15, 1990.

The Reimposition of U.S. Hegemony over Nicaragua

Harry E. Vanden
and Thomas W. Walker

Hegemony, the dominance of one state over another, is seen by many as a given in international relations. The concept assumes that a major power in a region has the right to dominate the politics of nearby weaker states. Until the late 1980s this was the attitude and role of the Soviet Union in Eastern Europe and Afghanistan. Similarly, French behavior toward the North African states of Tunisia and Algeria in the nineteenth century was that of a hegemonic state.

From the late nineteenth century onward, U.S. behavior toward Latin, and especially Central, America and the Caribbean—"our back-yard"—has been that of a hegemon. It is true that modern international law stresses the sovereign equality of all states (Article 2, UN Charter). And, especially after the Second World War, colonialism has come to be rejected by an ever-growing number of states, particularly in the Third World. Nevertheless, for the United States, old hegemonic instincts and reflexes, at least in regard to Central America, have survived to the present. Its behavior toward the Sandinista revolution in Nicaragua is a dramatic case in point.

For members of the Frente Sandinista de Liberación Nacional (FSLN), which overthrew the U.S.-backed dictatorship of Anastasio Somoza on July 19, 1979, U.S. hegemonic control—or Yankee imperialism, as they saw it—was an anathema, an affront to national sovereignty and dignity. Nicaragua, for them, had been the victim of U.S. meddling from the time of the American filibusterer William Walker in the 1850s to the U.S.-promoted overthrow of nationalist leader José Santos Zelaya in 1909 to the U.S. military occupation of their country from 1912 to 1925 and 1926 to 1933 to subsequent U.S. support for the dynastic dictatorships of the Somoza family from 1936 through 1979. Not surprisingly, they venerated Third World anti-imperialist leaders, most notably the martyred Nicaraguan guerrilla chief Augusto César Sandino, who had waged a successful guerrilla war against the U.S. occupiers in the late 1920s and early 1930s and for whom they named their movement. Having overthrown the U.S.-backed Somoza dictatorship, they were determined to exercise their sovereignty fully and defend Nicaragua's status as a nation-state equal to any other in the international community. They sincerely desired friendly relations with the United States, but ones based on sovereign equality rather than on traditional subservience.

Like a growing number of Latin American and Third World intellectuals, the Sandinistas viewed the region's acute social problems as a product of an international economic and political system that misused the means of production, generated income concentration, and created and reinforced the position of an intransigent privileged elite. For them, real social and economic change could not be achieved short of a sweeping revolution that would alter traditional class relationships and allow the new government to manage the country's domestic and international economic and political life for the benefit of the majority.

Washington's first response to this new agenda developed during 1978 and 1979 when the Sandinistas were in the final phases of defeating Somoza. The Carter administration reluctantly came to a policy of promoting what many termed "Somocismo without Somoza," which would have jettisoned the old client-dictator but preserved the old class relationships and political structures such as Somoza's praetorian army, the National Guard, and his Liberal party while essentially excluding mass-based organizations such as the FSLN.[1]

Even though the Carter administration had tried several tactics to stop the Sandinistas from coming to power, the inevitability of victory was finally acknowledged. Afterward, both sides sincerely tried to get along. For their part, the Sandinistas knew that they could ill afford to be excluded from the Western economic system. The Cubans had warned them that they should not isolate themselves unnecessarily from the United States, and the Soviets had let it be known that they were unwilling to shoulder the expense of another Cuba in the Americas. For its part, the Carter administration also was aware of these facts and did not want to be a party to the type of mutual overreaction that had occurred between Cuba and the United States two decades before.

Rather, it hoped that by being friendly and supplying aid it could moderate the revolutionary process and perhaps eventually defuse it, as the United States had done with the Bolivian revolution in the 1950s.

The inauguration of Ronald Reagan, however, was a watershed. From then on, although apparent efforts at accommodation would occasionally surface, the dominant theme was confrontation. The Republican administration came to office with an inflexible mind-set on Nicaragua. It was dedicated to removing the Sandinistas from power by whatever means necessary. As Walter LaFeber notes in the introduction to this volume, "the Reagan administration used war, not diplomacy, as its state policy." If the new government in Nicaragua could not be toppled by a well-orchestrated destabilization plan, as the United States had done in Chile in the early 1970s, then military activity by locals and the Central Intelligence Agency (CIA) would be used to overturn it, as had occurred in Guatemala in 1954.

The Sandinistas, however, who had fought their way to power with the help of the Nicaraguan people, also understood military force and enjoyed widespread popular support. They were dedicated to enlightened international relations and to the full use of the UN system. Moreover, they were aware of the nature of realpolitik and the fact that, under the UN Charter, nations were clearly granted the right of self-defense (Article 51). Thus, from the time it came to power, the Sandinista leadership was careful to make sure that it had a competent military force to protect Nicaraguan sovereignty.[2]

Reagan's election and inauguration triggered a precipitous increase in the manpower and armament strength of the Sandinista armed forces.[3] And, as though setting the stage for such action, the new administration in Washington already was accusing Nicaragua of being a totalitarian state and a platform for Soviet/Cuban-directed subversion in Central America. The Sandinistas' worst fears were soon confirmed when rumors of the new administration's CIA-directed counterrevolutionary program against Nicaragua were confirmed by fact and deed.

Although the Reagan and Bush administrations would fail in their immediate objective of defeating the Sandinistas militarily, the damage and cost exacted by the war and related U.S. machinations would ultimately so destabilize the Nicaraguan economy and, hence, its political system that the Nicaraguan people would vote in February 1990 to turn the Sandinistas out of power. Under the Washington-promoted government of Violeta Chamorro, U.S. hegemony would be restored. The techniques used by the United States in its anti-Sandinista campaign consisted of at least four dimensions: propaganda, military confrontation, economic war, and diplomatic intransigence.

Propaganda

From the outset the Reagan administration attacked the Sandinistas with propaganda. The purpose appears to have been to discredit them in the eyes of the Nicaraguan people,[4] to cause them to become condemned and isolated internationally, and to sway U.S. public opinion to support the contra war and other anti-Sandinista measures.

The tactics used were clever. To begin, the Communist label was misleadingly pinned on the Sandinistas. It mattered not in the least that neither the Sandinistas, nor major Communist regimes throughout the world, nor local Nicaraguan Communists considered the Sandinistas to be Communist. Nor was it important that they preserved a mixed economy in which private ownership predominated; subsidized parochial education and printed "In God We Trust" on all coins; created a political system in which, beginning in 1984, there were free elections based on West European practices;[5] and maintained a nonaligned foreign policy.[6] The fact that most Sandinistas were Marxist-Leninist in their interpretation of history, that Communist countries were among the many with which they developed and maintained good relations, and that, by default, they eventually became heavily reliant on Socialist-bloc weaponry—all these were taken out of context to justify pinning the Communist label on them. Once so labeled, the Sandinistas could be plausibly charged with committing a myriad of sins commonly associated in the popular mind with Communist regimes: holding sham elections, persecuting Jews, suppressing the Protestant and Catholic churches, abusing ethnic minorities, mishandling the economy, and so forth. Although virtually all of these charges were either wholly or largely groundless, they came to be believed by important audiences such as the U.S. Congress, citizens of other Central American countries, and even many Nicaraguans.

Some of the most important distortions concerned the alleged Sandinista military threat. The danger, so the argument went, was two-pronged. First, Washington argued that the Sandinistas had engaged in a massive arms buildup that was unrelated to its defense needs and therefore threatening to the stability of all of Central America. Second, from early 1981, when the State Department issued its famous White Paper on "Communist Support of the Salvadoran Rebels," the administration maintained that the Nicaraguan government was playing a major support role in the uprising in El Salvador.[7]

The charge that Nicaragua was providing important and continuous arms support to the Salvadoran rebels was never seriously substantiated during the Reagan administration. From the start, the Sandinistas did express their moral support for the Salvadoran rebels. However, although they later acknowledged that some arms may have passed through their country at the turn of the year 1980–81, they remained adamant that this traffic subsequently had stopped. The Reagan administration did an unconvincing job of documenting its arms-running charges against Nicaragua. The famous White Paper proved very little and was largely discredited shortly after it appeared. As Wayne Smith, chief of the U.S. Interest Section in Havana from 1979 to 1982, later said, that document "became a source of acute embarrassment to the Administration, primarily revealing shoddy research and a fierce determination to advocate the new policy whether or not the evidence sustained it."[8] Thereafter, many papers were issued but none set forth convincing evidence or proved the allegations.

To counter criticism about the lack of evidence, Reagan administration officials asserted that, although they had ample proof, they were unable to reveal it to the public because to do so would compromise their intelligence apparatus. Although this convinced many congressmen who were anxious not to appear "soft" on communism, it only increased the skepticism of most other observers. The fact is that for arms from Nicaragua to have gotten to El Salvador, they would have had to be transported by air, by water across the Gulf of Fonseca, or overland through Honduras. The Reagan administration was never able to document such traffic. The only arms-carrying plane ever captured during the Reagan years turned out to be of Costa Rican origin. In spite of a multimillion-dollar contra program designed explicitly to stop the alleged arms flow, no arms whatsoever were seized. Any significant and continuing flow of arms—by whatever route—logically would have resulted in frequent interception by U.S. or Salvadoran naval forces in the Gulf of Fonseca, by the Salvadoran or Honduran air forces, by Honduran ground forces, or by the contras themselves. It is hard to believe that if planes, boats, or overland smuggling parties had been intercepted, the Reagan administration would not immediately have called a press conference to present such evidence. Since such evidence was never offered, it thus seems reasonable to conclude that there was little, if any, arms flow. By 1988 the administration had tacitly acknowledged the weakness of its argument and had begun to offer other reasons for its continued support for the contras.

It is true that, during the Bush administration, evidence of Nicaraguan arms smuggling was allegedly discovered. Late in 1989, just in time to be used to discredit Daniel Ortega at a summit meeting in Costa Rica, weapons—conveniently wrapped in Nicaraguan newspapers— were discovered in a panel truck that allegedly had just crossed from Nicaragua into Honduras. Shortly thereafter, a plane loaded with arms allegedly crashed in El Salvador. Conveniently again, it bore a flight plan indicating that it had just come from Nicaragua. Once more, the timing was fortuitous for the U.S. side; the dramatic revelations served temporarily to deflect media attention from the Salvadoran military's recent massacre of six Jesuit priests, their housekeeper, and her daughter. Since deliberate disinformation is part of the modus operandi of the CIA and was used frequently as a tool against the Sandinistas, it is best to reserve judgment of the veracity of these alleged arms discoveries except to note that they came after over eight years of unsubstantiated charges.[9]

The charge that Nicaragua had created a military establishment that far exceeded its legitimate defense needs also was leveled at the government in Managua. It is undeniable that the Sandinistas continued to increase Nicaragua's armed strength. Their initial belief that their revolution might be put under siege by hostile forces soon was validated by increased attacks by the U.S.-controlled contras. Thus, by late 1983 the country had strengthened its armed forces to some twenty-five thousand men and women and had created a popular militia force in excess of sixty thousand. As the contra war intensified, the regular armed forces were increased to more than sixty thousand. Unable to secure the weapons they needed at prices they could afford from Western sources (the United States put substantial pressure on France and other Western suppliers not to sell to the Sandinistas at all), their armament came almost exclusively from the Socialist bloc. It included not only enough AK-47 and AK-M rifles for the Sandinista armed forces and the militia but also a number of Soviet tanks, antiaircraft guns, rockets, and eventually transport and Mi-24 Hind attack helicopters. And there were a few Soviet military advisers, some East German security personnel, and from two hundred (if you believe the Cuban version) to two thousand (if you prefer the Washington figures) Cuban military advisers in Nicaragua. In addition, a number of new military facilities were constructed and several airstrips were lengthened in preparation for the possible arrival of advanced fighter aircraft.

All of this sounds ominous when taken out of context, but it is necessary to probe deeper into the matter than was typical of the carefully staged media events organized by the U.S. government. To understand the Nicaraguan buildup, it is necessary to examine: 1) the historical context, 2) the Carter and Reagan administrations' policy toward Nicaragua, and 3) the offensive and defensive capabilities of Nicaragua's military establishment.

Historical Context

The leadership that came to power in Nicaragua in 1979 was reasonably well educated. Many of the new leaders had a deep interest in history, both national and regional. Besides being aware of Washington's historical hegemonic policy toward their own country, the Sandinistas were not unmindful of patterns of behavior that the United States had developed in the twentieth century to deal with revolutionary, leftist, or merely populist governments in the hemisphere that had endeavored to chart an independent course in their domestic and/or foreign policies. From 1911 through the 1930s the Mexican revolution had stimulated the United States to engage in heated rhetoric, a number of threats, and several military incursions, not to mention frequent claims that the revolution was Bolshevik. Later, a democratic attempt at reformist revolution in Guatemala (1945–1954) was also labeled Red and destroyed by a destabilization program and a surrogate exile invasion armed, organized, and directed by the CIA.[10] Likewise, the ill-defined populist revolution in Bolivia (1952–1964) seems to have been co-opted and ultimately derailed by U.S. economic and military assistance and advice. The Cuban revolution (1959 to date) had suffered CIA sabotage, economic destabilization, and the CIA surrogate invasion at the Bay of Pigs in 1961. The right-wing military coup that snuffed out a populist democratic government in Brazil in 1964 was the product, at least in part, of a U.S. destabilization program. In the Dominican Republic in 1965, a nearly successful revolt aimed at returning that country to democratic rule was blocked by direct U.S. military intervention. In Chile in the early 1970s, a CIA destabilization program set the stage for the military overthrow of that country's constitutionally elected government.[11] It seemed to the new Nicaraguan leaders that the United States was still very willing to enforce its traditional hegemony and engage in what they believed were clear examples of Yankee imperialism.

Carter Administration Policy and Reagan Campaign Rhetoric

Although the Carter policy toward the new government of Nicaragua seemed to be oriented toward cooperation rather than confrontation, there were matters in 1979 and 1980 that were highly disquieting to the Sandinistas. The Nicaraguans, for instance, were worried from the start by Washington's failure to convince Honduras to dismantle the encampments of Somoza National Guardsmen who had escaped across the border following the FSLN victory. Although not a significant military threat at that time, their presence was ominous. Some former guardsmen actually engaged in small-scale guerrilla activity and banditry in northern Nicaragua. In fact, in 1980, they killed eight literacy campaign volunteers.

In that same year the rhetoric of the U.S. presidential campaign offered scant cause for comfort. During the summer the Republican national platform "abhor[red] the Marxist Sandinista takeover" in Nicaragua and promised to cut economic aid to that country. Months before, some of candidate Ronald Reagan's top advisers had produced the famous Santa Fe Document that declared that World War III—a struggle between "freedom" and communism—already had begun and that the United States was losing in Central America for lack of decisive action.[12] During the campaign Reagan advisers continued to talk of the need for firm action in regard to Nicaragua; some even referred to the time-tested techniques of U.S. aid cutoffs, destabilization, and surrogate invasion.[13]

The exact nature of the hostile behavior of the Reagan administration immediately upon coming to power will be discussed later. However, it should be clear that given the events of 1979 and 1980, the Sandinistas would have been neglecting very legitimate security concerns had they not devoted significant attention and resources to defense matters. They felt compelled to take the necessary steps to convert their ragtag guerrilla army into a more modern fighting force that was at least capable of providing minimal defense of their territory and sovereignty.

Nicaragua's Offensive and Defensive Capabilities

If one looks dispassionately at the matter, it quickly becomes apparent that Nicaragua's military might in 1981—and, indeed, throughout the Sandinista period—was essentially defensive in nature. The Reagan administration itself was embarrassed in September 1982 when a subcommittee of the House Committee on Intelligence issued a staff report criticizing U.S. intelligence performance in Central America. It noted in particular that, while U.S. intelligence services were publicly trumpeting Nicaragua's supposed offensive capabilities and intentions, there had been "classified briefings whose analytical judgments about Nicaragua's intentions were quite distinct from those that appeared implicit in the briefings on the buildup."[14]

In that same month, before another committee of the House, Lt. Col. John H. Buchanan, USMC (Ret.), gave an assessment of Nicaraguan and neighboring armed forces based on extensive interviewing and field research in the area. He argued that Nicaragua was not liable to attack its most frequently mentioned target, Honduras. Unlike that country, he reasoned, Nicaragua had no jet air force and the tanks that it did have were probably not capable of making the long trip to Tegucigalpa without air cover along the only possible route: the winding, mountainous Pan-American Highway.[15]

Although additional weapons subsequently were acquired by both sides, the relative strength of either side did not change. This was particularly true in light of the continuing U.S. support for improving the training and weaponry of the Honduran armed forces as seen in the 1988 Honduran acquisition of F5 jet fighters. Accused by the Reagan administration of planning to acquire modern MiG jet fighters, the Nicaraguan government never did so.

The willingness of the United States to invade small countries was brought home by events in Grenada in 1983. Subsequently, the Sandinistas made even greater efforts to ensure that their defenses were adequate to make an invasion of Nicaragua very costly. As contra attacks increased in number and brutality and the United States brought six thousand troops into Honduras in military maneuvers (known as Big Pine I, II, and III), Nicaragua increased the size of its armed forces. By 1988 it had in excess of sixty thousand regular troops with a militia at least as large. This was a sizable force by Central American standards. However, even leaving aside the threat of U.S. invasion, Nicaragua confronted a major problem. The contras were exacting a huge toll in economic losses and human suffering. To be able to guarantee minimum security for its citizens, the Nicaraguan state had to secure the national territory from this menace. Military authorities around the world, including the Pentagon, generally agree that it takes a ratio of at least ten regular-army troops to one guerrilla to contain a guerrilla insurgency. Assuming the validity of such strategic thinking and given the fact that the United States had been able to impress and recruit up to fifteen thousand contra troops at the height of the war, Nicaragua's military manpower was only minimally adequate. Even with the increased troops and weaponry, Nicaraguan government forces did not begin to prevail over the contras until the mid-1980s, and it could not be said that the U.S.-backed forces were in large part defeated until 1988. Indeed, the contra leadership did not agree to a cease-fire and peace talks until their prospects for a battlefield victory had all but evaporated.

Thus, it is not surprising that even an important classified U.S. Army intelligence survey, conducted in 1984 after the major Sandinista buildup, would state flatly and in contradiction of public Reagan administration rhetoric that "the primary mission of the Nicaraguan Armed Forces is the *protection of the country from external aggression*, while also maintaining internal security and order during the consolidation of the Sandinista Revolution." Later, the same document would reiterate that "regular activities by counterrevolutionary groups has made the *protection of the country from external aggression* the primary concern."[16]

Military Confrontation

The question of whether or not the United States posed a military threat to Nicaragua is not a matter for debate. As early as 1983 there was massive evidence of the central and not-so-covert role of the Reagan administration in organizing large-scale counterrevolutionary military and sabotage activities against Nicaragua.[17] Subsequent revelations in the Iran-contra hearings showed how deeply—and often illegally[18]— White House staff members were involved in this enterprise. In addition, the United States had poured armament and advisers into neighboring Honduras (U.S. $285.5 million in military aid between 1982 and 1985), staged increasingly large and menacing joint military exercises just across Nicaragua's northern border, mined its harbors, blown up its oil-storage facilities, and held threatening naval maneuvers off Nicaragua's coasts. Likewise, U.S. high-altitude reconnaissance flights regularly violated Nicaraguan airspace.

The earliest manifestation of the U.S. military threat was largely verbal. Within weeks of President Reagan's inauguration, the verbal attacks on Nicaragua began. February saw the State Department's White Paper on alleged Nicaraguan support for the Salvadoran rebels. During that same month Secretary of State Alexander Haig blustered that the United States must "go to the source" to stop such subversion. Further, in the next few months there was talk that "various military contingencies" were being studied.[19] Meanwhile, early that year much-publicized paramilitary training camps for future Nicaraguan "freedom fighters" began to appear in the Florida Everglades and elsewhere in the United States.[20]

In March 1981 the White House issued an initial policy paper calling for stepped-up covert action in Central America.[21] At this time, William Casey, the new head of the CIA, started to organize the "secret war" against the Nicaraguan government.[22] This new thrust was to be the mainstay of U.S. policy toward Nicaragua for the next eight years. It repeatedly foreclosed negotiations to have its proxies pursue war. As former National Security Council staffer Robert Pastor observed, the administration "came to rely on the contras as its only instrument for pursuing U.S. interests."[23]

Casey and others in the Reagan administration did not appear to be concerned by the way in which the contras were treating Nicaraguan civilians. They were more interested in policy ends. By employing the services of nongovernmental sympathizers such as Richard Secord, and by enlisting the aid of third states such as Israel and Argentina, they remained somewhat removed from any excesses that might come to light and clearly gave themselves a basis for deniability.[24] Through contacts with the Guatemalan military, the remnants of the Somozan National Guard were introduced to a group of advisers whom the Argentine military had sent to Guatemala to aid that country in its fight against "subversives." The veterans of Argentina's "dirty war" (1976–1983) found that they had much in common with their Nicaraguan counterparts. Soon the Argentine Army's Battalion 601 was being deployed to train and organize a force that could be used to attack the new government in Managua. Many of the Nicaraguans were even sent to Argentina for special training.

Casey evidently took a personal interest in the project and even flew to Honduras in 1981 to check on its development.[25] The remnants of the old National Guard were combined with a few other Nicaraguans to form the Nicaraguan Democratic Force (FDN). By 1982 and 1983, Honduras became a beehive of contra activity. Over 10,000 counter-revolutionaries were "recruited" (often by kidnapping, threat, or bribery), paid, trained, armed, and disgorged into Nicaragua. As support from the United States increased, they began to mount larger attacks in Nicaragua. After their humiliating defeat in the Falklands War, however, the Argentine military eventually withdrew its advisers and the United States began to run the "secret war" more directly. They even recruited some Nicaraguan politicians who were free of identification with Somoza or the National Guard and integrated them into the FDN leadership to give it a facade of civilian democratic control. Those who were actually doing the fighting, however, were another story.

Most of the initial troops and virtually all of their officers were former guardsmen. Men known as *Suicida* (Suicide), *Cancer*, and *El Muerto* (The Dead One) led the fighters into the field. They had little or no respect for human life, often killing their own men for minor infractions. They hated the Sandinistas and all who worked with them. They seemed to believe that they could reduce support for the regime by brutalizing all who were connected with it. As civilian casualties reached the thousands, more and more reports of their abuses began to come out of Nicaragua.

Initially, international public opinion was diverted from contra abuses when the U.S. government focused attention on the documented abuses committed by some Nicaraguan military personnel following a poorly conceived operation to move the Miskito Indians from their traditional homelands to areas where the government could better protect them from the roving contra bands and the influence they might wield.[26] Although the government eventually admitted the abuses, reversed its policy of relocation, and curbed misbehavior by its functionaries, horrors by the contras increased. Gang rapes, emasculation, premortem skinning, and eye-gouging were common practice.[27]

A well-publicized report about the persistent attacks on Nicaraguan civilians suggests that this was part of a contra campaign of terror against the Nicaraguan population.[28] The counterrevolutionaries and their American supporters first denied and then minimized these actions. However, in a 1985 report on violations by both sides in the Nicaraguan conflict, Americas Watch concluded that "in combination, the Contra forces have systematically violated the applicable laws of war throughout the conflict. They have attacked civilians indiscriminately; they have tortured and mutilated prisoners; they have murdered those placed *hors de combat* by their wounds; they have taken hostages; and they have committed outrages against personal dignity."[29]

A report on Nicaragua by Amnesty International expressed concern about "the frequently reported torture, mutilation, and execution style killing of captives by irregular military forces opposing the Nicaraguan Government."[30] The contras had developed a policy of terrorizing the civilian population so they would be afraid to support the government or to help produce the badly needed export crops, or so they would simply abandon the countryside and flee to the cities where they would need to be maintained. Crops could not be harvested in northern areas of the country because of the danger to the farmworkers. Cooperative farms, private farms, food-storage facilities, and even schools, health clinics, and day-care centers became prime targets in the increasingly violent attacks. Workers, teachers, and health-care personnel were frequently kidnapped or murdered. Trucks, buses, and cars were machine-gunned or blown up by antitank or antipersonnel mines placed on rural roads.

Although not well covered by the U.S. press, terror by 1983 had become a means of achieving policy objectives in Nicaragua. Reports of a CIA manual for the contra leadership surfaced in October 1984. *Psychological Operations in Guerrilla Warfare* had been prepared by a CIA employee and distributed to FDN officers. In a section on "Implicit and Explicit Terror," the manual reminds the reader that "a guerrilla force always involves implicit terror because the population, without saying it aloud, feels terror that the weapons may be turned against them."[31] In the section on the "Selective Use of Violence for Propagandistic Effects," the manual is even more explicit: "It is possible to neutralize selected targets, court judges, *mesta* judges, police and state security officials, CDS chiefs, etc."[32]

Contra tactics offended even some of the civilian leaders whom the CIA had recruited for the contras. Edgar Chamorro, who had been hired in 1982 to be one of the civilian chiefs of the FDN and to act as their public relations spokesperson, eventually quit in disgust over the treatment of civilians and Sandinista prisoners. Having talked to unit commanders as they returned from the field, he concluded that "the atrocities ... were not isolated instances, but reflected a consistent pattern of behavior by our troops. There were unit commanders who openly bragged about murders, mutilations etc. . . . they told me it was the only way to win the war, that the best way to win the loyalty of the civilian population was to intimidate it and make it fearful of us."[33]

Throughout the war it was clear that civilian, rather than military, personnel and infrastructure were the primary targets of the contras. Thus, the focus on civilian targets was a fundamental element of a CIA plan for a 1987 spring offensive.[34] But even as early as 1984, FDN leader Adolfo Calero is on record as saying: "There is no line at all, not even a fine line, between a civilian farm owned by the government and a Sandinista military outpost."[35] Nor were foreign workers exempt from attack. After counterrevolutionary forces kidnapped eight West German volunteers in May 1986, a contra spokesperson proclaimed that "any foreigner who voluntarily aids in development and reconstruction projects is considered an enemy."[36] Such was the case for U.S. citizen Benjamin Linder who, in June 1987, became the ninth foreign civilian to be killed by the contras. Attacked while he was helping to develop a small hydroelectric project in northern Nicaragua, he was initially wounded by a grenade and then shot at point-blank range in the back of the head.[37]

The human cost of the contra war was staggering. According to internal government statistics divulged to Thomas Walker in January 1990, the death toll for the entire conflict (1980–1989) was 30, 865.[38] This included 21,900 contras and 8,965 individuals categorized by the government as "our people," made up of approximately 4,860 government troops and 4,105 others, mainly civilians. Among the civilians, peasants suffered the worst with 2,469 dead. It is also significant that 130 teachers, 40 doctors and nurses, 152 technicians, and 41 other professionals also fell victim to the war. Calculating roughly that the population of Nicaragua, which grew from 2.5 to 3.8 million in the period from 1979 to 1989, averaged 3.3 million during the war years, the over 30,000 dead represented .9 percent of the population. An equivalent loss for the United States would be 2.25 million, or over thirty-eight times the U.S. death toll in the entire Vietnam War. The contra war also produced 20,064 wounded, many of whom were so maimed that they would be wards of the state for the rest of their lives.

This great human toll in dead and wounded took a significant toll in morale as well. By the time of the 1990 election, the general population was demoralized from nine years of death and suffering. That the war could well continue unless they voted for the U.S.-sponsored candidate was made clear by a significant increase in contra activity in the electoral period from October 1989 to February 1990.[39] Many Nicaraguans were tired of the military draft that had been declared late in 1983. And they were disappointed that FSLN candidate Daniel Ortega had not followed through with his rumored intention to announce the end of the draft at his huge last rally before election day. It is likely that these factors significantly contributed to the outcome of the 1990 elections.

Economic War

Another aspect of the U.S. war on Nicaragua was economic strangulation. It appears that the United States had at least two motivations in trying to undermine the economy of the country. First, Washington was aware that an economic collapse in Nicaragua would destabilize and discredit that nation's new political system and might lead ultimately to its demise, just as the Nixon-Kissinger plan to "make the [Chilean] economy scream"[40] had done in that country less than a decade earlier. Second, no matter what the political outcome, the destruction of the Nicaraguan economy was good in and of itself as a way of demonstrating once again that any alternative to laissez-faire capitalism—especially one that U.S. officials would describe as Marxist-Leninist or "Communist"—could not work.

Having just suffered tremendous economic decline during the last two years of the Somoza regime, Nicaragua was in no position to withstand economic aggression from the most powerful nation on earth a little over two years later. Much of the country's agricultural, industrial, and commercial infrastructure had been damaged during the war. Its public coffers and private banking system had been brazenly looted by the departing dictator and his cronies. The country had been saddled with a foreign debt of over $1.6 billion and capital flight during the conflict had exceeded $500 million.[41]

Remarkably, however, Nicaragua was one of the very few countries in the region to show economic growth during the years from 1980 through 1983. According to statistics from the United Nations Economic Commission on Latin America, in these four years before the Reagan policy began to impact heavily, Nicaragua's economy experienced an overall per capita growth of just over 7 percent, while the economies of Central America as a whole declined by 14.7 percent per capita.[42] Part of this can be attributed to the jump-back effect—a return to normalcy after a disastrous decline. But some of it undoubtedly was due to the fact that the Sandinistas had not opted for the so-called Communist economic system for which they would be accused but rather had pursued the promotion of a mixed economy in which private production still accounted for over one half of total output. In addition, the redistribution of poorly utilized Somoza-owned resources into the hands of categories of people previously deprived of access to the means of production may have helped generate this growth.

This early period of growth, however, would be followed quickly by a disastrous decline as the Reagan administration's destabilization policies began to have their impact in the mid-to-late 1980s. Whereas the Carter administration had given foreign aid and loans to Nicaragua and had encouraged international lending agencies to do the same, the Reagan administration not only cut off all U.S. assistance to that country but also insisted that the Inter-American Development Bank (IDB) and the World Bank, upon whom most Latin American countries routinely rely for economic assistance, do the same. After 1982 virtually all IDB and World Bank assistance to Nicaragua dried up; this in spite of the fact that both institutions had enthusiastically supported

Nicaraguan recovery in the first year or so. Ironically, an IDB report in 1981 had noted that "the negative consequences of the war are far from over. Per capita income levels of 1977 will not be obtained, in the best of circumstances, until the late 1980s." While recommending considerable international financial support, the IDB warned that "any untoward event could lead to financial trauma."[43] By blocking IDB and World Bank aid, the Reagan administration would deliberately induce precisely this type of trauma.

Another aspect of the U.S. economic assault on Nicaragua was the severance of normal trade with that country. Prior to the Sandinista victory, Washington was Managua's leading trading partner. Within weeks of coming to power, the Reagan administration cut off all Nicaraguan access to American wheat; later came a threat to stop the import of Nicaraguan beef. In October 1982, Standard Fruit Company suddenly pulled its banana-buying operation out of Nicaragua. In May 1983 the United States cut the quota for the importation of Nicaraguan sugar by almost 90 percent. Finally, on May 7, 1985, President Reagan declared a state of national emergency and embargoed all trade with Nicaragua. Even at that point the country's economy had been closely tied to the United States: $58 million in Nicaraguan exports went to the United States, and $110 million in the latter's exports entered Nicaragua.[44]

The Reagan administration also put pressure on other countries to curtail or terminate trade and aid relationships with Nicaragua. Venezuela stopped while Mexico drastically curtailed its provision of oil at concessionary terms in the mid-1980s. In 1989 the Scandinavian countries convinced Nicaragua to implement a harsh austerity program in return for promises of renewed aid. However, the United States then pressured those Nordic benefactors to withhold their aid until after the 1990 elections. Anguished Nicaraguans commented bitterly that the whole affair was like undergoing major surgery without anesthesia. Even the Soviet Union, anxious to please its newfound American friends in the post-Cold War era, curtailed its 1989 assistance to Nicaragua.

Finally, the war itself also had a tremendous and multifaceted impact on the Nicaraguan economy. In addition to direct damage caused by the fighting and by CIA and contra sabotage, there was the loss in productivity in the war zones and the costly reallocation of resources from civilian economic and social projects to the war effort. Of necessity, the military budget grew in the mid-to-late 1980s to well over 60 percent of total spending. As a result there was a chronic shortage of foreign exchange that made it difficult to acquire any imported goods, including spare parts for automobiles or machinery and many essential materials for manufacturing and agriculture—all of which caused severe spot shortages of many goods and interrupted production and transport generally. Lacking real funds, the government then resorted to the printing of unbacked paper money, thus stimulating spasms of inflation that in 1988 reached over 33,000 percent.

The Sandinistas also made mistakes that added to the woes of their economy. These included the implementation of economically distorting pricing policies and multiple exchange rates as well as the promotion of unrealistically grandiose development projects.[45] But the damage caused by the Sandinistas was small in comparison to that inflicted by Washington's program of economic strangulation. In its suit against the United States in the International Court of Justice, Nicaragua claimed $17.8 billion in damages. Of that figure, some of the claim was for "damages to development and sovereignty, compensation for the dead and wounded, and 'moral damages.' " If, for the sake of argument, we exclude the latter categories, the cost for the war comes to over $9 billion in fairly tangible damages and setbacks.[46] If, on top of this, we are still very conservative and thus halve that sum again, we end up with $4.5 billion, a figure many times the total annual export earnings of Nicaragua, which, in the best of times, were only a little over $700 million and by the late 1980s had declined to around $200 million.

All of this meant that the standard of living of the average Nicaraguan declined sharply in the mid-to-late 1980s. Further, since each new measure adopted by the Sandinistas in order to stop the economic free fall was, for all practical purposes, predoomed to failure, the revolutionary government looked increasingly inept and foolish to its public. Lest they miss the point, Mrs. Chamorro's U.S.-financed opposition daily, *La Prensa*, was present during most of the period to place the blame for the economic disaster squarely on the shoulders of the Sandinistas. The U.S. role in the economic collapse of Nicaragua was consistently ignored. Of course, most Nicaraguans were aware that the United States had played a role in damaging their economy, but, ironically, even this fact gave candidate Chamorro an advantage over her opponents: After all, she alone could promise that a vote for her would help end Washington's economic embargo and open up the flow of multilateral aid. In the long run, it would appear that many desperate or disillusioned Nicaraguans voted their pocketbooks in February 1990.

Diplomatic Intransigence

Given that both Washington and Managua frequently announced their willingness to resolve their differences through peaceful means, one might have expected a high level of diplomatic interaction. In fact, this did not occur. Indeed, the Reagan administration was consistently reluctant to meet directly with representatives of Managua. Apart from a series of inconclusive meetings in Manzanillo, Mexico, in the election year of 1984, the Republican administration was loath to enter into any serious negotiations with the Sandinistas. Rather, it preferred to insist that Managua negotiate directly with the U.S.-controlled contras. Given the fact that the Nicaraguan leaders perceived the contras as paid U.S. proxies who lacked legitimacy, this was a very difficult demand for them to accept.

However, other Latin American nations realized that protracted conflict in Nicaragua and the ongoing guerrilla wars in El Salvador and Guatemala were very dangerous to the well-being and stability of the region. In January 1983 the foreign ministers of Venezuela, Colombia, Mexico, and Panama (meeting on the Panamanian island of Contadora) formulated their own plan to achieve peace. By the end of the year the four Contadora countries had convinced the five Central American nations to sign a document of objectives. These included: the prohibition of support for insurgencies in neighboring countries, a prohibition on foreign military bases, a phased reduction of foreign military advisers, limits on conventional military forces, and the necessity for national reconciliation among conflicting political groups within each country. In September 1984 the Central American nations were poised to sign a treaty concretizing these points. Nicaragua held out initially but surprised many by finally agreeing to sign the accord.

This treaty clearly would have satisfied all legitimate security concerns of the United States or the Central American states. It was not, however, consistent with Washington's traditional hegemonic stance (it was, after all, the result of a Latin, and not U.S., initiative) and would have ended the contra war with less than a total victory for the U.S. proxies. Thus, the United States successfully pressed its most dependent allies (El Salvador, Honduras, and Costa Rica) to reverse themselves and declare the treaty unacceptable. The Reagan administration declared its support for the Contadora process publicly but now did everything it could behind the scenes to block it.[47] This and similar Washington-inspired machinations prevented the Contadora process from ever coming to fruition. Further, it set the pattern followed by the Reagan administration in subsequent Latin-inspired negotiations.

The Central American states became increasingly concerned with the ongoing contra war and intransigent U.S. foreign policy in the region. Led by Oscar Arias, the newly elected president of Costa Rica, the area's presidents began to meet in 1986 and in August 1987 devised a plan for peace in Central America. Its general outlines were similar to the Contadora proposal, but it also called for setting up national reconciliation commissions, a cease-fire in those nations where insurgencies were occurring, democratization and free elections, and the granting of amnesty to political foes. The Reagan administration had been pushing its own peace plan, which it knew was totally unacceptable to the Nicaraguans, and seeking more military aid for the contras. On a more statesmanlike plane, House Speaker Jim Wright met with Nicaraguan President Ortega when he visited the United Nations. This suggested good faith on the part of the Democratic congressional leadership and seems to have been instrumental in the realization of the accords.

After President Arias won the Nobel Peace Prize for his diplomatic initiative, the Reagan administration was forced publicly to praise the new peace process. In Nicaragua this led to a series of initiatives beginning with the establishment of the National Reconciliation Commission and ending with direct negotiations with the contras and a temporary cease-fire. Indeed, by the second quarter of 1988 it seemed that the contra civilian leadership and the Nicaraguan government leaders were about to negotiate a mutually satisfactory end to the conflict. However, backed by the CIA and conservative sectors of the Honduran military who were close to the United States, hard-line contra military leaders won out over the more moderate political leaders. Led by former National Guard officer Enrique Bermudez, the new contra leadership followed U.S. suggestions and reneged on what had already been agreed to, thus sabotaging the peace process once again.

From then until June 1990, two months after the U.S.-sponsored Chamorro administration was inaugurated, the United States maintained the contras intact, in complete disregard of the various peace agreements. At first, the possible disbanding of the contras was used as a bargaining chip to persuade the Nicaraguan government to modify its already quite concessionary 1988 electoral law. For instance, the government was forced to agree to more free, uncensored television and radio time for opposition campaign programming. And, most notably, it was pressured into allowing foreign campaign funding for parties competing in the election (which is expressly prohibited in the United States and in most other Western democracies). In spite of these concessions, however, the United States then insisted that the contras must be maintained in order to ensure a free election. Once the free election had taken place, the contras then were maintained on the pretext that they were essential to ensure the inauguration of Mrs. Chamorro. And once that had taken place, they then were kept intact for another two months until the Chamorro government agreed to integrate many contras into the police force and turn over large tracts of national territory—much of it rainforest parkland—to be used as "development poles" by ex-contras.

The 1990 Election

On Saturday, February 25, 1990, the Nicaraguan people cast their ballots in what was clearly the most internationally observed election in the history of the Western Hemisphere. (Having seen the Reagan administration denounce their 1984 election as a Soviet-style farce, the Sandinistas had insisted on unprecedented levels of international observation in 1990.) By 9:00 P.M. that evening, three hours after the polls closed, both the United Nations and the Organization of American States' observer teams had projections, based on a stratified sampling of results from voting places throughout the country, which were accurate to within 1 percent of the final result. Within one-half hour, Mrs. Chamorro and President Ortega were informed of their findings. By early morning Ortega went on nationwide television and delivered a moving concession speech. Later that day he went to Mrs. Chamorro's residence, embraced and congratulated her, and offered to support her new government.

As it turns out, 86.1 percent of Nicaragua's electorate had voted. Of these, 54.7 percent had voted for Mrs. Chamorro and her National Opposition Union (UNO) coalition, 40.8 percent had voted for Ortega and the FSLN, and the rest had voted for candidates of other parties.[48] In the United States, officials and the media in general were ecstatic about this "victory for democracy" in the "first free election" held in Nicaragua since the "leftist Sandinista takeover" in 1979. What is more, pressure by the contras was credited with forcing the Sandinistas to hold the election.

In fact, a national election to be held in 1990 was written into the 1987 constitution. Moreover, that constitution was the work of a constituent assembly and a government elected in 1984. Further, the 1984 election, although denounced by the Reagan administration and largely ignored by the U.S. media, generally had been praised as free, open, and competitive by such diverse, disinterested, and credible observer groups as those sent by the British House of Commons and Lords, the

Irish parliament, the Dutch government, Willy Brandt representing European Social Democrats, and the Latin American Studies Association.[49] As in 1990 the 1984 electoral and party laws were very progressive in comparison with practices in the rest of Latin America. And in 1984 the background conditions for holding an election were markedly better in Nicaragua than, say, in El Salvador, where the U.S. government and press lavished praise on the process.

In reality, the most important difference between 1984 and 1990 was that, in the interim, Nicaragua had undergone slightly more than five additional years of war, destruction, and economic destabilization. Whereas officials in Washington were aware that no opposition group could win a fair election in 1984 against the still-popular Sandinistas, they were equally aware five years later that a united opposition might very well ride the tide of popular anguish to an electoral victory. Apparently, that awareness accounts for both the Reagan administration's intense opposition to the 1984 election and the Bush administration's promotion of a unified candidate in 1990 and its open funding of her campaign.

In the long run, however, it was not the Bush administration's multimillion-dollar covert and nearly $8 million overt support for the UNO forces that tipped the scale. Indeed, thanks to U.S. bureaucratic inertia, most of that aid did not even arrive in Nicaragua until early 1990—too late to have much impact. Nor did the UNO candidates outcampaign their FSLN opponents. To the contrary, the Chamorro campaign was troubled by open infighting (sometimes physical), amateurish television spots, and an inarticulate and awkward presidential candidate, while the Sandinistas ran a flashy modern campaign with lots of glitz, paraphernalia, and huge rallies. No, it is likely that the campaign itself was essentially irrelevant. What seems to have mattered most in shaping the outcome was the clear awareness in the minds of most Nicaraguans that they had a clear choice in 1990: Vote Sandinista and, in doing so, perpetuate the war and economic strangulation; or vote for the U.S.-sponsored candidate and, in doing so, end the war and economic aggression. They chose the latter.

Significantly, there was virtually no celebration in Managua in the wake of the UNO victory. Although joyous events from holidays to birthday parties are almost always marked in Nicaragua by the rattle of firecrackers and the boom of rockets, Managua was strangely quiet that night and for the next several days. Apparently, for many, a vote for the U.S.-sponsored candidates had been merely an unhappy expediency, a way to get the United States to stop inflicting war and economic suffering on them. Although they perceived that their suffering might now be eased, they were in no mood to celebrate.

Conclusion

The U.S. strategy of "low intensity conflict" had paid off. Through it, Washington had succeeded in reasserting hegemonic control over Nicaragua. Almost immediately after Mrs. Chamorro's inauguration, the process of agrarian reform that had benefited over one hundred thousand poor families under the Sandinista revolution began to be reversed. Public school textbooks that had taught an awareness of Nicaraguan sovereignty and patriotic history were replaced by imported texts recommended and paid for by the U.S. Agency for International Development. Contras were integrated into the national police force, the Sandinista People's Army was more than halved, and Mrs. Chamorro boldly announced her objective of eliminating the army entirely.

Once again, a Latin American experiment in national self-determination had been contained. The irony was that this reassertion of hegemonic control had come only shortly after the United States' archrival, the Soviet Union, had gracefully relinquished control over its East European empire. All this posed an important question: Was what had happened in Nicaragua simply a tragic last spasm of the dying Cold War or was the United States really bent on being the world's last imperialist power?

Notes

1.   For additional discussion of hegemony in the Latin American context see Guy Poitras, *The Ordeal of Hegemony: The United States and Latin America* (Boulder, 1989), and Abraham Lowenthal, *Partners in Conflict: The U.S. and Latin America* (Baltimore, 1988). For a more thorough description of U.S. policy in Nicaragua in 1978 and 1979 see William M. LeoGrande, "The United States and the Nicaraguan Revolution," in Thomas W. Walker, ed., *Nicaragua in Revolution* (New York, 1982), 63–77.

2.   For a thorough discussion of the Sandinista armed forces see Thomas W. Walker, "The Armed Forces," in his edited work *Revolution and Counterrevolution in Nicaragua: A Comprehensive Overview* (Boulder, forthcoming in 1991).

3.   Ibid.

4.   For detailed discussion of the U.S. use of the anti-Sandinista media in Nicaragua see Angharad Valdivia, "The U.S. Manipulation of Nicaraguan and Other Latin American Media," in Walker, ed., *Revolution and Counterrevolution*.

5.   For a discussion of the evolution of political institutions in Nicaragua see Andrew Reding, "The Evolution of Formal Governmental Institutions," in Walker, ed., *Revolution and Counterrevolution*.

6.   See Waltraud Queiser Morales and Harry Vanden, "Relations with the Nonaligned Movement," in *Nicaragua: The First Five Years*, Thomas W. Walker, ed. (New York, 1985), 467–84; and Mary Vanderlaan, *Revolution and Foreign Policy in Nicaragua* (Boulder, 1986).

7.   "Text of State Department Report of Communist Support of the Salvadoran Rebels," *New York Times*, March 9, 1981.

8.   Wayne Smith, "Dateline Havana: Myopic Diplomacy," *Foreign Policy* 48 (Fall 1982): 162.

9.   For some examples of deliberate CIA disinformation against Nicaragua see Walker, "The Armed Forces."

10.   For one of the best accounts of this matter see Richard H. Immerman, *The CIA in Guatemala: The Foreign Policy of Intervention* (Austin, 1982).

11.   For ample documentation of the Chilean operation see U.S. Congress, Senate, Staff Report, Select Committee to Study Governmental Operations with Respect to United States Intelligence, *Covert Action in Chile*, December 18, 1985.

12.   Committee of Santa Fe, *A New Inter-American Policy for the Eighties* (Washington, DC, 1980).

13.   "Reagan's Advisors Step Up Search for the 'Responsible Right,' " *Latin American Weekly Report* (September 26, 1980): 5.

14.   Staff Report, Subcommittee on Oversight and Evaluation, Permanent Select Committee on Intelligence, *U.S. Intelligence Performance on Central America: Achievements and Selected Instances of Concern*, September 12, 1982 (mimeograph).

15.   Lieutenant Colonel John H. Buchanan, USMC (Ret.), Prepared Statement before the Subcommittee on Interamerican Affairs, U.S. House of Representatives, Committee on Foreign Affairs, U.S. House of Representatives, "U.S. Military Aid to Honduras," September 21, 1982 (mimeograph).

16.   Department of the Army, United States Army Intelligence and Threat Analysis Center, United States Army Intelligence and Security Command, *Army Intelligence Survey: Nicaragua, Volume III–Armed Forces (U)* (Washington, DC, May 1984), 1–5 (emphasis added).

17.   Those wishing to find more information on different facets of the U.S. war against Nicaragua should see Thomas W. Walker, ed., *Reagan versus the Sandinistas: The Undeclared War on Nicaragua* (Boulder, 1987); Peter Kornbluh, *The Price of Intervention: Reagan's War against the Sandinistas* (Washington, DC, 1987); Jonathan Marshall, Peter Dale Scott, and Jane Hunter, *The Iran-Contra Connection: Secret Teams and Covert Operations in the Reagan Era* (Boston, 1987); and Holly Sklar, *Washington's War on Nicaragua* (Boston, 1988).

18.   In the mid-1980s, Nicaragua sued the United States before the World Court for having mined its harbors and promoted the contra war. Although it refused to recognize the court's jurisdiction, the United States was found guilty. Accordingly, "under general principles of humanitarian law, the United States was bound to refrain from encouragement of persons or groups engaged in conflict in Nicaragua to commit violations of common Article 3 of the four Geneva Conventions of 12 August 1949." Louis Henkin et al., *International Law: Cases and Materials* (St. Paul, 1987), 722, in particular, and 633–50, 708–36, in general. There is also evidence indicating that drug

money may have been used to finance the contras; see Jonathan Kwitny, "Money, Drugs and the Contras," *Nation* (August 29, 1987): 145–66; Leslie Cockburn, *Out of Control: The Story of the Reagan Administration's Secret War in Nicaragua, the Illegal Arms Pipeline, and the Contra Drug Connection* (New York, 1987); and *Inside the Shadow Government: Declarations of Plaintiffs' Council Filed by the Christic Institute, U.S. District Court, Miami, Florida, March 31, 1988* (Washington, DC, 1988). For a good general treatment of the relationship among drugs, organized crime, and the CIA see Jonathan Kwitny, *The Crimes of Patriots: A True Tale of Dope, Dirty Money, and the CIA* (New York, 1987).

19. "Haig Voices Concern on Nicaragua," *Washington Post*, November 15, 1981.

20. Eddie Adams, "Exiles Rehearse for the Day They Hope Will Come," *Parade Magazine* (March 15, 1981): 4–6.

21. Christopher Dickey, *With the Contras in Nicaragua* (New York, 1985), 104.

22. Ibid. See also Harry E. Vanden, "Law, State Policy, and Terrorism in Central America: The 1980s," *New Political Science* 16/17 (Fall/Winter 1990).

23. By 1987 the administration had given more money to the contras to overthrow the Nicaraguan government than the United States had given to all five Central American countries from 1962 to 1980. Ibid.

24. "Casey's Secret CIA Disclosed," *Tampa Tribune*, July 11, 1987.

25. Ibid.

26. Americas Watch, *Violations of the Laws of War by Both Sides in Nicaragua, 1981–1985* (New York, 1985), 4.

27. Ibid.

28. Reed Brody, *Contra Terror in Nicaragua: Report of a Fact-finding Mission: September 1984–January 1985* (Boston, 1985).

29. Americas Watch, *Violations of the Laws of War*, 6.

30. Amnesty International, *Nicaragua: Human Rights Record* (London, 1986).

31. *Psychological Operations in Guerrilla Warfare*, trans. by the Congressional Research Service, October 15, 1984, 11.

32. Ibid., 4.

33. "Affidavit of Edgar Chamorro," Submitted to the International Court of Justice, in re Nicaragua v. United States of America, September 5, 1985, 23. Obtained through the Central American Historical Institute, Georgetown University, Washington, DC.

34. Joel Brinkley, "CIA Gives Contras Detailed Profiles of Civilian Targets, Raids Planned in Spring," *New York Times*, March 19, 1987.

35. "Assassination of U.S. Volunteer Part of Contra Drive," Central American Historical Institute *Update* (May 11, 1987): 3.

36. Ibid.

37. "Linder Died by Gunshot, Report Says," *Tampa Tribune*, June 6, 1987.

38. These and the statistics in the rest of this paragraph are from eight pages of charts provided by the Nicaraguan Ministry of the Presidency, January 1990.

39. Coauthor Thomas Walker is in a particularly good position to attest to this upsurge in contra activity. As a member of the Latin American Studies Association's election observer delegation he was specifically assigned to observe and investigate the campaign and election in the war zone of northern Nicaragua in late 1989 and early 1990.

40. From Seymour Hersh, "The Price of Power: Kissinger, Nixon and Chile," *Atlantic Monthly* 250 (December 1982): 11.

41. Michael E. Conroy, "Economic Legacy and Policy: Performance and Critique," in Walker, ed., *Nicaragua: The First Five Years*, 232.

42. Ibid., 220.

43. The IDB report as quoted in ibid., 233.

44. E. V. K. FitzGerald as cited in John A. Booth, "United States Policy toward Central America," *Current History* 85, no. 515 (December 1986): 407.

45. For sharp criticism of these mistakes see Joseph Ricciardi, "Economic Policy," in Walker, ed., *Revolution and Counterrevolution.*

46. For a table with a good breakdown of the $17.8-billion damages claimed by Nicaragua see Kent Norsworthy with Tom Barry, *Nicaragua: A Country Guide* (Albuquerque, 1990), 59.

47. For more details about the long search for peace see William Goodfellow and William Morrell, "From Contadora to Esquipulas to Sapoa and Beyond," in Walker, ed., *Revolution and Counterrevolution.*

48. Both authors were in Nicaragua to observe the elections. The Latin American Studies Association delegation, of whom Walker was a part, produced a lengthy report (*Electoral Democracy under International Pressure: The Report of the Latin American Studies Association Commission to Observe the 1990 Nicaraguan Elections*, Pittsburgh, March 15, 1990), which is available for purchase by contacting: LASA Secretariat, William Pitt Union, 9th Floor, University of Pittsburgh, Pittsburgh, PA 15260. See also Harry E. Vanden and Gary Prevost, *Democracy, Socialism, and the State in Nicaragua* (Boulder, forthcoming).

49. For a description of those elections and bibliographical reference to the election reports see Thomas W. Walker, *Nicaragua: The Land of Sandino* (Boulder, 1986), 51, 52, 54, 116–19.

U.S. FOREIGN POLICY
AND THE CRISIS

Vietnam, Central America, and the Uses of History

George C. Herring

More than fifteen years ago, toward the end of the Vietnam War, the Harvard historian Ernest May examined a series of case studies from World War II through Vietnam. He concluded that, in responding to foreign policy crises, policymakers and the public were invariably guided by history, especially by their memory of the recent past. He went on to say that, equally invariably, they used history badly. Their historical knowledge was at best superficial. Their historical reasoning was "thoughtless and haphazard." Indeed, he specifically argued that such reasoning had been a major cause for American involvement in Vietnam.[1]

Similar to the case studies May considered, from the time Central America became a major national issue it was inextricably linked to Vietnam. It is instructive, therefore, to consider the ways in which Vietnam and Central America have been compared, to analyze the extent to which and the reasons why they are in fact analogous, and, proceeding from there, to discuss how history can be useful in dealing with today's problems. In general, it should be noted that history and, in particular, the analogy with Vietnam have been no better used in dealing with Central America than in the instances May studied, and this has been true of those who have opposed U.S. involvement as well as those who supported it.

In looking first at how Vietnam and Central America were joined in public discussion in the Reagan years, no matter what the point of view, analogies were discovered, memories evoked, and lessons drawn. To start at the beginning, and at the top, there are indications that the Reagan administration, in undertaking its initial, firm commitment to El Salvador in 1981, thought that it could win a quick victory and in so doing erase the stigma of defeat in Vietnam and exorcise the so-called Vietnam syndrome—the perceived public reluctance in the wake of Vietnam to take on commitments in the Third World.[2]

When the quick victory turned into an illusion and the commitment aroused the popular apprehensions it was supposed to dispel, President Ronald Reagan and his advisers immediately sought to distance themselves from Vietnam. Secretary of State Alexander M. Haig, Jr., went to great lengths to show that Vietnam and El Salvador were drastically different. The United States had clear-cut—indeed, obvious—vital interests in El Salvador, he insisted, which had not been the case in Vietnam (a statement that must have come as a shock to the generation of policymakers who had based an escalating commitment in Vietnam on precisely the opposite grounds).[3] Since early 1981, President Reagan repeatedly stated that there was "no comparison with Vietnam and there's not going to be anything of that kind [in El Salvador]."[4] Reaganites such as Ernest Lefever echoed this refrain, arguing that the United States failed in Vietnam because it did not act decisively and implying at least that Reagan would not make that mistake in El Salvador. The more apt analogy, Lefever insisted, was Greece where, under the Truman Doctrine, the United States turned back an insurgency between 1947 and 1949. Other Reagan supporters insisted that the Dominican Republic, where Lyndon B. Johnson successfully intervened in 1965, was more relevant.[5]

American conservatives supported the president's commitment in El Salvador, but, where Reagan attempted to evade the Vietnam issue, his conservative brethren pronounced numerous lessons from Vietnam to guide policy in El Salvador. Columnist George Will harked back to Woodrow Wilson to find that the cause of American problems in Vietnam, El Salvador, and Third World countries generally was the effort to force-feed democracy to nations that simply were not ready for it. The United States had pressed elections on Vietnam, he warned, and Saigon "is now Ho Chi Minh City."[6] Henry Kissinger emphasized different lessons. Never an admirer of the American democratic system, he proclaimed, upon accepting chairmanship of the president's commission on Central America, that "it is imperative [in dealing with problems there] that we avoid the bitter debates that characterized the Vietnam period."[7] Norman Podhoretz, editor of *Commentary*, added another lesson; namely, that "fighting a war on the cheap is a sure formula for defeat." If in Central America U.S. military power was called for and was not used or was used halfheartedly, he noted, we will "reveal ourselves as a spent and impotent force."[8] Along the same lines, the Kissinger Commission Report evoked memories of Vietnam when it warned of the dangers of a stalemate in El Salvador. In words almost identical to those used by Kissinger in his famous 1969 *Foreign Affairs* article on Vietnam, the report stressed that "the insurgency is winning if it's not losing, and the government is losing if it's not winning."[9]

On the other side of the political spectrum, liberal critics of Reagan's policies gloomily forecast a replay of Vietnam in El Salvador. The Coalition for a New Foreign and Military Policy, responding to the president's "no comparison" statement, pointed to the long history of oppression in El Salvador and an unpopular regime backed by U.S. money and insisted that the comparisons were all too obvious.[10] To George Ball, Johnson's in-house critic on Vietnam, El Salvador's "music and words sound like plagiarization. I have the feeling that we've heard it all before but in another setting."[11] Liberal journalist Tad Szulc warned that, if the United States persisted in its present course in El Salvador, it would become bogged down "in an endless, Vietnam-style guerrilla war in the Salvadorean mountains and jungles," a "scenario for absolute disaster."[12]

Outside the formal debate, similarly, discussion of El Salvador invariably began with, or came back to, Vietnam. When Congress discussed El Salvador, one legislator conceded that Vietnam was a "ghostly presence; it's there in every committee room, at every meeting."[13] Many of the top U.S. advisers in Central America, men such as Ambassador John Negroponte and General Paul Gorman, were old Vietnam hands, and most of the U.S. military advisers had served apprenticeships in Indochina. The programs being applied by American advisers often seemed to be retreads of ones that had worked in Vietnam or programs modified in the light of Vietnam failures.

The military brought to El Salvador an exceptional amount of Vietnam baggage. "All I want to do is win one war, that's all, just one," an adviser told a reporter, as though wars, like baseball, were tallied in win-loss columns. "It'll be like winning the World Series for me." Another adviser expressed fear of a repetition of the final days of April 1975. "If the sense spreads that the U.S. will desert them," he said of the Salvadorans he was working with, "I don't know what they'll do. It's Vietnam all over again."[14] Among senior U.S. military officers, Adam Smith wrote in 1983, Vietnam was a "silent obsession. It lurks in nuances and ellipses, even when the discussion is about something else."[15] They were unwilling to undergo in Central America what they had experienced in Vietnam. They were reluctant to see the army committed, as General Edward Meyer affirmed in the fall of 1983, unless the nation itself was committed.[16] The presence of Vietnam in the military mind was clearly manifested in September 1983 in the famous Freudian slip of Marine Corps Commandant General P. X. Kelley who, before a committee of Congress, inadvertently used the word Vietnam when he meant to say Lebanon.[17]

In November 1984, Secretary of Defense Caspar Weinberger set forth a series of "tests" for the use of American military power that seemed squarely based on the lessons of Vietnam and clearly designed for Central America. At one point, Weinberger explicitly stated that the administration would not permit U.S. military forces, as in Vietnam, "to creep—or be drawn gradually—into a combat role in Central America." Stressing that the administration's policies were designed to avoid the need for direct involvement, he went on to warn that, if U.S. forces were required, "we must commit them, in sufficient numbers, and we must support them, as effectively and resolutely as our strength permits. When we commit our troops to combat, we must do so with the sole object of winning."[18]

If the polls mean anything, the American public, at least partly because of Vietnam, had little stomach for any such commitment. Polls taken in the spring and summer of 1983 revealed that a solid majority of Americans (75 percent) saw the likelihood that U.S. involvement in El Salvador would turn into another Vietnam, and a smaller majority (54 percent) opposed sending troops even if the government was about to be defeated by leftist forces.[19]

Wherever one turned, then, discussion of El Salvador invariably referred back to Vietnam and discussion of Vietnam invariably moved forward to El Salvador. A 1983 political cartoon portrayed President Reagan, waist deep in quicksand, rifle held above head, doggedly plunging forward, while a nervous Uncle Sam inched along cautiously behind. "Quit grousing!" Reagan orders Sam, "I'm telling you it's not Vietnam!" "It doesn't look like Munich, either," a still-wary Sam replies.[20] In her book *The March of Folly*, even Barbara Tuchman, who once said that the purpose of history was "not to instruct but to tell a story," set out to find "lessons" from Vietnam and wondered how the United States could continue in El Salvador the "imbecility" it had practiced earlier in Southeast Asia.[21] The discovery of lessons was not limited to Americans. A representative of the Salvadoran right wing, protesting U.S. interference in his country's internal politics, exclaimed in frustration that El Salvador should "fight the war without the influence of foreign advisers who were defeated in similar conflicts and have nothing to teach the valiant Salvadoran soldiers."[22]

In the second Reagan administration the focus of the debate on Central America shifted to Nicaragua, but the Vietnam analogy remained an integral part of it. On the tenth anniversary of the fall of Saigon in

April 1985, Secretary of State George Shultz used the lessons of Vietnam to justify U.S. support for the efforts of the Nicaraguan contras to overthrow the leftist Sandinista government. "Broken promises. Communist dictatorships. Refugees. Widened Soviet influence, this time near our very borders," the secretary warned. "Here is your parallel between Vietnam and Central America." Shultz appealed for aid to those "freedom fighters" who were trying to save the people of Nicaragua from the fate of Cuba, South Vietnam, Cambodia, and Laos. He blamed domestic critics of the Vietnam War for the outcome and warned that history might repeat itself in Nicaragua. "Those who assure us that these dire consequences are not in prospect are some of those who assured us of the same in Indochina before 1975."[23]

In congressional debates on aid to the contras, supporters of the administration took much the same line. Representative Robert Dornan (R-CA), recently returned from visits to Hanoi and Managua, spoke of the "frightening similarities" between the two in terms of economic decay and political oppression and warned that the United States would be "sealing the fate" of eleven thousand to thirteen thousand people if it refused to aid the contras.[24] Responding to those who warned of another Vietnam in Central America, administration supporters insisted that nothing was more likely to force U.S. military intervention than the consolidation of an aggressive, pro-Soviet regime in Managua.[25] Blaming Congress for the fall of South Vietnam, Representative Newt Gingrich (R-GA) warned that the same people who were now opposing aid to the contras "were wrong about South Vietnam and watched it become a dictatorship and watched the boat people flee . . . , were wrong about Cambodia and watched 'The Killing Fields.' "[26]

Opponents of aid to the contras also resorted to the Vietnam analogy. Reading newsclippings from 1964 indicating that no troops would be needed and reports from 1966 that more troops would be required, Representative Andrew Jacobs (D-IN) proclaimed: "Here we go again. Gulf of Tonkin Day . . . We ought to know by now that when they send the guns it does not take long before they send the sons."[27] Others warned in Vietnam-like terms of a "slippery slope," of step-by-step escalation into a jungle quagmire in Central America.[28] "Again and again," columnist James McCartney wrote, "as the debate reached a climax on the House floor, the spectre of American troops bogged down in an indecisive war haunted many members of the House."[29] Even when the House finally passed the aid package in June 1986, the influence of Vietnam was evident. By a vote of 215 to 212, the representatives also passed an amendment to bar U.S. personnel from providing training or other assistance to the contras within twenty miles of the Nicaraguan border.

Affirming that the Vietnam syndrome was still very much alive, Representative David Bonior (D-MI), himself a Vietnam veteran, insisted that the "experience was so intrusive into the lives of our generation that it will be with us forever and ever."[30]

Since Vietnam and Central America were so often joined in public discussion, it is not only appropriate but also essential to examine the analogy closely, to determine the ways in which they were similar and the ways they differed. On the surface, at least, the conflicts seemed strikingly similar. In each case the perceived enemy was a revolutionary regime that appeared to threaten the interests of the United States and the small nations to which it was allied in a region deemed critically important. In each case significant support for the nation opposing the United States came from its number-one adversary, the Soviet Union. In El Salvador, at least, the analogy could be carried a step further. There, much as it did in Vietnam, the United States supported an established government against a leftist insurgency with some external support in a small, underdeveloped country in a tropical region.

The differences were much greater. The conflicts occurred in very different parts of the world in different historical settings and political cultures.[31] War originated in Vietnam in 1945 as a nationalist revolution against French colonialism. The conflicts in Nicaragua and El Salvador originated in response to narrowly based reactionary regimes, with varying degrees of support from the United States. Both conflicts became internationalized in their early stages. In Vietnam, however, the major "outside" power, North Vietnam, was fanatically committed to liberating its southern brethren and unifying the country and, with assistance from China and the Soviet Union, provided the bulk of external aid to the southern insurgency. Cuba and the Soviet Union have provided primary support to Nicaragua and, along with Nicaragua, have given some aid to the Salvadoran rebels. Neither has had the same level of interest or commitment that the North Vietnamese had in Vietnam.

There were also profound differences in the internal situations in each of the conflicts. The National Liberation Front of South Vietnam appears to have been more tightly knit and more deeply committed to its goal than the loose coalition of groups that made up the opposition in El Salvador. The Catholic church was an important player in each of the conflicts, but its role was strikingly different. The church represented the one solid base of support for the Ngo Dinh Diem and Nguyen Van Thieu regimes in South Vietnam. In Latin America generally, however, the church in recent years identified with the poor and oppressed. In El Salvador, it was split between support of the government and support of the insurgents. In Nicaragua, it opposed the Somoza regime and the Sandinista government. Also in Nicaragua, of course, the fundamental difference was that the role of the United States was reversed: it supported the counterrevolutionary contra insurgency against an established government, precisely the opposite of what had happened in Vietnam. The conflicts were thus very different, and the revolutions and wars in Central America took quite different courses from that in Vietnam.

Given these similarities and differences, does the Vietnam analogy have any value in dealing with the problems of Central America today? It is clear, as Ernest May concluded of the period from 1945 to 1965, that thus far history has been badly used. Each side in the debate was extremely sensitive to the Vietnam analogy, especially since that war was so close and fresh in the popular mind. But the analogy misled rather than guided, obscured rather than clarified. Conclusions on both sides were based on superficial historical knowledge and faulty historical reasoning. Each side blatantly abused history for partisan purposes, and each demanded more than history could possibly deliver by asking it to forecast outcomes.

The Reagan administration stretched credulity to the breaking point by asserting that there was no comparison between El Salvador and Vietnam. The comparisons were all too obvious, and, more important, to say that El Salvador was not another Vietnam did not, as the president seemed to wish, eliminate the need for further discussion. To reject the Vietnam analogy for an analogy with Greece in the 1940s or the Dominican Republic in the 1960s, moreover, was the most blatant form of argument by historical expediency, of selecting the example that had the desired outcome and using it.

The effort to apply lessons from Vietnam to Central America was equally misleading. It violated what historian David Hackett Fischer has called "the didactic fallacy," the attempt to extract specific lessons from history and apply them literally to contemporary problems without regard to the differences in time, space, and historical circumstances.[32] The lesson that we failed in Vietnam because we did not use our power decisively, and therefore in Central America we had to apply it quickly and without stint, breaks down at several points. We cannot be sure that a different application of U.S. military power in Vietnam would have produced better results; it might have provoked a nuclear war. The relevance of this lesson for the distinctly different situation in Central America was, in any event, open to question.

On the other hand, the opposition's ominous warning that El Salvador or Nicaragua would become another Vietnam was as much an abuse of history as the Reagan administration's arguments and, indeed, as the so-called Munich analogy was for American involvement in Vietnam. It violated another of Fischer's fallacies, that of "the perfect analogy"—the "erroneous inference from the fact that A and B are similar in some respects to the false conclusion that they are the same in all respects."[33] Vietnam and Central America were different in important ways, and it was highly unlikely that the outcome would be the same. As Fischer suggests, each historical situation is unique, and we cannot make superficial comparisons and draw facile conclusions that, because such and such occurred before, the same or the reverse will happen this time.

Even more important, the Vietnam analogy inhibited discussion of Central America on its own merits and terms. Rather than indulging in the nondebate of whether Central America would become another Vietnam, we should have addressed the major issues in Central America itself. What was the nature of the struggle there? In what ways, if at all, did it threaten our vital interests? Could we morally justify intervention in support of the existing government in El Salvador and the contras in Nicaragua? Could we tolerate doing nothing? What were the possible consequences of deeper involvement, including military intervention? All of these questions were raised at one time or another, but they were never really confronted in a systematic or sustained way.

Does this mean, then, that history has nothing to teach us, or, more specifically, that the Vietnam analogy is useless in dealing with problems in Central America or elsewhere? Obviously, this is not the case. History in general, and the history of American involvement in Vietnam in particular, have much to teach us, but we must use them with discretion and caution and not demand too much from them.

We could have learned a lot that was of value from the study of the unique histories of El Salvador, Nicaragua, and other Central American nations, and from the study of our traditional relationships with these nations. Discussion of the crisis in Central America was almost totally devoid of historical context, an alarming and dangerous omission given its importance. Such analysis might have provided us with a much clearer picture of the origins and nature of the difficult and distinctive problems in each of the Central American nations. Understanding of its traditional role might have made the United States more sensitive to the ways in which Central Americans viewed it. It might have suggested a great deal about the extent of our influence there and the possible responses to programs initiated by us.

Although history does not offer specific lessons, it can provide a desperately needed perspective on contemporary problems. From studying our involvement in Vietnam, for example, we could learn much about ourselves and how we deal with other peoples. The mindset that got us into Vietnam is quite similar to that which undergirded the Reagan administration's policies in Central America and therefore is worthy of critical analysis. Many scholars believe that in dealing with the Vietnamese we consistently worked from a base of ignorance and cultural blindness. We must be sensitive to the same errors in our dealings with Central Americans today. Study of the interplay within the Moscow-Beijing-Hanoi triangle during the Vietnam War can shed light on, although obviously it will not foretell the direction of, the relations among the Communist nations in dealing with Central America.

When used cautiously and with due regard to its limitations, the Vietnam analogy might even have provided guidance, if not outright lessons, that could have been useful in handling specific problems in Central America. U.S. relations with the Saigon government, for example, suggest, seemingly paradoxically, that the deeper our commitment the smaller our leverage in getting that government to take necessary actions for what we believe are necessary for its survival.[34] Policymakers should at least have been alert to this possibility as U.S. involvement in El Salvador and other Central American countries became more and more complex.

Above all else the Vietnam experience suggested the centrality of local circumstances in international conflicts. From the outset, American policymakers defined the problem in Vietnam in the context of the Cold War. To a considerable degree, however, local forces explained the origins, the peculiar dynamics, and the outcome of the war. By wrongly attributing the conflict to external forces, the United States drastically misjudged its internal dynamics. By intervening in what was essentially a local struggle, it placed itself at the mercy of local forces, a weak client, and a determined adversary. What might have remained a localized struggle was elevated into a major international conflict, with enormous and fateful consequences for Americans and especially for the Vietnamese. The circumstances in Central America are different, and the outcome will certainly not be the same. But the point should be clear: we ignore local forces at our own peril.[35]

Without suggesting to us outcomes that are foreordained, the study of history might also teach us a healthy caution. "History does not teach lots of little lessons," Gordon Wood has written, "it teaches only one big one: that nothing ever works out quite the way its managers expected or intended."[36] In the final analysis, however, one of the most important functions of history, or the historian, may be to expose false analogy. As a wise Englishman, James, Viscount Bryce, once put it, "The chief practical use of history is to deliver us from plausible historical analogies."[37]

Let us study Vietnam and study it carefully and with an open mind. But let us be conscious that the purpose of our study is to gain perspective and understanding, not hard and fast lessons. With tongue planted firmly in cheek, the historian and Vietnam policymaker James Thomson once proposed that we should learn one central lesson from Vietnam: never again to "take on the job of trying to defeat a nationalist anticolonial movement under indigenous Communist control in former French Indochina"—a lesson of "less than universal relevance," he quickly and redundantly added.[38] Thomson obviously overstated for effect, but again the point should be clear. Each historical situation is unique, and the use of analogy is at best misleading; at worst, dangerous.

Writing in 1970 about the misuse of historical analogy in dealing with Vietnam, Fischer suggested that the problem had to be "studied and solved in its own terms, if it is to be solved at all."[39] Perhaps the best way to conclude this analysis of the use of the Vietnam analogy in the debate on Central America would be to paraphrase Fischer and change the point of reference. As valuable as an understanding of Vietnam may be to us, the problems of Central America and other foreign policy problems can best be studied and solved in their own terms if they are to be solved at all.

Notes

1.   Ernest R. May, *"Lessons" of the Past: The Use and Misuse of History in American Foreign Policy* (New York, 1975), x, xi, 190.

2.   *New York Times*, September 25, 1983.

3.   See, for example, Alexander Haig's testimony before the House Committee on Foreign Affairs as reported in ibid., March 3, 1982.

4.   Reagan statement quoted in ibid., July 26, 1983.

5.   Ibid., July 31, 1983.

6.   George Will, "Woodrow Wilson's Ghost in El Salvador," *Herald-Leader* (Lexington, KY), July 31, 1983.

7.   *New York Times*, July 25, 1983.

8.   Ibid., July 24, 1983.

9.   Kissinger Commission Report as summarized in *Herald-Leader*, January 8, 1984.

10.   *New York Times*, July 24, 1983.

11.   Quoted in Robert G. Kaiser, "El Salvador: A Rerun of Vietnam Movie?" *Courier-Journal* (Louisville, KY), March 14, 1982.

12. Tad Szulc, "El Salvador Is Spanish for Vietnam," *Penthouse* 15 (September 1983): 58.

13. James McCartney, "El Salvador and the Ghost of Vietnam," *Herald-Leader*, May 1, 1983.

14. *New York Times*, November 8, 1982.

15. Adam Smith, "Will You Go to El Salvador?" *Esquire* (September 1983): 12. See also Drew Middleton, "Vietnam and the Military Mind," *New York Times Magazine* (January 10, 1982): 34.

16. See especially Richard Halloran, "Vietnam Consequences: Quiet from the Military," *New York Times*, May 2, 1983. This "lesson" is emphasized in the study by Harry G. Summers, Jr., *On Strategy: The Vietnam War in Context* (Carlisle Barracks, PA, 1981), which sets forth what has become the new conventional wisdom in the army.

17. *New York Times*, October 2, 1983.

18. Ibid., November 28, 1984. See also Caspar W. Weinberger, "The Uses of Military Power," *Defense* (January 1985): 2–8.

19. "Public Opinion on Central America," *Public Opinion* 6 (August–September 1983): 25; *New York Times*, July 25, 1983.

20. Tony Auth in Detroit *News*, May 20, 1983.

21. Gordon Wood review of Barbara Tuchman's *March of Folly* in *New York Review of Books* 31 (March 29, 1984): 8.

22. *Newsweek* 103 (January 16, 1984): 27.

23. George Shultz, "The Meaning of Vietnam," U.S. Department of State *Bulletin* 85 (June 1985): 13–16.

24. *Congressional Record*, 99th Cong., 2d sess. (March 18, 1986): H1216.

25. Ibid.

26. Ibid., H1408.

27. Ibid., 99th Cong., 2d sess. (March 19, 1986): H1329.

28. James McCartney column, *Herald-Leader*, March 22, 1986.

29. Ibid.

30. *New York Times*, May 25, 1986, and June 29, 1986.

31. For extended commentary on the importance and role of political culture in the Vietnamese revolution see John T. McAlister, Jr., and Paul Mus, *The Vietnamese and Their Revolution* (New York, 1970); Frances FitzGerald, *Fire in the Lake* (New York, 1972); and David Marr, *Vietnamese Tradition on Trial* (Berkeley, 1982). For comment on the role of political culture in Central American revolutions see Richard Morse, "Toward a Theory of Spanish-American Government," in Howard Wiarda, ed., *Politics and Social Change in Latin America* (Amherst, 1974); and Eldon W. Kenworthy, "Dilemmas of Participation in Latin America," *Democracy* 3 (Winter 1983): 72–83.

32. David Hackett Fischer, *Historians' Fallacies* (New York, 1970), 157.

33. Ibid., 247.

34. Lawrence E. Grinter, "Bargaining between Saigon and Washington: Dilemmas of Linkage Politics during the War," *Orbis* 18 (Fall 1974): 837–67.

35. Stanley Karnow, "Vietnam as an Analogy," *New York Times*, October 4, 1983.

36. Wood review of Tuchman in *New York Review of Books*, 10.

37. Fischer, *Historians' Fallacies*, 242.

38. Quoted in Richard Pfeffer, ed., *No More Vietnams? The War and the Future of American Foreign Policy* (New York, 1968), 258.

39. Fischer, *Historians' Fallacies*, 250.

The Permanent Campaign's Impact on U.S. Central American Policy

Eldon Kenworthy

That politicians borrow techniques from advertising to get themselves elected hardly is news. Nor is it news that such techniques work. "The simple story of [the 1988 presidential] election is that the Bush commercials have worked and the Dukakis commercials have not," claimed veteran pollster Louis Harris.[1] Less is written, however, about the selling that politicians do in between elections, particularly the selling that affects foreign policy. Yet it would be naive to think that those elected by what Walter Dean Burnham calls "television advertising, continuous polling and consent-massaging"[2] would set those techniques aside once in office or that these techniques would respect the old adage that (partisan) politics stops at the waters' edge.

Complaints over the "selling of the presidency," so evident after the 1988 presidential campaign,[3] have not been accompanied by comparable attention to what such selling means for policymaking, particularly U.S. policy toward Latin America. Of the Washington insiders concerned about this region, only the losers have been willing to discuss the extent to which policy may be driven by domestic political calculations, while many critics of U.S. policies toward Latin America, being outsiders to the world of the Beltway, gravitate to interpretations in which the Central Intelligence Agency (CIA), or some secret team linked to that agency, or large multinationals and banks, drive policy. This article explores the insights to be gained by viewing recent episodes in Washington's Central American policy as driven by domestic political considerations, including the opinion-manipulation techniques developed by the current generation of U.S. politicians and their handlers.

Early in the Reagan years, reporter Sidney Blumenthal noted a "permanent campaign" being conducted by a president adept at "applying in the White House the techniques he employed in getting there."[4] Every night was election night as White House staffers watched to see if the stories they had planted that morning dominated the evening news—or if they had been able to put their "spin" on news they could not control. Major policies were chosen and important speeches written using sophisticated software that predicted different constituencies' reactions to various positions and power phrases. As stock market reports are to business leaders, so the almost daily readings of the president's standing in the polls became the barometer by which the White House staff judged the success of its work and charted its next moves.[5]

Not that Team Reagan lacked an agenda of its own or was unwilling to pursue unpopular policies. Through what came to be known as strategic polling (that is, opinion polling married to demographic analysis, and eventually to trials in test markets), the Reagan White House developed the ability to present the public with choices that it could not refuse. U.S. military support for the contras (Nicaraguan exiles intent on overthrowing the Sandinista government of their homeland) was sold as combating communism, as striking back at international terrorism, as halting the flow of illegal drugs into the United States, or as supporting a worldwide transition to democracy. Which of those "explanations" was featured in administration rhetoric depended upon the pollsters' reading of what was making the public fearful or angry at that moment. "Permanent campaign," therefore, is best understood as the unrelenting, skillful attempt to mobilize public emotions around "solutions" (be they candidates or policies), preselected by political elites, with those techniques well hidden from public view.

Approaching the midpoint of George Bush's first term as president, the permanent campaign does not appear to be an artifact of the Reagan years. (Shaped in the volatile and image-conscious politics of California, and capitalizing on its leader's acting skills, Team Reagan struck some observers as a unique phenomenon unlikely to be repeated.) Indeed, many of those most adept at managing public and congressional opinion through media events, sound bites, and strategic polling moved from the Reagan administration into key positions in the Bush White House and cabinet, including Bush's campaign manager, Secretary of State James A. Baker III. Nine months into the Bush presidency, the

New York Times wondered: "What kind of foreign policy will the United States ultimately have if you can take Mr. Baker out of the campaign but cannot take the campaign out of Mr. Baker?"[6]

Others quickly caught on. Driven by the tenfold increase in money spent on electoral campaigns over the past decade and one half, and by the professional advertising skills such money buys, the permanent campaign spread like Kurt Vonnegut's ice-9 through the system. "Now both ends of Pennsylvania Avenue seem immobilized by a politics of avoidance," observed the *New York Times* in a three-article series taking note of the permanent campaign, "where poll-takers and advertising producers are more influential than economists or engineers." Echoing Blumenthal, the *Times* reported that "public-opinion measurement has become a key tool not only of modern politics but of government."[7] From Madison Avenue and Hollywood to presidential electoral campaigns, and from those campaigns into the policymaking process itself, a technology has spread whose generic name is advertising.

More than other regions, Central America and the Caribbean lend themselves to an advertising-driven approach to policymaking. Proximity, visible in the migration to the United States of many whom the media stereotype as poor or criminal, causes these countries to seem more threatening to the public than they are by any objective reckoning. Eruptions of Marxism, revolution, and anti-*yanqui* nationalism revive that fear and loathing in the dominant North American culture that persisted beneath a post-1930s veneer of Pan-Americanism. These are lands still depicted by political cartoonists and by Hollywood as tropical jungles inhabited by hot-blooded *mafiosos*, either sinister or laughable. Some Latin elites play upon those fears to manipulate Washington into protecting their interests, in the process reinforcing many North Americans' conviction that they know what "these people" need even when they know neither their culture nor history. As the 1980s demonstrated, U.S. reactions to Central America and the Caribbean marry strong emotions to little information. From an advertiser's point of view, that is the perfect combination.[8]

Add geopolitics to this imbalance in the public's response and we can understand why Central America and the Caribbean provide unmatched opportunities for U.S. presidents to launch bold positions and to experiment with dramatic actions. The allies and enemies who most matter to Washington concede the Caribbean Basin to it as a U.S. sphere of influence. Thus, the region serves as a theater in which American politicians project their ambitions, their ideologies, and their desire for the limelight at little risk. This is the place to showcase U.S. solutions for Third World underdevelopment or to warn other nations of the U.S. resolve to halt Communist expansion or to undergird democracy. This is the place where an ambitious unknown, say, a young vice president, can make his mark.

Not all of the region is risk free, of course. When Ronald Reagan sought to demonstrate that the United States was back from defeat in Vietnam and humiliation in Iran and once again standing tall, he did not follow his first secretary of state's proddings to go to the source of Central American insurgencies, presumed to be Cuba, for Cuba enjoyed the explicit military protection of the Soviet Union. The Reagan administration made its statement, rather, by invading Grenada at a time when the Marxist rulers of that tiny republic were engaged in fratricide. When George Bush sought to lay to rest the image of indecisiveness that had dogged him through the 1988 presidential campaign and into the presidency, he invaded Panama, again toppling the unpopular government of a small state weakened by a U.S. economic blockade.

Both military interventions were designed to minimize loss of U.S. lives through massive surprise attacks, a strategy that tends to increase casualties in the recipient country. Both interventions were celebrated within the United States as proving something to the world. In function, if not in cost, these were media events not unlike those staged in Nicaragua by the CIA to demonstrate that the contras were a viable fighting force. That is, these were attention-catching events orchestrated by the White House to make a point to the U.S. public and Congress, and to the world at large—that undifferentiated world out there which (the U.S. public is told) validates U.S. credibility.

Obviously, we are too close to the December 1989 invasion in Panama to offer a balanced analysis. But if a plausible case cannot be made for the role of domestic politics in an intervention fresh in readers' memories, then this analysis will not convince many. After reviewing what is known about Panama, we will turn to a more frightening and complex example of the permanent campaign, one in which advertising techniques were used to override the well-grounded doubts of Congress and the public regarding a Central American policy. The Reagan administration's selling of its support for the Nicaraguan contras from 1984 to 1987 provides a clear case of modern advertising techniques being used not to communicate public opinion but to dominate it, by mobilizing emotions and identities that had little to do with the case at hand.

Invading Panama

Within days of the invasion of Panama, mainstream U.S. media discarded the officially cited motives of protecting U.S. lives, promoting democracy through ridding Panama of its dictator, defending the canal, and attacking drug trafficking and associated money laundering. What made this invasion so tempting to the decision makers, according to the best journalistic accounts, were the botched attempts at a negotiated solution and at an internal coup that preceded it. The invasion was a quick fix for previous failures in the formulation and execution of U.S. policy toward Panama and its ruler, General Manuel Antonio Noriega.

In November 1989 the Bush administration found itself with the (perceived) choice of intervening militarily or of appearing weak and indecisive. Given Bush's image problems at the time, the latter option was unacceptable, so the word went out in early November to prepare for a military intervention. "It shouldn't have come to this," commented *Newsweek*. "Whatever one thinks of last week's American assault, it was the product of failure." The *Wall Street Journal* agreed, saying the invasion was "necessitated as much by previous American policy mistakes as by Manuel Noriega's own provocative actions of recent weeks."[9]

Fearing the repercussions of striking a deal with Noriega during his 1988 presidential campaign, Vice President Bush and Secretary of the Treasury Baker (soon to be Bush's campaign manager) in high-level policy deliberations opposed President Reagan and Secretary of State George Shultz's willingness to negotiate with the Panamanian strongman. A deal almost concluded in May 1988 would have sent Noriega into exile in exchange for Washington's effectively dropping drug charges against him in U.S. courts. Once past the elections, Bush was willing to negotiate a similar package, especially after the Panamanian coup of October 3 failed—a failure many observers laid to administration bungling. Negotiations once more proved too belabored for White House temperaments, and Bush told the Joint Chiefs of Staff to proceed with preparations for a massive military intervention.

"At bottom," concluded *Newsweek*, "a large part of the rationale was simple frustration and embarrassment at being bested by a thug." Concurring, the *Washington Post* described how "getting rid of Noriega" had become "a test of U.S. manhood." Members of Bush's own party were ridiculing the White House for not taking action. While denying he was "questioning anybody's particular manhood," New York Republican Senator Alfonse D'Amato said, "We are being perceived as cowards, lacking the resolve to deal with . . . a tinhorn drug dealer by the name of Noriega." At press conferences Bush acknowledged his "enormous frustration," while a longtime friend of the president told the *New York Times* that Bush was "obsessed" with Noriega and a close aide noted that a "personal vendetta" affected the president's decision to intervene.[10]

President John F. Kennedy had been similarly vexed with Fidel Castro and President Reagan with Muammar al-Qaddafi. Nothing annoys U.S. presidents as much as upstart leaders of small countries acting in the world arena, not buckling under to Washington's diplomatic and economic pressure. Reagan's 1986 bombing of Libya boosted his public opinion ratings, as a secret White House poll predicted it would.[11] In a similar fashion, President Bush converted diplomatic ineptitude in Panama into a public relations success.

Following the invasion, Bush's approval rating rose to 79 percent, higher than any that Reagan had achieved, while the pollsters noted that "Bush's image was helped significantly by his decision to invade Panama." To Republican National Committee Chairman Lee Atwater, a key player in developing the permanent campaign under Reagan, in Panama Bush hit the "political jackpot." Among Americans under thirty years of age, the invasion was the only news in December to eclipse the National Football League play-offs, despite such dramatic developments in Eastern Europe as Nicolae Ceausescu's bloody overthrow in Romania. Sixty percent of the entire U.S. public said they followed events in Panama closely (twice as many as the next cited story), while General Noriega led the list of the names in the news freely recalled by those polled. The Panama invasion was the fourth most closely watched story in the four years that the Times Mirror Center has taken such a measure, and various polls showed that eight out of ten Americans liked what they saw.[12]

The Panama invasion mimicked prime-time entertainment in its high-tech shoot-'em-up followed by the suspense of tracking down Noriega. Confrontations between U.S. authorities and other embassies, including Nicaragua's and the Vatican's, added to the drama. This was world politics reduced to face-to-face conflict, spiced with the link to illicit drugs and revelations of Noriega's voodoo room. Topping it off were the gratifying images of Panamanians welcoming American GIs. Just as polls indicate that many Americans form their opinions about drug policy from watching such shows as "Miami Vice," so the Panama invasion captured and gratified a mass audience by mimicking entertainment.

Invasions such as Grenada and Panama are not only popular with the public but also are endorsed by leaders of the opposing political party. If few U.S. soldiers are killed, if an unpopular regime is toppled, if the troops are not trapped in a lengthy occupation, if the story disappears from the news before the troubling complications of the cleanup and rebuilding become evident—the word "cleanup" containing insight into U.S. views of what follows such interventions—then the operation will be pronounced a success. That Americans will rally behind their president in such situations had become such an axiom of U.S. politics that candidates seeking to unseat an incumbent president fear nothing so much as a surprise of this kind.

To achieve this feel-good result, however, Washington must structure the situation so that Uncle Sam can appear the aggrieved party pushed beyond the limits of patience and decency. The desired image is that of the lawman in movie westerns who is not looking for a fight but, when provoked, proves he is the fastest gun in town, or that of the aging gunfighter who comes out of retirement to help the weak preyed upon by the depraved. Without apologizing for Noriega, whose vices led him into the trap laid by Washington, we can make note of that trap, which in other situations would be called a sting.

It is now known that detailed plans for the U.S. attack were approved on November 3 and sent to the U.S. Army's Southern Command. From that day onward, helicopters and tanks were secretly shipped to U.S. bases in Panama and other preparations laid. The final go-ahead was given by President Bush on December 17, and the attack launched in the early hours of December 20. Between the November decision and December implementation, a series of provocations occurred in the form of U.S. troop movements. Without denying the Panamanian contribution to this escalation, it can be said that U.S. actions drew the incident that occurred on December 16, when a marine lieutenant was killed after running a Panamanian roadblock in a restricted zone and a navy officer was beaten and his wife harassed by Panama Defense Force members, many of them apparently drunk. Escalating provocations had brought Noriega the previous day to assert that a state of war existed between the two governments. Lacking the cool displayed by Sandinista leaders in similar situations, Noriega and his troops fell into the trap.

Run through the administration's public relations mill, Noriega's statement was transformed into a declaration of war on the United States, while the killing of the U.S. serviceman was presented as an attack out of the blue. The stage was set: The president could intervene to protect U.S. lives, as his predecessors had in invading the Dominican

Republic (1965) and Grenada (1983). According to one presidential aide, Bush "saw an opportunity this time he didn't want to miss." Said another high-level participant, "I'm not sure Bush wasn't looking for an excuse at that point."[13] In his televised speech to the nation seven hours after the attack had begun, the president said he had acted because "the lives of American citizens were in grave danger," a statement repeated in later press conferences.

The public bought it. Few thought to ask why an invasion was needed to protect American lives given the routine presence of some twelve thousand U.S. troops in Panama. Few pondered why it required the largest U.S. military operation since Vietnam to remove Noriega when one State Department lawyer had almost achieved that objective in May 1988, before short fuses in Washington blacked out negotiations still in progress. America at the service of the worldwide movement toward democracy was the theme struck by official Washington, to which the public responded without reflecting that East European peoples were achieving democracy by throwing out regimes imposed on them by military force. To the president, Panama was "another campaign streamer" added to a "roll call of glory" that bears Yorktown, Gettysburg, and Normandy. "Just as the world has in the past welcomed the departure of Somoza, Duvalier, Marcos, and, more recently, Honecker, Zhivkov, and Husák," Bush's envoy to the Organization of American States (OAS) told that body on December 22, "it is time this organization put itself on the right side of history."[14] Apparently no one in the OAS was so impolitic as to point out that it had not taken military intervention by Washington to bring down Haiti's Jean-Claude Duvalier, the Philippines' Ferdinand Marcos, East Germany's Erich Honecker, Bulgaria's Todor Zhivkov, and Czechoslovakia's Gustav Hosák. Collectively and individually, most Latin American governments went on record opposing Washington's unilateral overkill.

General Frederick F. Woerner, Jr., the senior U.S. military commander in Panama whose mid-1989 replacement facilitated planning for the invasion, inasmuch as he opposed it, in retrospect offered the opinion that the intervention was not driven by strategic considerations, or by other foreign policy objectives, so much as by U.S. domestic politics.[15] Noriega's connection to drug trafficking and to the CIA, an agency once headed by Bush, catapulted the dictator into an issue in the 1988 presidential campaign. (Democratic candidate Michael Dukakis preferred this issue to the more consequential one of Central American conflicts, since on the latter his Arias-like position might appear to be too "soft" on communism.) The ineptitude of both the Reagan and Bush administrations in removing Noriega by regional diplomacy, bilateral negotiations, or even covert action left President Bush with an image problem that the invasion solved at a stroke.

Less evident in the journalists' reconstruction of events is a cluster of motives no less linked to domestic politics, although to bureaucratic turf and budget battles more than to the president's image. During the year prior to the invasion, the Pentagon's position shifted from a reluctance to invade—Noriega not being worth a single U.S. soldier's life, it was said—to enthusiasm for the invasion if it could be big enough. As national security adviser to Reagan in 1988, General Colin Powell "generally opposed the use of force to remove Noriega." As chairman of the Joint Chiefs of Staff under Bush from October on, however, Powell emerged as one of the invasion's staunchest supporters, coming up with a battle plan that made it appear less risky to the president because it was more massive and quick. Among various explanations for the general's reversal, Bob Woodward of the *Wash ington Post* cites the weeks spent by Powell preceding the invasion in "dealing with proposals for sharp reductions in the U.S. defense budget."[16]

The period leading up to the invasion of Panama saw Communist regimes collapse in Central and Eastern Europe, leading to calls in Congress to cut defense spending. The chairman of the Senate Budget Committee, Democratic Senator James Sasser, argued that eliminating $15 billion from the $300 billion defense budget would not threaten national security "unless you plan to take the B-2 and bomb Colonel Qaddafi's tent with the darned thing."[17] Six Stealth fighter-bombers (F117As) were deployed in Panama, two of them to drop one-ton bombs. While many in Congress were advocating scaling back production of the hyperexpensive Stealth fleet—each F117 cost $100 million—Stealth technology played a role in the "successful" invasion of Panama.

Testifying before the House Armed Services Committee three months after the invasion, Army Chief of Staff General Carl Vuono touted his service's freshly demonstrated ability to bring an "overwhelming application of combat power" to bear on conflicts in the Third World and to restore order afterward with its "civil affairs" units.[18] Denied previous justifications by trends in Europe and in the Soviet Union, which was disengaging from the Third World, the Pentagon now offered its services in solving other problems overseas, including drug trafficking and dictatorship. Noriega being both a dictator and drug trafficker, taking him out by military force with little loss of

U.S. life helped the Pentagon market its new post-Cold War mission, just as it helped Bush bury the same image of indecisiveness that had proved costly to President Jimmy Carter.

Selling the Contras

A good test of the permanent campaign's role in Central American policy is the Reagan administration's 1985–86 effort to secure military funding for the Nicaraguan contras from a Congress that had turned down a similar request on four occasions since 1983. Unlike the Panamanian invasion, there was no clear crisis that could rally the public around the president, no innocent U.S. citizens to be saved, and little likelihood of producing quick and dynamic "successes." By 1985, in fact, Congress was growing tired of the divisive contra-aid issue while the general public remained indifferent. Most Americans polled still were uncertain which side Washington supported in which conflict in Central America, while clear majorities opposed anything that smacked of greater military involvement by the United States.[19]

Ronald Reagan had been propelled into the presidency by a conservative coalition with a heterogeneous agenda. The religious right focused on banning abortion and promoting prayer in the public schools, while business supporters sought deregulation and tax reform. Led by Cuban exiles and wealthy Texans, vocal Sunbelt conservatives stressed the dangers and opportunities in Central America and found a champion in the president's first secretary of state, Alexander Haig, and Director of Central Intelligence William Casey. "Mr. President, this is one you can win," Haig is reported to have told Reagan, while to small, elite audiences Casey spelled out what came to be known as the Reagan Doctrine.[20]

Deeply formed by their experience of World War II and the first decade of the Cold War, Casey and Reagan still viewed the globe as two great blocs locked in mortal combat. Civil wars and rebellions in Asia, Africa, the Middle East, and Latin America were only extensions of a fundamental encounter between a free world led by the United States and a Communist-cum-terrorist movement led by the Soviet Union. "Freedom fighters" the world over were waging the same struggle inside what Casey called "the occupied countries—Afghanistan, Cambodia, Ethiopia, Angola, Nicaragua—in which Marxist regimes have been either imposed or maintained by external force." Reagan stated that the 1983 "events in Lebanon and Grenada, though oceans apart, are closely related." Behind each was the hand of Moscow, he continued, "provid[ing] direct support through a network of surrogates and terrorists."[21] A Republican position paper on Latin America spoke of World War III having already begun and, due to the previous Democratic administration's indecision, of the Kremlin currently winning.[22] The Reaganites were determined to turn this tide, if not immediately in Afghanistan or Cambodia, then immediately in Central America and the Caribbean where surely, with sufficient will, Washington could prevail. Their goal was nothing less than the rollback of Marxism there.

Thus, when President Reagan called the contras "freedom fighters" and compared them to the French Resistance, that rhetoric revealed his underlying view of international affairs. Under Reagan the debate over Central America became a debate over U.S. values and experience, not Central America's. The Reaganites warned of another Munich while calling for the hemispheric equivalent of the 1947 Truman Doctrine; their opponents in Congress warned of another Vietnam while agreeing with the White House that Americans could not tolerate another Cuba. Traditional U.S. anticommunism confronted traditional U.S. isolationism around a replay of past U.S. mistakes.

Central American policy was driven by an ideology that rallied a diverse conservative coalition around a common stance toward communism and a common commitment to restoring Washington's standing internationally, not by economic interests in any concrete or proximate sense. U.S. business played little role in policy formation, in contrast to the Nixon-Kissinger attack on Chile in the early 1970s, nor is it clear that business was served by the economic warfare and political tensions engendered by the Reagan policy in the Caribbean Basin. Similarly, it is hard to find a trained analyst of U.S. strategic concerns, in or outside the government, who took seriously the administration's invocations of Caribbean choke points and fears of Soviet bases in this region. Most analysts understood that, having a satellite in Cuba, the Kremlin neither needed nor wanted similar commitments elsewhere in a region so far from its heartland, for these commitments carry costs.[23] Indeed, in its refusal to embrace the Contadora treaty process led by its ally Mexico, the Reagan White House demonstrated its lack of interest in reaching international understandings that could have limited Soviet and Cuban military activities in Central America in exchange for similar limitations on Washington. Thus, Washington sought a free hand in Central America because it desired the one thing international agreements rarely produce: the overthrow of a sitting government.

Powerful political and economic interests within the Reagan coalition worried that the president's ideologically driven preoccupation with Central America would derail efforts to reorder the economy, privatize public agencies, and deliver the coup de grace to the Democrats' New Deal coalition. Under Chief of Staff James Baker's direction, Central American policy took a back seat to the domestic agenda during the first term. The most influential White House staffers played down the antagonisms with Congress that Central America invariably evoked and sought to smother the trigger-happy image that the president had brought into the White House. To the magicians of the permanent campaign during the first term—several of whom moved out of the White House after Reagan's reelection to take more prestigious or lucrative positions—Central America was a sideshow. They supported Reagan's second secretary of state, George Shultz, when he encouraged experienced diplomats to explore negotiated solutions that might obviate divisive U.S. military involvements to the south.

Whenever these diplomatic explorations approached success, however, as they did in mid-1984, those whom Washington insiders called "the ideologues" rallied from second-level positions at the National Security Council (NSC), the Department of Defense, and other agencies, and used their access to the president through CIA Director Casey, United Nations Ambassador Jeane Kirkpatrick, or Defense Secretary Caspar Weinberger to torpedo negotiations. In his account of these battles, ideologue Constantine Menges takes pride in the seven times such timely intervention prevented President Reagan from following Shultz and National Security Adviser Robert McFarlane into what Menges considered the "cunning Mexican-Cuban-Nicaraguan false treaty trap."[24]

With this division at the White House blocking the diplomatic track, Casey pursued a covert military track largely on his own, with the president's enthusiastic but disengaged support. (As everyone who intimately worked with Reagan did, Casey complained about the president's inattention to details and lack of follow-through.) The CIA essentially bought, then expanded, a contra force created by Nicaraguan ex-National Guardsmen after Anastasio Somoza was overthrown, a force backed by the Honduran military with assistance from the Argentine army. (*Contra* is one half of the Spanish word for counter-revolutionary.)

CIA direction and provisioning of the contras was secretly but legally approved by Congress in 1981–82, followed by public appropriations in the following fiscal year. This funding was accompanied by understandings between Congress and the executive eventually written into law as the Boland amendments, which restricted the appropriated funds to objectives provided by the Reagan administration to Congress in its secret presidential findings (for example, the first finding claimed that the purpose of supporting the contras was to interdict arms the Sandinistas were sending to Salvadoran Marxist rebels). By the middle of 1984, however, a pattern of events had persuaded many in Congress that these restrictions were being ignored by Casey. In October 1984, therefore, Congress cut off all further funding and explicitly prohibited U.S. military and intelligence personnel from aiding the contras.

The 1987 Iran-contra hearings revealed the administration's response to this 1984 reversal. The White House solicited secret donations from foreign governments and private individuals and shifted coordination of the contras from the CIA to the NSC, where Lieutenant Colonel Oliver North took on the task. But this was only a fall-back strategy, a way to "hold the resistance together body and soul" (as Reagan charged National Security Adviser McFarlane to do) until Congress could be turned around. The Democrat-controlled House's refusal to back administration policy not only limited the possibilities of expanding the contra army but also gave Central Americans pause over Washington's ultimate intentions. Vulnerable U.S. allies, such as the Honduran government, feared being left with disgruntled contras on its soil should the Sandinistas prevail or Washington pull out. Secret funding could not buy the policy the legitimacy it needed.

By the spring of 1985, therefore, the Reagan administration had decided to mount a coordinated advertising campaign that would make use of the president's popularity, then at its height following the 1984 landslide reelection. Key elements of the economic agenda had been passed by Congress, reducing the consequences of antagonizing Democrats. New Chief of Staff Donald Regan, who had learned marketing skills on Wall Street, was more willing than his predecessor to "let Reagan be Reagan" on foreign policy, including Central America. With North managing the secret contra operation and fellow ideologue Elliott Abrams exercising wide latitude as the new assistant secretary of state for Inter-American Affairs—Shultz having cut his losses and turned his attention elsewhere—the ideologues moved from veto power to operational control of Central American policy.

The campaign sought to light a fire beneath wavering and undecided legislators through direct appeals to their constituents, using a battery of techniques ranging from prime-time presidential speeches to paid thirty-second spots in selected media markets, from ghostwritten op-eds to staged tours of contra leaders and Sandinista defectors. By the summer of 1985 the administration had reached a consensus on going for broke, settling for nothing less than full military aid to the contras even if that required hardball attacks on opponents who stood in the way, such as Red-baiting the liberal Democrats.

Since it took awhile to coordinate the multiple tasks performed by various private and governmental agencies, the full impact of the campaign was not felt until the early months of 1986. Among the many participants coordinated by interagency working groups largely run out of the NSC were the Office of Public Diplomacy for Latin America and the Caribbean (nominally in the State Department), the president's speechwriters and pollsters, and various private foundations, grass-roots organizations, and consulting firms that provided cutouts for illegal lobbying and fund-raising activities. (Consultants paid for activity X through noncompetitive contracts from the Office of Public Diplomacy, for instance, would engage in Y, an activity that the office could not legally sponsor.)[25]

It worked. In the wake of the Iran-contra scandal, it is easy to lose sight of the Reagan administration's success in boxing enough members of the House into a corner where, to avoid appearing "soft" on communism in an election year, they voted in June 1986 for more contra military aid in one year than Congress had appropriated in all previous ones. Ben Bradlee, Jr., correctly described the 1986 campaign as "a dramatic extension of earlier White House efforts to blend public relations with policy on the Central American front."[26]

Stalled by the Democratic leadership's parliamentary tactics, full military funding for the contras did not pass the Republican-controlled Senate until August and did not reach the president's desk until October. But, no matter. Signed into law on October 25, this legislation permitted the CIA to resume its old roles of guiding and supplying the contras while legitimating the base building and military exercises in Honduras that the Pentagon had continued, activities that served the contra cause in multiple ways. At the time it was estimated that the $100 million voted by Congress actually released some $400 million in contra support.

To Secretary of State Shultz, the campaign marked a "shift of view" in the nation. "We are seeing a growing breadth of support for the basic policy in Central America," he said after the climatic June 25 victory in the House.[27] While the extent of the shift in grass-roots public opinion was slight, the administration did succeed in altering the terms of the debate in both the mainstream media and Congress. The campaign succeeded in portraying the Sandinistas as Communists controlled by Moscow and in making members of Congress define themselves on that issue. Were they anti-Communist or pro-Communist? Attention was shifted from the abysmal human rights record of the contras to the behavior of the Sandinistas. In a tactic known within the administration as "gluing black hats on the Sandinistas," the threat presented by a nationalist-Marxist regime in Central America was transmuted into the quite different question: Do you approve of the Sandinistas? Sweeping charges of Sandinista attacks on religion, mistreatment of Indians, and associations with drug traffickers were pieced together from decontextualized bits of information. Finally, in a time-honored Washington tradition, the campaign positioned Reagan policy as the only prudent middle course between two unacceptable alternatives: If we do not support the contras now militarily, we soon will face a Central America overrun by Communists and then our only options will be capitulation or the deployment of U.S. troops.[28]

Analysts in and outside the government noted the shifts in Soviet behavior, as Mikhail Gorbachev accelerated his predecessors' disengagement from revolutionaries in lands that held no strategic importance for the Kremlin, but this did not stop the White House from playing up the historic fear of communism among the U.S. public and heightening that fear with references to Central America's proximity. Secret polls purchased by the Republican National Committee kept the campaign planners up to date on which issues would work in the home districts of wavering representatives. Memorandum traffic between National Security Adviser McFarlane and his deputy North contains a detailed plan of action leading up to a congressional vote on contra aid in the spring of 1985, suggestive of the planning carried to fruition later that year and the next. "Conduct public opinion poll of America [*sic*] attitudes toward Sandinistas, freedom fighters" to "see what turns Americans against Sandinistas"; "prepare a 'Dear Colleagues' lu [letter] for signature by a responsible Democrat which counsels against 'negotiating' with the FSLN," the Sandinista party. North envisaged hiring British mercenaries to stage attacks in Nicaraguan cities timed to influence the 1985 congressional vote, with such actions attributed to the contras to demonstrate new-found strength in urban areas.[29]

This is not the place to describe in detail the tactics through which the executive lobbied Congress without most representatives being aware of it, or the methods by which newspaper and television editors were duped into accepting manufactured stories as news and op-eds as genuine. From presidential speeches hammering the whose-side-are-you-on theme to congressional remarks ghostwritten by the Office of Public Diplomacy, from television ads showing Soviet ICBMs rising from Nicaraguan silos to official White Papers full of misinformation, the American public, press, and legislature were propagandized. Here it is sufficient to point out the coordination behind this campaign, which mirrored that of recent presidential electoral campaigns.

With this campaign's success, two years of supporting the contras on the sly and of lying about it could come to an end. National Security Adviser John Poindexter talked of transferring North to the CIA, to deflect the attention that the hyperkinetic colonel was beginning to attract at the NSC. A collective sigh of relief must have arisen from those, such as Poindexter and North, who had had to keep *this* from Shultz, *that* from the president, a great deal from Chief of Staff Regan, and almost everything from Congress. Even the CIA officer responsible for the Central American region was kept out of the loop.

Ironically, just as the policy could go public, a skeleton fell from its closet. On what would have been one of Project Democracy's last clandestine flights over Nicaragua to resupply the contras, its plane was shot down. Captured was a U.S. mercenary and a paper trail that eventually led to North's office and to a CIA operative at the U.S. embassy in Costa Rica. The English-speaking press did not make much of this, however, until Attorney General Edwin Meese revealed a few weeks later that the secret contra supply effort—conducted while the second Boland amendment remained in effect—had been funded from profits made by the Enterprise in selling U.S. missiles to Iran. (The Enterprise was the name given by North and retired Air Force General Richard Secord to their arms business; Project Democracy was North's term for the clandestine operation resupplying the contras in which the Enterprise played a leading role.) In shredding hundreds of incriminating documents, North missed one that alluded to the secret diversion of funds from Iran to Central America, and Meese's assistant found it. Without that tenuous link, it is not at all certain that the Iran arms-for-hostages scandal would have brought Reagan's Central American policy down with it.

Investigations into the Iran-contra scandal provide a window onto this otherwise hidden advertising and lobbying campaign that turned Congress around in 1986. We can see that the executive branch has three ongoing sources of propaganda techniques. The first is in the "psych-war" wings of the intelligence and military agencies. Walter Raymond, a CIA expert in such matters, organized the campaign from his post at the NSC, while the Office of Public Diplomacy borrowed similar talent from the military. Two investigators concluded that the Reagan administration "was indeed running a set of domestic political operations comparable to what the CIA conducts against hostile forces abroad."[30]

A second source of opinion manipulation consists of a White House staff peopled with pollsters, speechwriters, advance men, public relations hacks, and press secretaries—a stable of strategists who learn opinion manipulation in electoral campaigns. Linked to this is a third center in the national offices of the two main political parties and their associated consultants and contractors. Thus, the knowledge and skills necessary for mounting high-pressure advertising campaigns around foreign policy survived the fall of the point personnel, such as North, and of the point agency. While Congress shut down the Office of Public Diplomacy in the wake of the scandal, it did not amend the regulations that failed to prevent that or any other agency from waging a permanent campaign around a foreign policy.

Having a legalistic culture, Americans focus on "dirty tricks" that break the law while overlooking practices that corrupt the democratic process despite their legality. When the air cleared from the Iran-contra scandal, the Government Accounting Office, Congress's investigative arm, decided that the Reagan administration had engaged in "prohibited, covert propaganda activities" but did not recommend prosecution or legislative remedies.[31] Given the narrow focus in existing federal regulations on the funding of lobbying activities, much of the campaign had been technically legal. A president can solicit private contributions that buy television spots targeted at specific members of Congress or specific bills before Congress. He can even attract those contributions by offering donors a private meeting with him at the White House. Ronald Reagan did the above, knowingly. But as long as no congressionally appropriated funds are used in the making of those television commercials, this mockery of regulations intended to prohibit the executive from lobbying the legislature is legal.[32]

Legal or not, the use of advertising practices to manipulate policymaking undermines such bedrock principles of American government as separation of powers, Congress's coequal responsibility for foreign policies that involve war, and an autonomous and informed citizenry. Abolishing the Office of Public Diplomacy hardly addresses the issue of how responsible democracy meshes with the permanent campaign; it merely papers over the problem. Such constitutional concerns are not abstract. In this instance the emphasis on selling policy by manipulating consent led to bad policy and lack of learning.

The Legacy of Policy by Permanent Campaign

As Roy Gutman documents, while Reagan policy toward Nicaragua from 1984 through 1988 rested almost exclusively on the contras, top U.S. decision makers never reached consensus on an endgame. Would the contras overthrow the Sandinistas? Few analysts at the Pentagon or the CIA believed they could. Would the contras merely pressure the Sandinistas into negotiating a solution Washington could live with? The administration never settled on a negotiating strategy or agreed on its basic objectives. Instead, ideologues and dreamers such as North, Casey, and Reagan pulled the rug out from under experienced diplomats whenever the latter approached realistic agreements with the Sandinistas.[33]

This administration went through four assistant secretaries of state for Inter-American Affairs and a like number of special presidential envoys to the region. By projecting onto Congress its frustrations for its inability to speak with one voice, the Reagan White House overlooked work only it could do. Eventually, the administration was marginalized by this failure to define an achievable policy. From mid-1987 on, Congress threw its support behind the five Central American presidents who, through a series of meetings known as the Esquipulas II peace process, worked out a negotiated solution that finally fell into place at the beginning of 1990. To its credit, the Bush White House supported this Central American-driven outcome, hoping to sidestep the divisiveness associated with the Reaganites' insistence on having their way.

Similar inattention to an endgame was apparent, however, in the Bush administration's planning for the invasion of Panama. Again, military means overwhelmed political considerations in plans that concentrated on removing Noriega with little loss of U.S. life. The planners gave little thought to what would happen after the United States installed in the presidency Guillermo Endara, a Noriega opponent who had been robbed of an election the previous May. Would Washington restructure the Panamanian military and police, combined in the PDF, if this required a U.S. presence that compromised Endara's fragile legitimacy? Three months after Operation Just Cause, as Washington pompously called its invasion, Congress balked at voting the economic aid that the White House had promised the Endara government. In the absence of an overall strategy, many members of Congress, including Senate Majority Leader George Mitchell, believed that the money would be wasted.[34]

An axiom of business is that the less likely a product is to sell itself, the more it needs advertising. In policymaking, the opposite also is true: the more attention paid to selling, the less thought given to the policy's content. As conveyed by the medical metaphor "Vietnam syndrome," the Reagan White House viewed the public's reticence to support its Central American policies as a defect in the buyer to be circumvented, not as an indication that something might be wrong with the policy. The administration's "success" in 1986 lay in finally presenting the buyers with packaging they could not refuse—but that did not make the policy objectively any better. The danger of foreign policymaking by permanent campaign lies precisely in the split between the feedback leaders pay attention to—the manipulated manifestations of U.S. public opinion—and the real world in which policy ultimately succeeds or fails, in this case Central America.

Is the United States any the wiser for having lived through a period in which Central America was so widely discussed? President Reagan expended much rhetoric on this region, including a televised address to a rarely called joint session of Congress, arguing that the "vital national security" of the United States was on the line in Central America. The Bush administration's claim to support democracy by invading Panama, along with the public's ready acceptance of that claim, is evidence of lack of learning. Not only did the U.S. discourse on Central America not advance from Carter to Reagan to Bush, but it retreated to Woodrow Wilson's imperial insistence on teaching those Latins to choose good leaders, by military intervention if need be.

In this official Washington view, when dealing with Central America at least, democracy consists of the right people who, when placed in power, make democracy happen. It does not much matter how these people come to power. The Reagan White House talked of the contras bringing democracy to Nicaragua despite top contra military commanders' history of supporting the Somoza dictatorship and their intolerance of power sharing within their own organization. The Reagan administration invested more in the military overthrow of the Sandinistas than in the civilian internal opposition, whose nationalist legitimacy was undercut by Washington's role. Ideologues in the Reagan administration continually shot down negotiated solutions with the Sandinistas because, they claimed, those treaties could not deliver "genuine democracy." "Democracy" became a code word for imposing on Nicaragua the government of Washington's choice.

It was with greater plausibility that Bush endorsed Endara's party in Panama as democratic. But democracy ultimately is a process, not a group or a party. Democracy requires agreement on the rules of political contestation, a level of trust between all major participants in that competition, along with those habits of compromise and negotiation that yield a loyal opposition rather than rebellion or a coup. Imposing a government on a nationalistic Central American country by force, especially by foreign arms, works against that trust and those habits. It is hard to think of more nationalistic populaces than those of Nicaragua and Panama, both of which have rebelled against U.S. tutelage in the past. Crowds welcoming U.S. soldiers is no more an answer to this contradiction of Washington imposing democracy by force than is the behavior of a codependent spouse an assurance of a lasting marriage.

No less committed to democracy than U.S. leaders, throughout this period Costa Rican President Oscar Arias kept insisting that lasting democracy could not be imposed by outside force, since those means undermine that end. "If we democracies of the world show ourselves to be afraid of . . . using our own tools, such as dialogue and persuasion, we will be following the methods of the tyrants," Arias said on several occasions, sometimes adding that "nothing new and lasting" is likely to arise from civil war or military intervention.[35] A highly educated political scientist, Arias articulated what every U.S. leader ought to know: that democracy is grounded in process, not in the substitution of one group for another, and that the legitimacy of democratic governments is tied to sovereignty and self-determination.

Additional evidence of lack of learning can be read in the way that Reagan policies toward Central America were discarded. In the last two years of this administration, opponents of contra aid mimicked some of the techniques used by Oliver North and Carl Channell in the 1986 campaign, albeit with a broader base of donors and volunteer workers. Opponents of Reagan policy used phone banks to solicit money for ads on radio and television opposing continued aid to the contras. "You've got to make TV and radio spots such that people can read in their own point of view," commented one consultant to this campaign, suggesting that if this means playing to the public's isolationism and even racism, so be it. The public opposition to contra aid that such organizations as Neighbor to Neighbor tapped, according to a pollster working with those groups, stemmed in no small part from "a strong aversion to the region that goes from misinformation to racism."[36]

Thus, administration advertisements tapping America's rich lode of anticommunism were countered with ads that tapped an equally extensive, equally visceral isolationism. So structured, the "debate" over Central America was conducted through metaphors that had little to do with the region in the 1980s. "Another Europe 1947" (Truman stopping the Soviets in Greece rather than repeating Munich 1938) was pitted against "another Vietnam" (Americans dying in a distant war fed by nationalisms poorly understood). At times the debate degenerated into arguments over costs, as if price could justify goals. While Reagan closed out his presidency with words of trust and friendship for Soviet leader Gorbachev, his last address on Central America repeated the litany of the "growing Soviet-Cuban presence" in Nicaragua, with the Kremlin's goal still that of "establish[ing] a Soviet beachhead on the American mainland."[37]

Central America virtually disappeared from the 1988 presidential campaign as Republican candidate Bush understandably sought to distance himself from the Iran-contra scandal, while Democratic candidate Dukakis escaped the "wimp" label that adheres to advocates of negotiations and multilateralism by avoiding mention of his position on the region's conflicts. Dukakis preferred to shift the debate to Panama, Noriega, and drugs, where he could take a more aggressive stance. In the end, issues scarcely mattered. Bush won the election by using Baker's "news management strategy," which is to "control your message by keeping reporters and their questions away from a scripted candidate [and] capture TV's attention with prefabricated, photo-opportunity events that reinforce the campaign's chosen 'line of the day.'"[38] When the candidates stopped talking about Central America, so did the media. In this atmosphere of benign neglect, the Esquipulas II peace process progressed, although both Sandinistas and contras put their bilateral negotiations on hold until the new U.S. administration defined its position.

It is apparent, then, that ads rarely engage other ads. Central America died as an issue in U.S. politics without resolution, just as the Iran-contra scandal faded without serious public debate over its meaning for the American political process. The public ends up liking position X more than the position Y but without being able to articulate a reason that will inform future choices. With much less formal schooling, ancestors of this public could follow a discourse as complex as the Lincoln-Douglas debates, which mirrored similar debates periodically held in Congress. During the Reagan years, however, not even the foreign affairs committees of the two houses of Congress mounted full-scale debates into the goals and assumptions of the policy toward Central America.

It is easy to blame the citizenry for this atrophied discourse. If, after eight years of an administration's shouting that "vital security interests" are at stake in Nicaragua, one half of the U.S. public still did not know which sides Washington supported in which Central American conflicts, perhaps the United States is getting the discourse it deserves.

Irritated and bored with politics except when it offers shoot-'em-up entertainment or exposes the private lives of the rich and famous, large numbers of Americans no longer vote. Disproportionately present among the nonvoters are those persons young enough to have grown up watching sixteen thousand hours of television before they reach voting age.[39]

Blaming an undifferentiated public diverts attention from the fact, however, that 26 percent of U.S. adults (36 percent of those who do vote) display both the level of interest in national and international affairs and the information needed to sustain a better discourse than witnessed over Central America. A debate that had engaged this "attentive public" would have been lively, for it is not a single group but three. While the largest sector consists of "Enterprise Republicans," 96 percent of whom voted for Reagan in 1984, outnumbering them is a combination of "Sixties Democrats" and well-educated independents inclined to vote for the Democrats but capable of switching parties. On many issues the opinions of these groups bracket the national average, with at least one group to each side of the most popular (or mean) position.[40]

Reactivating such a discourse, however, would require politicians willing to speak to the issues instead of grabbing the cheap victory to be had in advertising to the pool of the tuned-out, yet manipulable, citizens. It is partly a matter of leaders placing democracy's need for a critically involved public over the immediate payoff of electoral victory, and partly a matter of leaders believing they can make sense to a national audience if deprived of the doublespeak of advertising, cue cards, and carefully scripted encounters. Carried to the highest office by the practitioners of the permanent campaign, George Bush admits that he does not excel at "this vision thing." He does not even complete his sentences. One of the most successful campaigns in commercial advertising is Marlboro, the best-selling cigarette in the world. Recent Marlboro ads do not even mention the product; they merely show the Marlboro man, an image that triggers the positive but irrational association smokers have with this product. Similarly, a political discourse in which "read my lips" substitutes for argument serves leaders who would rather not explain their positions.[41]

While one factor promoting advertising in politics is the tendency of politicians to carry into policymaking the techniques learned in campaigning for office, another is the fear they may have that the public will not support costly foreign policies in defense of the far-flung U.S. interests. The public's understanding of "security" and "defense" is rooted, naively, in elemental concepts of survival and of preserving an "American way of life" on North American soil. This way of life may require Washington to be more of a global policeman than the public understands (making sure, for example, that Europe gets its Middle Eastern oil). Rather than explain that, however, politicians use advertising techniques to move the emotional charge attached to security and defense from one set of symbols (home, American way of life) to a more diverse and remote set of symbols (defense of the free world, U.S. credibility abroad). Reagan's dramatic image of a worldwide Communist threat made this transfer relatively easy to accomplish in 1986, as easy perhaps as flashing the Marlboro man before a smoker. But the same advertising techniques can use new threats to market old policies, as may be seen in Bush's "war" on drugs. If a cowboy can sell a cigarette named Marlboro and democracy can sell military intervention, what limits does this process have?

Such speculation should not seem out of place in a discussion of U.S. policy toward Central America and the Caribbean because that policy, this article has argued, is shaped by concerns that have more to do with the smoke and mirrors of domestic U.S. politics than with what is happening in those regions. Unfortunately, foreign policy by permanent campaign trades future flexibility for today's sale, for it atrophies the political system's ability to think its way out of old positions. Updating Washington's relations with its historic sphere of influence has been made more difficult by the politicians' recent reiteration of "doorstep," "democracy," "backyard," and "soft underbelly." As a method of legitimating foreign policy, political advertising limits choice and encourages nostalgia. In this way, the medium becomes the message. The "permanent campaign" does not just legitimate a policy, it deforms it.

Notes

1. "TV's Role in '88 . . . ," *New York Times*, October 30, 1988.
2. "Don't Blame Registration in Low Voter Turnout," ibid., November 24, 1988.
3. The term "selling of the president" first appeared in Joe McGinniss's book on the Nixon campaign, *The Selling of the President, 1968* (New York: Pocket Books, 1970). McGinniss reminds us that the techniques singled out in this analysis antedate the Reagan era. This is not the place, however, to chart their origins.
4. "Marketing the President," *New York Times*, September 13, 1981. For more thorough exposure to Blumenthal's analysis see his *The Permanent Campaign* (New York: Simon and Schuster, 1982), 283–334.

5. Perhaps the best book in the burgeoning literature on how the Reagan administration manipulated the press, public, and Congress is Jane Mayer and Doyle McManus, *Landslide: The Unmaking of the President, 1984–1988* (Boston: Houghton Mifflin, 1988).

6. "Baker's World," *New York Times*, September 21, 1989.

7. "America's Politics Loses Way as Its Vision Changes World," ibid., March 18, 1990.

8. For evidence for this view, which otherwise may strike the reader as contentious, see George Black, *The Good Neighbor* (New York: Pantheon Books, 1988).

9. "For Bush, the Best of a Bad Bargain?" *Newsweek* (January 1, 1990): 23; "U.S. Policy Errors May Have Forced Nation to Undertake Massive Invasion," *Wall Street Journal*, December 21, 1989.

10. "For Bush, the Best of a Bad Bargain?" 23; "Countdown to an Invasion," *Washington Post National Weekly Edition*, January 22, 1990; "Bush's Obsession," *New York Times*, December 26, 1989. The press conference occurred on December 18, 1989.

11. Mayer and McManus, *Landslide*, 221–23.

12. "The Public Says Bully for Bush," *Washington Post National Weekly Edition*, January 22, 1990; "Times Mirror News Interest Index, January 1990," a news release of the Times Mirror Center for the People and the Press, January 11, 1990. Atwater's comment was quoted by a reporter at the presidential press conference covered by the *Washington Post*, January 6, 1990.

13. "The Aftermath of a Quick Strike," *Washington Post National Weekly Edition*, January 1, 1990.

14. "U.S. Reports Latin Trend to Restore Panama Ties," *New York Times*, March 9, 1990; "Panama: A Just Cause," *Current Policy* 1240 (Washington, DC: U.S. Department of State, Bureau of Public Affairs).

15. "Countdown to an Invasion," *Washington Post National Weekly Edition*, January 22, 1990.

16. "The Conversion of Gen. Powell," *Washington Post*, December 21, 1989.

17. "Bush Willing to Accept Big Cuts in the '91 Military Budget," *New York Times*, March 18, 1990.

18. "Split between Army and Marines Surfaces in Debate on 3d World," ibid., March 15, 1990.

19. Norman Ornstein et al., *The People, Press and Politics* (Reading, MA: Addison-Wesley, 1988). This analysis commissioned by the Times Mirror Company was based on polls conducted by the Gallup Organization in April-May 1987, p. 54. See also "Relax, Democrats: The Public Supports You on Nicaragua," *Washington Post National Weekly Edition*, April 7, 1986; and "American Opinions on Aid to Contras," *New York Times*, April 20, 1986. As late as 1987 only 45 percent of the nation's adults knew that Washington supported the opposition in Nicaragua, while 39 percent responded "not sure" or "don't know."

20. Laurence Barrett, *Gambling with History* (Garden City: Doubleday, 1983), 207; Bob Woodward, *Veil: The Secret Wars of the CIA* (New York: Pocket Books, 1988), 426.

21. Woodward, *Veil*, 332, 462.

22. Committee of Santa Fe, *A New Inter-American Policy for the Eighties* (Washington, DC: Council for Inter-American Security, 1980).

23. Peter Clement, "Moscow and Nicaragua: Two Sides of Soviet Policy," *Comparative Strategy* 3, no. 1 (1985): 84–85. For additional analysis of the security rationale see Lars Schoultz, *National Security and United States Policy toward Latin America* (Princeton: Princeton University Press, 1987), pts. 2, 3.

24. Constantine Menges, *Inside the National Security Council* (New York: Simon and Schuster, 1988), 133–37, 155–57, 166.

25. U.S. Department of State, Office of Inspector General, "Audit Report No. 7PP-008: Special Inquiry into the Department's Contracts with International Business Communications and Its Principals," July 1987; Peter Kornbluh, "The Contra Lobby," *Village Voice*, October 13, 1987. Kornbluh is responsible for the earliest and best reporting on the campaign to turn around the Congress on contra aid.

26. Ben Bradlee, Jr., *Guts and Glory: The Rise and Fall of Oliver North* (New York: Donald Fine, 1988), 221.

27. "Winds of War Blow through Washington," *Washington Post National Weekly Edition*, July 28, 1986.

28. For a more complete analysis of how the campaign framed the debate see Eldon Kenworthy, "Where Pennsylvania Avenue Meets Madison Avenue," *World Policy Journal* 5 (Winter 1987/88): 107–27.

29. "Marketing Reagan," and "White House Propaganda Activities," *Propaganda Review* 1 (Winter 1987/88); Roy Gutman, *Banana Diplomacy* (New York: Simon and Schuster, 1988), 281. Creating events in Central America to influence debates in the United States was by no means limited to this scheme, which North failed to pull off. For other examples see Woodward, *Veil*, 293, 314–17; and "A U.S. Frame-up of Nicaragua Charged," *New York Times*, February 4, 1988.

30. Robert Parry and Peter Kornbluh, "Iran-Contra's Untold Story," *Foreign Policy* 72 (Fall 1988): 4. Raymond's title was special assistant to the president and director of international communications. This veteran of CIA disinformation campaigns overseas coordinated the Central American Working Group on Public Diplomacy out of the NSC.

31. "State Dept. Linked to Contra Publicity," *New York Times*, October 5, 1987; Comptroller General of the United States (GAO), "Report to Congressman Dante Fascell, Chair of the Foreign Affairs Committee, House of Representatives," September 30, 1987 (B-229069).

32. The U.S. Code (18, 1913) prohibits use of "money appropriated by any enactment of Congress . . . directly or indirectly to pay for any personal service, advertisement, telegram, telephone, letter, printed or written matter, or other device, intended to influence in any manner a Member of Congress." President Reagan's role is described by Kornbluh in "The Contra Lobby" and by Bradlee in *Guts and Glory*, in the chapter entitled "Blue Rinse and Ham Hocks & Dogs."

33. Gutman, *Banana Diplomacy*, chaps. 10–12.

34. "House Approves Latin Aid; Senate Troubled by Priorities," *New York Times*, April 4, 1990; "Funnel, Don't Flood, Aid to Panama and Nicaragua," ibid., April 10, 1990.

35. Oscar Arias, *El camino de la paz* (San José: Editorial Costa Rica, 1989), 144, 319–20.

36. David Moberg, "The Grassroots Push to End Contra Aid," *In These Times*, September 2, 1987; John Judis, "We Love the Contras, We Love Them Not," ibid., September 30, 1987.

37. "Central America at a Critical Juncture," U.S. State Department *Current Policy* 1007 (October 1987).

38. Mark Hertsgaard, "Electronic Journalism," *New York Times*, September 21, 1988.

39. Neil Postman, *Amusing Ourselves to Death* (New York: Viking Penguin, 1986), chaps. 4, 9.

40. Ornstein, *People, Press and Politics*, 42, 53–55.

41. George Bush clarified his views on drugs during the first presidential candidates' debate by referring to the movie *Crocodile Dundee*. Ann Crigler's research suggests that, in this, Bush resonates with the public whose views on drug policy are heavily influenced by the entertainment media ("Political Experts Offer 3 Views," *New York Times*, October 29, 1988).

Conclusion: Toward a New Central American Policy

Kenneth M. Coleman
and George C. Herring

The essays in this volume reject what appears to be the prevailing conventional wisdom, that the confrontational and interventionist policies of the Reagan and Bush administrations have brought success for the United States in Central America. The authors argue, to the contrary, that the United States misperceived the causes of conflict in the region and developed policies that were wrongheaded in their assumptions and basic premises and costly and disastrous in their consequences. Even apparent successes in Nicaragua and Panama, the authors concur, resulted from earlier policy failures and only superficially dealt with the fundamental problems in those countries.

The Central American crisis of the 1980s was rooted in deep-seated and long-standing indigenous problems. The fundamental causes were the political, social, and especially economic inequities that have long afflicted the region, problems to which the United States, through its quasi-imperial role in many of the countries, has contributed. Billie DeWalt and Pedro Bidegaray make clear the way in which Central America's current economic problems derive from such factors as concentration of land ownership and dual labor markets. Kenneth Coleman highlights the polarized political systems that have limited the attainability of the centrist governments that the United States professes to support. By analyzing the changing role of the Catholic church in Central America, Kathleen Blee illustrates the extent to which new forces are at work in the region. And Ilja Luciak illustrates how Nicaraguans in the 1980s debate the concept of democracy in ways not well comprehended in the United States.

The authors further agree that the United States developed policies based on false assumptions. Throughout the Reagan years, the Central American crisis was portrayed in the language and imagery of the Cold War: intervention by the United States was justified to prevent the entrenchment of Communist influence along its southern border. The Soviet Union supported the Sandinista government in Nicaragua, to be sure, and that government in turn provided limited and sporadic support to the insurgency in El Salvador. But to depict the crisis in Central America as essentially a Cold War struggle ignored the more important indigenous sources and grossly exaggerated the external causes.

America's stake in the region also was distorted. The Reagan administration repeatedly claimed that U.S. vital interests would be threatened by additional Communist takeovers in Central America. For the most part, however, these interests were defined only vaguely in terms of geography and credibility, with the administration warning that acquiescence in Communist triumphs so close to home would undermine the prestige of the United States and drastically weaken its influence throughout the world. Some of the contributors to this volume might concede that U.S. strategic interests could have been endangered by the establishment of a Soviet satellite in Central America. They reject, however, the simplistic notion that the Sandinistas in Nicaragua or the FMLN in El Salvador ever served as mere instruments of Soviet policy—a notion that seems even more preposterous now with the collapse of the Soviet empire in Europe—and they emphatically deny that a Marxist government that emerged in any of the Central American countries would have been a Soviet satellite.

The authors disagree or at least differ in emphasis regarding the wellsprings of U.S. policy. Taking the long historical view, Walter LaFeber finds the Reagan policies of support of the status quo and military interventionism deeply rooted in tradition. Throughout the twentieth century, he argues, the United States has supported reactionary oligarchic governments that have served its economic and political ends in Central America, and it has used military force to put down popular uprisings that threatened those interests. From a shorter perspective, George Herring contends that the Reagan policies were partly motivated by a desire to exorcise the Vietnam syndrome, the alleged malaise that gripped the American people in the aftermath of that debacle and presumably limited foreign policy initiatives. Eldon Kenworthy also finds the Reagan policies rooted in domestic factors.

Central America has served as a "theater," he notes, "in which American politicians project their ambitions, their ideologies, and their desire for the limelight at little risk." Using the same advertising and propaganda techniques that get them elected, they underwrite a "permanent campaign" to sustain their popularity and maintain domestic support by launching bold policies in areas such as Central America.

The contributors generally concur that, having defined the problem incorrectly, the Reagan and Bush administrations developed solutions that have been notably unsuccessful, in many instances counterproductive, and disastrous for Central America. For the region as a whole, the decade of the 1980s was an era of massive economic and military intervention. From 1981 the United States pumped into a small, impoverished region billions of dollars in economic assistance, much of it military hardware. The infusion of outside aid further dislocated already vulnerable economies. It prolonged and rendered more bloody already bitter military conflicts. During the period from 1978 to the present, an estimated two hundred thousand to three hundred thousand Central Americans died in wars largely financed by the United States. In a more general sense, leaders of other Latin American countries complained of the "Centralamericanization" of U.S. policy at the expense of more pressing issues, most notably the spiraling debt that threatened the entire hemisphere.

The pattern of U.S. intervention varied. In El Salvador, as William LeoGrande points out, the Reagan administration sent advisers and massive military aid to assist in the suppression of a left-wing insurgency, and it backed the futile efforts of centrist José Napoleón Duarte to establish a stable and responsible government. In Nicaragua, as Harry Vanden and Thomas Walker have shown, under the aegis of the Reagan Doctrine, the administration created virtually from scratch the contra insurgency to overthrow the Sandinista government and used legal and extralegal means to sustain it.[1] Honduras was militarized to serve as a base in Washington's not-so-covert war against Nicaragua. And in Panama, after abortive efforts to destabilize the government and unseat dictator Manuel Noriega, the Bush administration in December 1989 resorted to modern-day gunboat diplomacy, dispatching twenty-four thousand troops to capture Noriega.

The results also varied. El Salvador proved the validity of Coleman's thesis. Despite $3.5 billion in U.S. aid between 1980 and 1989, the army could attain no more than a stalemate in its bloody, seemingly interminable struggle with the FMLN. And the center, instead of getting stronger, grew weaker. Stricken with cancer, Duarte lost his effectiveness. His Christian Democratic party lost its legislative majority to the right-wing ARENA party in early 1988 and lost the presidency to ARENA's Alfredo Cristiani in 1989. After nearly a decade of struggle, the situation remained more polarized than ever, and an estimated seventy-two thousand Salvadorans died at the hands of right-wing death squads and the military that the United States supported so lavishly.[2]

In Nicaragua also, the Reagan policies produced a decade of bloody struggle. The U.S.-backed contras were never strong enough to eliminate the Sandinista regime, but their insurgency destabilized the government, kept the country in turmoil, and produced extraordinary economic distress. Eventually both sides wearied of the struggle, and in March 1988 they agreed to a cease-fire. In a shocking turnabout in 1990 the Sandinistas were defeated in elections, but U.S. claims for success seemed at best strained. The victory of Violeta Chamorro resulted primarily from war-weariness and a desperate hope for economic improvement. Yet the sources of domestic conflict had not been removed, and a decade of war left the nation in dire economic straits.

Even in Panama, claims of victory seemed grossly exaggerated. The Bush administration was able to prove its toughness, to be sure, and it removed in the form of Noriega a large and sharp thorn from its side. But the means used seemed to many critics disproportionate to the ends attained. As Richard Millett points out, moreover, intervention brought the United States much ill will in the hemisphere and did nothing to resolve Panama's pressing economic and political problems.

Thus, after more than a decade of large-scale U.S. intervention, the Central American crisis persists. The great majority of the thirty million Central Americans are worse off today than in 1980. Poverty is pervasive, and social and economic imbalance the norm. In El Salvador, for example, despite massive U.S. aid, wealth is more concentrated than ever. The poorest 20 percent of the population earned less than 4 percent of the country's income in 1985, while the richest earned 55 percent.[3] The gap between rich and poor is larger now than in 1970.

Central America also experienced the most rapid military buildup in its history. In El Salvador, Nicaragua, Honduras, and Guatemala, the armed forces doubled between 1981 and 1986, and in all four countries the military constituted a shadow government with vast political power. In three of those countries, civilian government existed in name only. Leaders in El Salvador, Guatemala, and Honduras were powerless to rein in entrenched interests, especially on the political right, and were afraid to tackle fundamental issues such as disarmament, land reform, and human rights.

In Guatemala, El Salvador, and Nicaragua, conflict persisted, at great economic and human cost. The advent of civilian government in Guatemala in 1986 had given hope to that troubled nation, and for a time there was notable improvement in respect for human rights. By the end of the decade, however, President Vinicio Cerezo increasingly deferred to the military, and human rights abuses were on the rise again. Reliant on the Guatemalan army to fight its own war against the drug trade, the United States seemed increasingly reluctant even to protest its assaults on human rights.[4]

In El Salvador the civil war continued unabated. Efforts to negotiate a settlement failed, and President Cristiani's attempt to negotiate with the insurgents and his shift toward the political center provoked an angry backlash from ARENA and its militant leader Roberto D'Aubuisson. American officials increasingly talked of "Lebanonizing" El Salvador, by which they meant withdrawing from a situation that their own involvement had greatly worsened.

Nor was there peace in Nicaragua. President Chamorro struggled to hold together the unwieldy coalition that had brought her to power and to deal with her country's grinding economic problems. She enjoyed little success and found herself embattled and often isolated. The political right resented her alleged appeasement of the Sandinistas. The latter seemed to be making good their vow to "govern from below" by demanding what appeared to be a virtual veto power over government policy and by launching a series of crippling general strikes.[5]

Thus, although it no longer dominates the front pages of U.S. newspapers, the Central American crisis continues. And the question remains: What can or should the United States do? It is always easier, of course, to indicate what is wrong with a set of policies than to propose alternatives, but criticism bears with it an obligation to do just that.

An initial step is to refrain from reasoning by analogy. Foreign policy failures and "successes" of the recent past, such as Vietnam, the 1989 Panamanian invasion, and the 1990 Nicaraguan elections, do not provide explicit lessons for other settings, and facile historical analogies mislead. The history of each Central American state is unique, as is its relationship with the United States, and insightful and effective U.S. policy must take into account the differing origins of Costa Rican, Nicaraguan, Panamanian, and Salvadoran "democracies."

The Cold War mind-set that shaped the Reagan administration's approach to Central America was inappropriate in the 1980s, and it has no relevance whatever in the 1990s. Eastern Europe has moved toward competitive political systems and market economies. The Soviet Union itself is threatened with separatist movements in the Baltic region and on its southern flank and has experienced a degree of political opening and economic change that Americans would have found inconceivable as recently as 1988. Even more dramatic, Presidents Mikhail Gorbachev and George Bush have formally pronounced the end of the Cold War, thus removing the rationale for four decades of U.S. foreign policy. In this context the possibility of Soviet intervention in Central America is negligible to nonexistent, and it will be impossible even for the most rabid anti-Communist to argue that conflict in that region stems from outside forces.

Paradoxically, just when the threat of external intervention is lowest, the United States may be most inclined to intervene in Central America. Conservatives committed to an activist role may well conclude that intervention in Grenada, Nicaragua, and Panama produced greater democratization and greater respect for the United States. Persuaded in the aftermath of Washington's victory in the Cold War that the tide of history is running on the side of democratic capitalism, they may well conclude that overt U.S. intervention is the way to resolve the Central American crisis.

We reject these premises and conclusions. The United States did unseat dictators in Grenada and Panama, and U.S. intervention did contribute to the Sandinista defeat in 1990. That this intervention brought genuine and stable democracy in Grenada and Panama is open to serious question, however. And in Nicaragua, internal forces were perhaps more important than external ones in producing the outcome, as was the unprecedented decision of a revolutionary party to submit to elections and accept defeat. Whatever its intentions, moreover, the United States has been unable to curb the right-wing forces that are the major obstacles to political democracy and economic reform in Guatemala and El Salvador. Intervention of the sort that characterized U.S. policy in the 1980s is not the answer.

What, then, are the possible U.S. responses to the persisting crisis in Central America? Three options appear plausible. First, the United States can continue to respond to military crises as they emerge in Central America, letting local conservatives set the agenda. Second, it can pursue more aggressively a conservative vision of democratic capitalism in Central America on the premise that if a system is not capitalist it is not democratic. Or third, it can promote peace as the essential condition for democratic compromise, letting each Central American country work out its own model of political economy.

The first option seems somewhat less likely under Bush than it did under Ronald Reagan. President Bush has at least proven himself capable of joining with congressional Democrats in forcing groups such as the Nicaraguan contras to disarm and accept the results of competitive elections won by the "other side."[6] Yet this choice is the easiest for the U.S. policymakers. Washington's traditional posture toward Central America and the Caribbean has been to ignore the region until local conservatives argue that there is a "Red threat." A military response under these circumstances is unlikely to arouse significant opposition at home (witness public acquiescence in Guatemala in 1954, the Dominican Republic in 1965, Grenada in 1983, and Panama in 1989). Regrettably, U.S. disinterest in and misunderstanding of Central America remain sufficiently strong, and the national inability to understand that crimes committed in the name of anticommunism can be more heinous than those committed by Marxists makes this response possible in the presidency of George Bush or any of his successors.

Given the recent electoral success of Republicans in presidential politics, the United States might attempt to foment a revolution of democratic capitalism throughout Central America. In this second option, inducements might be furnished to the region's governments to engage in privatization and open their borders to U.S. exports and capital and to U.S. investors to direct their capital to "friendly" Central American states. If conflict were to ease, then Central American and U.S. private capital might return to the area.

This policy would face major problems. The lack of dynamism in Central American economies rarely results from excessive governmental bureaucratization. These economies have not been as highly "statized" as those elsewhere in Latin America, partly because they are less industrialized. Rather, insufficient dynamism has resulted from small market size, eased somewhat during the heyday of the Central American Common Market (1961–1972), ill-distributed purchasing power, political conflict, and attendant capital flight.

The greater the U.S. presence in the economies of Central America, the more likely that political conflict would erupt over whose interests were being served by foreign investors who shipped profits outside the country. Hence, the more visible the resurgence of U.S. capital in the region, the greater the chance of political conflict over the terms of foreign participation in the local economy.[7] Temporary respites from political conflict may prove to be self-limiting.

Finally, the Central American economies may be influenced less by the policy choices of their governments than by their external relationships. For example, export-oriented economies may be conditioned most fundamentally by tariff-free access to U.S. markets. In addition, barriers against the immigration of labor migrants who seek to use sojourns in the United States to earn small amounts of capital that can be invested in microenterprises in their home countries will influence Central Americans profoundly.[8] The United States is unlikely to open fully its own borders to Central America's leading exports: agricultural products and human labor. Thus, the prescriptions of U.S. conservatives for Central America are likely to be applied inconsistently, thereby eroding their potential for fomenting a democratic-capitalist revolution.

A third option for the United States would be to permit the region's countries to solve their own problems. Peace came to Nicaragua primarily through the efforts of Central American presidents to construct principles for domestic negotiations. Oscar Arias Sánchez, then president of Costa Rica, was instrumental in formulating the framework and lobbying for its implementation. Yet the meetings of the five Central American presidents may have been equally important. By assembling frequently between 1986 and 1990, they developed tolerance for those who might have been adversaries. Conventionalist presidents from Honduras and El Salvador (under Cristiani), would-be reformist presidents constrained by right-wing armies in El Salvador (under Duarte) and Guatemala, and reformist President Arias negotiated with revolutionary President Daniel Ortega of Nicaragua. When the time came for Ortega to give up power, the transition proved easier than had been predicted.

This third option assumes that democratic institutions will not look the same in all circumstances, that they will emerge from local political forces, and that they will be able to supersede and control local conflicts. Allowing local forces to assess their own conflicts and develop their own institutions may be the United States' best contribution to democratization. Washington should indicate that it does not care who wins or loses so long as the losers are protected and have a meaningful opportunity to compete and win another day.

That choice is difficult for conservatives and some liberals in the United States. Those who believe that democracy and capitalism are inextricably linked regard elections as democratic only if capitalists prevail. If socialists win, then elections immediately become undemocratic. But that reasoning must be rejected. In the long run, the United States can contribute to democratization only if it keeps firmly in mind two essential principles: It must make clear that it will have warm and friendly relations only with regimes that 1) support electoral account-ability and 2) preserve minority rights. If both conditions are present, then any choice—including that of economic systems—can be made or unmade. The United States should seek positive relations with such regimes, even if economic relationships must be reordered. It has nothing to fear from democratic regimes that choose socialist economic principles. But if either socialist or capitalist regimes become un-democratic, then it should be cool toward them to the extent that they deviate from electoral accountability and fail to protect essential minor-ity rights.

To do that, Washington must rely on observers other than its own diplomats. U.S. diplomats accredited to other governments will never be fully apprised of human rights violations. The United States must listen carefully to reports by international agencies such as the Inter-American Commission on Human Rights of the Organization of American States and private nongovernmental international groups such as Amnesty International and Americas Watch. These agencies as well as those monitoring electoral compliance can assess independently both dimensions of democracy.[9]

Should democracy be found not to exist, the United States must not impose it by force. It legitimately might cut off economic or military assistance to indicate its opposition to nondemocratic regimes, but it always should leave to a country's own citizens the decision of how best to free themselves from repression. The people may find such mechanisms, as in Augusto Pinochet's Chile and the Communist re-gimes of East Germany, Poland, and Romania; or they may not, as in the People's Republic of China. In each case, the United States played a secondary role.

Ultimately, the United States must realize that genuine democrati-zation will come to Central America only if democratic principles of compromise are valued by Central Americans. Those principles will be valued in turn if they help address and resolve fundamental economic, political, and social issues. Rather than proselytize in an area that it does not understand, the United States must let Central Americans themselves decide which institutions best permit an effective attack on the persistent poverty of the region, as well as which best provide for government responsiveness while preserving the human and political rights necessary to reorient government policy. The choice of political institutions and economic frameworks will vary from country to coun-try. Decision makers in Washington are least likely to know which choices are most appropriate. Hence, they should neither attempt to impose constraints nor undo choices made by Central Americans themselves. Only by permitting the Central Americans to make their own choices can the United States contribute to a real and lasting peace in the region.

Notes

1.   On the origins of the contras see Christopher Dickey, *With the Contras* (New York, 1985).

2.   See John A. Booth and Thomas W. Walker, *Understanding Central America* (Boulder, CO, 1989), 85.

3.   *New York Times*, June 24, 1990.

4.   Ibid., July 5, 1990.

5.   See *Envío* 9 (August-September 1990), a special issue on the "100 Days of UNO."

6.   Should forces favoring socialism or statism win an election in Central America, it is less clear that President Bush or other U.S. conservatives would accept the results. As with President Reagan in 1984 in Nicaragua, they might seek to discredit an election process that produces an inappropriate victory.

7.   U.S. citizens should note that as increasing Japanese investment occurred in the U.S. economy in the 1980s, concern about "domestic content" legislation and other forms of economic nationalism surfaced in this country.

8.   On the importance of profit remittances from abroad to the health of local economies in another Latin American setting see Merilee S. Grindle, *Searching for Rural Development: Labor Migration and Employment in Mexico* (Ithaca, NY, 1988).

9.   U.S. decision makers, however, should feel free to judge whether the choices made by Central Americans are sufficiently in accord with the values of the North American people that the U.S. public would be willing to invest its scarce resources in supporting such governments economically.

Index

Latin American Silhouettes
Studies in History and Culture

William H. Beezley and
Judith Ewell
Editors

Volumes Published

William H. Beezley and Judith Ewell, eds., *The Human Tradition in Latin America: The Twentieth Century* (1987). Cloth ISBN 0-8420-2283-X Paper ISBN 0-8420-2284-8

Judith Ewell and William H. Beezley, eds., *The Human Tradition in Latin America: The Nineteenth Century* (1989). Cloth ISBN 0-8420-2331-3 Paper ISBN 0-8420-2332-1

David G. LaFrance, *The Mexican Revolution in Puebla, 1908–1913: The Maderista Movement and the Failure of Liberal Reform* (1989). ISBN 0-8420-2293-7

Mark A. Burkholder, *Politics of a Colonial Career: José Baquíjano and the Audiencia of Lima* (1990). Cloth ISBN 0-8420-2353-4 Paper ISBN 0-8420-2352-6

Kenneth M. Coleman and George C. Herring, eds. (with Foreword by Daniel Oduber), *Understanding the Central American Crisis: Sources of Conflict, U.S. Policy, and Options for Peace* (1991). Cloth ISBN 0-8420-2382-8   Paper ISBN 0-8420-2383-6

Carlos B. Gil, ed., *Hope and Frustration: Interviews with Leaders of Mexico's Political Opposition* (1991). Cloth ISBN 0-8420-2395-X Paper ISBN 0-8420-2396-8

Charles Bergquist, Gonzalo Sánchez, and Ricardo Peñaranda, eds., *Violence in Colombia: The Contemporary Crisis in Historical Perspective* (1991). Cloth ISBN 0-8420-2369-0   Paper ISBN 0-8420-2376-3

Heidi Zogbaum, *B. Traven: A Vision of Mexico* (1992).   ISBN 0-8420-2392-5